Strangers
in Our Midst

David Miller

Strangers in Our Midst

THE POLITICAL PHILOSOPHY OF IMMIGRATION

Harvard University Press

CAMBRIDGE, MASSACHUSETTS, AND LONDON, ENGLAND   2016

First printing

Library of Congress Cataloging-in-Publication Data

Names: Miller, David, 1946- author.

Title: Strangers in our midst : the political philosophy of immigration / David Miller.

Description: Cambridge, Massachusetts : Harvard University Press, 2016. | Includes bibliographical references and index.

Identifiers: LCCN 2015039092 | ISBN 9780674088900 (alk. paper)

Subjects: LCSH: Emigration and immigration—Political aspects. | Emigration and immigration—Philosophy. | Emigration and immigration—Government policy. | Immigrants—Government policy. | Immigrants—Civil rights. | Human rights.

Classification: LCC JV6255 .M55 2016 | DDC 325/.101—dc23

LC record available at http://lccn.loc.gov/2015039092

For Margaret, with love

Contents

Strangers
in Our Midst

Introduction

THIS IS A BOOK ABOUT IMMIGRATION: how to think about it, and what to do about it. Should we encourage immigrants to join our societies, or try to keep them out? If we are going to take some in but refuse others, how should we decide which ones to accept? Or does everybody have a human right to enter in the first place? What can we ask of immigrants once they arrive? Should they be expected to assimilate, or can they properly demand that we make room for the different cultures they bring with them? And so on.

Many people today are asking these questions. Immigration has become a hot political topic, especially in Western liberal democracies where citizens often feel that they are no longer in control of the movement of people across their borders. It is also highly divisive. Generally speaking, members of the public are anxious about the effects of immigration and are much more likely to want to reduce the numbers of people coming in than to increase them. There is, however, considerable variation between countries. In European societies, large majorities of citizens wish to see levels of immigration reduced. In the United Kingdom, for example, an opinion poll in late 2013 found that 80 percent of those who were asked thought that current levels of net inward migration were too high, 85 percent thought that immigration was putting too much pressure on public services such as schools, hospitals, and housing, and 64 percent thought that over the last decade immigration had not been good for British society as a whole.[1] Even the long-established principle of free movement *within* Europe is coming under pressure. A Swiss referendum in early 2014 found a slight majority in favor of imposing numerical caps on all forms of immigration, including from European Union (EU) countries.[2] Opinion in the United States is more evenly divided between supporters and opponents. In 2013, 40 percent wanted immigration to remain at its current level, 35 percent wanted it to fall, and 23 percent were in favor of it rising—though over the past decade as a whole the proportion wanting fewer immigrants has hovered between 40 and 50 percent.[3]

Critics will dispute the significance of such figures. They will argue that people are poorly informed both about the number of immigrants arriving and about the impact of immigration. What the public tends to overlook, in particular, are the economic benefits that immigrants bring with them and their willingness to undertake essential jobs (such as agricultural labor or care for the elderly) that few natives will perform. The critics will also hint darkly that immigrants are being made scapegoats for social problems, such as housing shortages and poorly performing schools, that have little or nothing to do with immigration as such. And we often hear expressed the view that opposition to immigration stems ultimately from prejudice, or even simple racism.

So the public debate on immigration generates much heat, but little light. Some academic commentators believe that the attention currently being paid to immigration is exaggerated. It is said that migration is simply an unavoidable part of the much larger process of globalization. We live in a world characterized by ever-increasing flows of capital, goods and services, and communications across national borders—flows whose overall effects are largely benign. When everything else is in flux, people will move too. Indeed they must move because the other components of globalization can't operate unless they do. Workers must move to the offices and factories where their skills are needed, students to the universities where cutting-edge research is being carried out, entertainers to the places where their audiences await them, and so forth. Some people may move on a temporary basis, but others will choose to stay. The issue we should be addressing is not so much how to control migration by restricting the numbers coming in but how to make it work as smoothly and efficiently as possible.

Another more skeptical view points out that population movements have been occurring throughout recorded history, and that although the numbers migrating may have increased in recent decades, it remains the case that the overwhelming majority of people still live in their country of birth. In 2013, the global migrant stock was 231 million, about 3 percent of the world population.[4] Admittedly this figure conceals some big differences—at one extreme, immigrants make up 70 percent of Qatar's population and 94 percent of its workforce[5]—but in most societies immigrants only make up a small fraction of the population. So why all the fuss?

The problem with downplaying the issue in this way is that it relies on a snapshot taken at the present moment, in circumstances where most migration is already subject to quite severe restrictions, and doesn't look at what might happen in the future were these controls to be relaxed or lifted altogether. The dynamics of immigration are quite complicated. A recent study by Paul Collier suggests that because immigrants are drawn to places where they can join a community of earlier immigrants from a similar cultural or national background, the size of the diaspora and the speed with which it integrates into the host country are important factors.[6] As the size of the (unassimilated) diaspora grows, its pulling power increases, and the rate of immigration will tend to increase indefinitely if there are no effective controls. This scenario of course assumes that potentially a very large number of people would choose to move to one of the advanced liberal democracies if they had the opportunity. This assumption is plausible, given the sheer size of the economic gap between rich and poor countries and the several decades (at least) that it will take to close that gap significantly—even if the global economic order is reformed and poor countries succeed in adopting pro-growth policies. Polling by Gallup, for example, suggests that 38 percent of those living in sub-Saharan Africa and 21 percent of those living in the Middle East and North Africa would prefer to migrate permanently.[7] So if we are going to have a discussion of immigration with all the policy options on the table (which means including "fully open borders" as one extreme position), then we must allow that immigration flows might be many times higher than those that we are currently experiencing.

At this point it is worth looking a little more closely at why immigration, even at quite a modest level, might create difficulties for the receiving societies. Voters rank it highly among the political issues that concern them, and unscrupulous politicians can win significant support by promising ever-harder crackdowns both on immigrant admissions, especially on those entering illegally, and on the various welfare entitlements that immigrants receive. No doubt some part of this response simply reflects prejudice and scapegoating. But to get a full grasp of the problems currently posed by immigration, it is worth making a short historical detour to see how the relationship between liberal states and immigrants has changed over the last couple of centuries. We can better understand our own predicament by comparing it with earlier periods in which immigration was, if not positively encouraged, at least regarded with relative indifference.

If we ask how immigration was generally viewed by members of liberal states in the mid-nineteenth century, the answer would be that states were regarded as having an unrestricted right either to accept immigrants or to refuse them entry as one aspect of their sovereignty, but in practice movement was often left unregulated. Controlling immigration only became an issue when the numbers arriving became large, or when the newcomers were regarded as undesirable on economic, moral, or racial grounds (or combinations of these). Thus in the United States, the first significant restriction imposed at federal level was on Chinese immigrants in 1882, in response to concerns that Chinese men were competing with native workers for jobs, and Chinese women were working as prostitutes.[8] In the United Kingdom, the Aliens Act of 1906 was aimed primarily at Jewish emigrants from Eastern Europe, though Chinese seamen were also targeted.[9] In both cases supporters of immigration controls used a rhetoric that denounced the low morals of the allegedly inferior races. Immigrants were acceptable, in other words—or in the U.S. case even positively to be welcomed—so long as they were of a type that posed no threat either to the morals or to the economic interests of existing citizens. And they were expected to fend for themselves. The state took no responsibility for the welfare of immigrants, who typically struggled for survival in the lowest depths of the society. The overall attitude of the receiving society toward the incomers was nicely summed up earlier in the century by the Chartist journalist Joshua Harney: "The exile is free to land upon our shores, and free to perish of hunger beneath our inclement skies."[10]

A further implication of the state's rights of sovereignty was that it could impose whatever conditions it liked on those seeking to enter, at least so long as these did not amount to brutal treatment. The liberal philosopher Henry Sidgwick spelled out the state's rights in a relatively brief discussion of the immigration question in his *Elements of Politics,* first published in 1891.[11] Sidgwick took it as axiomatic that states had the right to decide whether to accept any immigrants at all, the only qualification to this arising in the case of states whose borders enclosed large tracts of unoccupied land; so they must also have the right to decide on the terms of admission:

> A State must obviously have the right to admit aliens on its own terms, imposing any conditions on entrance or tolls on transit, and subjecting them to any legal restrictions or disabilities that it may deem expedient. It ought not, indeed, having once admitted them, to apply to them suddenly, and without warning, a harsh differential treatment; but as it may legitimately exclude them altogether, it must have a right to treat them in any way it thinks fit, after due warning given and due time allowed for withdrawal.[12]

Sidgwick also thought that states had good reason to be selective in deciding whom to admit, because "the governmental function of promoting moral and intellectual culture might be rendered hopelessly difficult by the continual inflowing streams of alien immigrants, with diverse moral habits and religious traditions."[13] He concluded that so long as immigration policy was assessed from the national perspective of the receiving state, it was morally acceptable for the state to balance the economic interest it might have in admitting immigrants with special skills against the threat they might pose to "the internal cohesion of a nation" and maintaining "an adequately high quality of civilised life among the members." There was, in other words, no duty to consider the interests of the immigrants themselves.[14]

I have cited Sidgwick as a representative of liberal attitudes toward immigration at roughly the moment at which large-scale immigration was becoming a political issue in Europe and North America in order to highlight the ways in which our thinking has changed in the hundred or so years since he wrote. Some of these changes have helped to support the claims of potential immigrants, while other changes have had the effect of burdening them. So first we have seen the rise of an international human rights culture that imposes far greater responsibilities on states in their treatment of immigrants than a philosopher in Sidgwick's time could possibly have envisaged.

States are now seen as having positive duties to take in those whose basic rights are being threatened in the places where they currently live—refugees especially. And even in the case of those who do not qualify for the special protection afforded to refugees, states are constrained by international law in the procedures that they use when selecting among applicants for admission and removing those who do not qualify but have arrived anyway. Of course these legal strictures are not always complied with in practice, but nonetheless states feel bound either to conceal or to justify their behavior when they take steps that violate human rights conventions, since these apply to all human beings regardless of nationality, including incoming migrants.

Next, when immigrants are admitted to liberal states, they benefit from the much wider scope of toleration that is now afforded to those whose lifestyles deviate from the social mainstream, and in fact they can benefit positively from the support that multicultural policies give to minority cultural practices. In other words, the pressure to assimilate to the dominant culture that was quite severe a century ago—at least for all those immigrants who wanted to rise out of the ghettos to which they were initially consigned—has been replaced by social norms that encourage many cultural flowers to bloom and that seek to remove barriers to opportunity for members of the minority cultures. In liberal democracies today, no idea is more powerful than equality of opportunity. Thus, on the one hand, if the state decides to use its resources to support cultural or recreational activities, it must do so evenhandedly (e.g., if string quartets are going to be subsidized, so also should steel bands and mariachi groups). On the other hand, individual opportunities to work and to advance up career ladders should not be affected by a person's cultural background. So we now have antidiscrimination law, we have an education system that is either strictly secular or else makes room for faith schools that cater to minority religions, and so forth. All of these changes make it easier for immigrants to live in their new home without having to abandon their inherited culture and indeed very often under conditions in which they are encouraged to celebrate that culture as part of the multicultural potpourri.

But there are other equally significant changes in the political culture that make the position of immigrants, especially newly arrived immigrants, more difficult. The first is the importance that is now attached to the idea of national citizenship. People mostly identify themselves politically with national communities that stretch backward and forward over the generations, and this membership is regarded as lifelong: it begins at the moment of birth and ends only with death. How, then, should newly arrived immigrants fit into this picture? Are they to be treated as candidate members who are expected in due course to integrate fully and then be treated in exactly the same way as native-born citizens? Or are they to be regarded as temporary associates, short-term residents trying to accumulate some capital before returning home, or desperate people seeking sanctuary while their own countries are torn apart by civil war? For societies that aspire to live up to liberal-democratic principles, it is intolerable for there to be a class of persons consigned permanently to hold a subordinate status within their borders. So all the immigrants who are destined to remain must be given the opportunity to gain rights of residence and eventually full rights of citizenship, while the others must be encouraged to leave when it is convenient and safe to do so. The state cannot simply adopt a laissez-faire attitude as it might have done a century and a half ago. Moreover, in the case of those embarking on the road to citizenship, it has a significant interest in their political education. Being a citizen is not just a matter of having a bundle of rights, such as the right to legal representation and the right to vote, important though these are. It also involves responsibilities and norms that define how citizens should behave. For example, a citizen should be willing to cooperate with the police in upholding the law and catching criminals. In a democracy, it involves accepting majority decisions, taken according to proper procedures, as authoritative until they are reversed. So in becoming a citizen, one also has to accept such responsibilities and embrace the corresponding norms. Moreover, in order to function as a citizen, a person must also align herself with the political system of which she now forms a part. To play the role adequately, she must respect its institutions and take on board at least some of the beliefs that lie behind them.

Exactly how far the new citizen must go in identifying with her adopted state is a matter of some dispute, as is also the nature of the required identification. Should it be narrowly political, in the sense of acknowledging the authority of a body of rules and principles, such as those embodied in the state's constitution? Or does it require a fuller type of identification with the nation that the immigrant has joined, which will include recognizing and embracing national symbols, speaking the national language, accepting some version of the "national story," and acknowledging the preeminent position of certain cultural features, including possibly a particular religion, within the national consciousness? These are questions that we will need to return to later in the book. In practice, there is a widely shared assumption that immigrants should at least be strongly encouraged to adopt more than a narrowly political identity. One sign of this is the growing popularity of citizenship tests that require the applicant to know something about the history and culture of the country he is joining. Of course these tests cannot by themselves make the immigrant adopt any particular attitude toward that society. But besides familiarizing him with some practical information about how the society works, their underlying purpose is to signal an expectation that he will integrate culturally as well as economically and socially.

For immigrants who have inherited their culture from nonliberal societies, this expectation may cause inner conflicts. To embrace the political culture of the receiving society, they may have to jettison some of their most firmly held beliefs. Reactions to this challenge may vary greatly, from exaggerated patriotic commitment to the new society at one extreme to rejection and alienation at the other. The problem perhaps becomes most acute when the receiving society is involved in conflicts within the region from which the immigrants originate, as has been happening since the time of the Iraq War in the case of immigrants from the Middle East. In these circumstances the new arrivals may come under pressure to support the state's policy, in order to avoid being labeled disloyal or even treacherous. That this should happen may seem strange, since democracies are supposed to be committed to freedom of expression and open critical debate on government policy. But these principles operate on the tacit assumption that all those involved in the debate identify with the political community and have its best interests at heart. Immigrants cannot count on this assumption being made in their case. So for them, speaking up against the government carries risks that native citizens do not have to face.

The point, then, is that being admitted to a national society as a prospective citizen imposes certain costs as well as conferring benefits. In earlier times, as I observed, immigrants were left to their own devices so long as they did not become involved in illegal or antisocial behavior. What they believed and how they felt about the society they had joined were of no particular interest. The contemporary democratic state cannot take such a hands-off view: it wants and needs immigrants to become good, upstanding citizens. And achieving this may involve encouraging or even requiring them to shed some of the cultural baggage they bring with them. Just how the balance is to be struck between supporting cultural pluralism and ensuring that there is a core set of beliefs that almost everyone subscribes to is one of the main problems facing states with large immigrant communities. Later in the book we will need to explore some of the pressure points where multiculturalism and citizen identity come into conflict.

Because most contemporary democracies are also welfare states (whether they self-apply the label or not), committed to implementing policies of social justice, a second set of problems arises. On the one hand, they try to achieve equality of opportunity; on the other, they provide income support and a range of social services intended to provide all citizens with the means for a decent life. Immigrants are among the beneficiaries of these policies, but they are also required to contribute to making them effective. Again, this requirement may involve complying with social norms—for example, ensuring that male and female children are given equal opportunities in education and employment—which may be at odds with the cultural or religious beliefs of some immigrants. Furthermore, social justice is normally thought to involve a lifelong scheme of social cooperation where most people are net contributors (through taxation) during certain periods of their lives, and net beneficiaries at other times, when they fall ill or reach the age of retirement, for instance. Immigrants typically join the scheme partway through their lives, raising the question whether they should immediately be entitled to the full range of welfare benefits or whether they need to earn their membership by a period of net contribution first. Popular resentment of immigrants often appears to be fueled by a perception, accurate or not, that they enter in order to receive benefits without having made an adequate contribution beforehand.[15] This issue, again, could not have arisen at an earlier time when the state provided rather little beyond basic protection to its subjects. Immigrants now have to be taken in not just as future citizens, but as members of an elaborate scheme of resource distribution that relies upon its members adhering to principles of contribution (e.g., making a genuine effort to find work) and principles of equality (e.g., seeing to it that jobs are given to the most qualified candidates, regardless of gender, race, or religion).

My point here is not that immigrants are unable or unwilling to become members of the scheme: there is no reason to believe that. The point rather is that the receiving state has to take active steps to integrate newcomers if the scheme is not to be weakened by the perception that they are not playing their part. Redistributive welfare states rely upon trust among citizens that each will behave fairly under the terms of the scheme, paying taxes honestly and not drawing benefits to which they are not entitled. There is evidence, unfortunately, that as societies become more diverse, ethnically or culturally, levels of trust tend to decline;[16] and this in turn makes it harder to win support for policies that may in practice benefit some groups more than others, even if this is not their intention.[17] The upshot is that we may face a trade-off between higher levels of immigration and creating or maintaining a strong welfare state, assuming the latter is one of our goals. The evidence about this is not always easy to interpret. In recent decades, relatively high levels of immigration to the advanced democracies have occurred during a period in which levels of welfare expenditure have risen for independent reasons, so the question is not whether immigration has reduced welfare spending in absolute terms, but whether it has slowed its growth. An analysis of social spending in eighteen Organisation for Economic Co-operation and Development (OECD) countries reaches the following conclusion:

> International migration does seem to matter for the size of the welfare state. Although no welfare state has actually shrunk in the face of the accelerating international movement of people, its rate of growth is smaller the more open a society is to immigration. The typical industrial society might spend 16 or 17 percent more than it does now on social services had it kept its foreign-born percentage where it was in 1970.[18]

The evidence referred to here is evidence about what has happened in the past. It does not preclude the adoption of countermeasures to overcome the dampening effect of immigration on welfare state expenditure. My point is just to underline that there is an issue that has to be faced squarely when significant numbers of immigrants enter an established welfare state, especially when cultural differences create a degree of mistrust between native and newcomer. Earlier I cited evidence of popular anxieties about immigration and also the views of critics who argue that these anxieties are ungrounded. What I have tried to suggest is that whichever side finally proves to have the better of the argument, there is an argument to be had. There is a real question about what the impact of immigration is on receiving societies, where the balance between costs and benefits lies, and also how the benefits and costs to the immigrants themselves should be entered into the equation. Should they be given equal weight, or is it legitimate to tilt the scales in favor of the existing members of the political community?

These are difficult questions (if they weren't, there would be no need for this book). In public forums, the debate about immigration is often conducted in rather narrow economic terms. Contributors try to estimate the net effect of immigration on the gross domestic product (GDP) of the receiving society. Usually this effect turns out to be positive, but it is small. However, it also seems important to examine how immigration affects the relative shares of national income going to different groups within the society, and here there is some evidence that immigration tends to exacerbate inequality by reducing the incomes of low-skilled workers, as an effect of increased competition for their jobs.[19] This outcome, of course, depends on the distribution of skills among the immigrant cohort; a more optimistic view holds that where immigrants are selected on the basis of their qualifications, as they are in many OECD countries, the main impact of immigration is slightly to raise unskilled wages because of complementarity between high- and low-skilled workers.[20] Where economists disagree, political philosophers should not try to adjudicate. All sides to the debate agree that the effects on wage levels are relatively small. Moreover, even if we confine our attention to the economic effects of migration, we need also to consider the impact on sending societies, where the effects, for good or ill, may be greater. Is there a danger that "brain drain" may have seriously harmful consequences for the societies that highly educated migrants are leaving? And if so, what weight should we give to this impact? This latter question immediately takes us beyond economics to political philosophy. For the questions it raises are, first of all, whether states are obliged to weigh the interests of all human beings equally when deciding upon their policies, or whether they are legitimately allowed to give more weight to the interests of their own citizens. And then, if they are indeed allowed to attend first to their own citizens, what are the limits to this partiality? What burdens, if any, are they allowed to place on outsiders, and what more positively must they do to help noncitizens whose human rights may be endangered? Answers to these very basic questions must be given before we can begin to formulate a coherent view on the claims of immigrants, and so Chapter 2 of this book will attempt to tackle them.

Economists themselves may be ready to concede that the main questions raised by immigration are not narrowly economic.[21] Another disciplinary group with a strong interest in questions of immigration are legal theorists and especially human rights lawyers. For, on the face of it, immigration policy as it is currently practiced raises serious concern about human rights. Consider the physical methods used by some states to prevent immigrants from entering their territory illegally, such as the practice of sending out patrol boats to intercept vessels carrying migrants before they reach shore—even though these vessels are often unseaworthy. Or consider the ways in which states try to prevent refugees from applying to them for asylum, by deterring airlines and other carriers from transporting them to the border where they could otherwise lodge their asylum claims. Or, finally, consider the position of those who do enter illegally and then, lacking the protection that the state would normally provide, find themselves having to take on work under very unsafe conditions. In the United States, an Associated Press investigation found that, in southern and western states, Mexican workers were four times as likely as the native born to be killed on their jobs.[22] In the United Kingdom, we remember the twenty-three exploited Chinese workers caught and drowned by the rising tide while collecting cockles in Morecambe Bay.[23] So if we look at immigration exclusively through the lens of human rights law, we are very likely to conclude that states should not only accept more migrants but take the task of protecting their human rights far more seriously than they currently do. A concern for human rights may not entail demolishing all border controls, but might it mean moving much closer to the open borders end of the spectrum?

The human rights perspective on immigration, like the economic perspective, makes an important contribution to our understanding, and in later chapters of this book I will look in some detail at the human rights questions posed by refugee admissions, selective immigration policies, temporary migration schemes, and so forth. But it still remains a partial perspective because it fails to consider other values that rightly play a central role in debates about immigration. These values are often collective, having to do with the general shape and character of the society that immigrants may be seeking to enter—for example, the overall size of its population, its age profile, the language or languages spoken by its inhabitants, or its inherited national culture. These are often matters of great significance to current citizens.[24] There will rarely be a full consensus about them, but in democratic societies a collective preference can emerge through free exchange of opinions in the media and political forums. People want to feel that they are in control of the future shape of their society. They have an interest in political self-determination, which includes being able to decide how many immigrants should be allowed to enter, who should be selected if more than this number apply, and what can reasonably be expected of those who are allowed in. A human rights approach to immigration cannot accommodate such collective values. A human rights lawyer may argue that human rights are always trumps, and therefore that any acceptable immigration policy must respect the human rights of potential immigrants, no matter what the democratic majority may think. But as we shall see later, things are not so simple. We are once again in the territory of political philosophy—this time looking at how, if at all, democracy within the state can be reconciled with the human rights of those beyond its borders.

So to get a proper grasp of the immigration issue, we have to start with some fundamental questions of political philosophy, but to look at them from a new angle. A shift of perspective is needed because political philosophy, say from the time of Hobbes onward, has largely been concerned with the internal relationship between the state and its citizens. All of the questions that we normally ask—How is the state's authority established? What rights do citizens possess against the state? Should government be democratic or oligarchic? What does social justice demand? And so forth—rest on the assumption that we already know who is to be included in the political community. All are equally subject to the authority of the state, even if (as in the case of women) they have historically been excluded from full citizenship. Alongside this rich tradition of state-centric political philosophy ran a smaller stream of international political theory, developing principles to regulate the behavior of states toward one another, and this has recently swollen to become a torrent, with works on cosmopolitanism, global justice, and related topics pouring from the presses. But neither tradition has found it easy to cope with the specific issue of immigration. The topic itself hardly appears in the classic texts of political philosophy. It receives no mention at all in John Stuart Mill's comprehensive study of government in *Considerations on Representative Government* or in Hegel's equally comprehensive *Philosophy of Right*, for example. We have to come forward to the end of the nineteenth century to find a philosopher such as Sidgwick devoting a small amount of space in a large book to the subject of immigration, and then, as we saw, arguing that states have almost unlimited discretion to admit or to reject migrants and to decide on the terms of their admission.

It is sometimes claimed that one exception to this rule is provided by Kant, who in his essay *Perpetual Peace* of 1795, spoke of the principle of "cosmopolitan right" that required those who arrived on the territory of a foreign state to be received without hostility.[25] Kant called this requirement "the natural right of hospitality," and some commentators have used this idea to develop a case for more open borders.[26] According to Kant himself, however, the right has a limited scope: it amounts essentially to the liberty to attempt to establish a relationship with the inhabitants of a country, especially for purposes of commerce, and moreover these inhabitants are entitled to turn the stranger away "if this can be done without causing his death."[27] It is explicitly *not* the right to settle, which according to Kant would require a specific contract with the natives. Kant, therefore, recognizes no general right to immigrate, although he does make use of the idea of the common ownership of the earth to justify the right of hospitality.[28]

Coming forward in time, the most influential work of political philosophy written in the later twentieth century, John Rawls's *A Theory of Justice*, avoids the issue of immigration altogether by assuming that the principles of justice it defends are to apply to a society whose membership is already fixed.[29] As he later put it, his theory was meant to apply to a "well-ordered society," conceived as "an ongoing society, a self-sufficient association of human beings which, like a nation-state, controls a connected territory . . . a closed system; there are no significant relations to other societies, and no one enters from without, for all are born into it to lead a complete life."[30] When in his late work *The Law of Peoples*, Rawls turned to consider principles to govern interactions between states, he continued to set aside the issue of immigration, arguing that the causes that produce large-scale immigration in the world today would no longer exist in a world that complied with the principles he was setting out: "The problem of immigration is not, then, simply left aside, but is eliminated as a serious problem in a realistic utopia."[31] Rawls's reluctance to address the topic is fairly easy to understand. His entire political philosophy was centered on the idea of a social contract between people who cooperated to their mutual advantage, treated one another as equals, and sought to discover principles that all could agree to live by. Immigrants do not fit into that picture, since the first question that needs answering is whether they should be invited to join the social contract in the first place. There is no obvious way to extend the principles that should apply *within* "a system of social co-operation designed to advance the good of those taking part in it"[32] to those who are not yet members.

Rawls wrote from within the state-centric tradition of political philosophy. One might expect that those who now depart from this tradition to take up a global perspective would find the issue of immigration more tractable, because they are likely to consider the distinction between those inside the state and those outside as morally irrelevant at a fundamental level. However, they too may have difficulty in getting to grips with the *specific* relationship between immigrant and receiving state. For the immigrant is not just an outsider. Someone who is actively seeking to enter the United Kingdom or the United States is not in the same position as someone currently residing in Bangladesh, say, who at best might be the beneficiary of a general responsibility to provide aid shared by all the citizens of rich countries. By arriving at the border, or indeed crossing it illegally, the migrant is putting herself at the mercy of the receiving state. What happens to her next will depend very largely on what the state decides to do—accept or reject her application to enter, and, if her application is unsuccessful, return her to the place she came from or send her to a third country. Because she has made herself vulnerable to the state's power in these respects, she also has moral claims against it that her cousin who has stayed behind in Bangladesh does not have. (This is an assumption to be justified later on in the book.) So although a cosmopolitan political philosophy might be expected to reach conclusions that are supportive of the claims of all (actual and prospective) migrants, it may have little to say about the specific cases of those who are actively attempting to immigrate.

This point can be illustrated by considering the most comprehensive treatment of immigration from a cosmopolitan perspective to date, Joseph Carens's *The Ethics of Immigration*.[33] Carens has much that is important and insightful to say about the treatment that immigrants are owed by the states they enter, but in order to do so he brackets off his cosmopolitanism for most of the book and assumes that states are justified in controlling their borders, selecting those who enter, and extending special treatment to their own citizens. In the closing chapters, he switches perspective and presents the case for open borders on cosmopolitan grounds. He makes it quite clear why he adopts this approach. In order to say something relevant to public policy in a world in which states do in fact guard their borders quite jealously, he argues, one needs to work within a statist framework. Nevertheless, there is a potentially a deep problem of inconsistency here.[34] If one's underlying commitments are indeed cosmopolitan, then it will be difficult to take seriously the justifications that are usually given to support policies such as requiring immigrants to take citizenship tests or affirm their loyalty to the state they have joined. One can assess how onerous these requirements are, and judge their acceptability on that basis, but underneath one must find all such practices unjustified. Imagine someone who is fundamentally opposed to marriage being asked for advice on a friend's wedding arrangements. It will be hard to make suggestions that are not in some way colored by the thought that the whole enterprise is a mistake. At best the advice will amount to damage limitation.

In Chapter 2, I discuss cosmopolitanism in general terms as a background to the debate over immigration. Here I simply want to indicate why, even if one is convinced by the general arguments in its favor, it may be less helpful than one might suppose in thinking about the practice of immigration, where this involves not only the question "should borders be open or closed?" but a much wider set of issues about the selection of immigrants, the treatment of refugees, integration policy, and so forth. Thinking about cosmopolitan approaches is, however, a good way of focusing on the question of what we should take as given and what we should regard as amenable to change when discussing immigration. How realistic or idealistic should we be? For example, should we take for granted a world made up of separate states in the first place? Should we assume that global inequalities will be roughly as large as they are now? How else might the current international order be changed?

The argument for swallowing a considerable dose of realism here is simply that the immigration *issue* would either disappear altogether or at least become much less pressing in a world that was configured quite differently from our own. Suppose there were no separate states, but simply administrative districts accountable to a world government of some sort. There would then be no immigration in the sense in which we understand it. People would still move from district to district, just as they do between regions in a federal state now, and it might be necessary to have policies that deterred or encouraged these movements, but nobody would enjoy a fundamental change of status by virtue of migration. Or suppose that states remained the basic sources of political authority, but the world was "distributively just" insofar as conditions of life—civil and political rights as well as economic living standards—were more or less the same everywhere.[35] Under these circumstances, there would still be some movement between states, as people found particular reasons for wanting to live in one rather than another, but (1) the volume of movement would predictably be much smaller than in a world such as ours, disfigured by gross economic inequalities, and (2) movements would be multilateral and largely reciprocal because there would be no general reason (climate or natural beauty aside) for preferring to live in one state rather than another. If we assume a fully just world, there would be no refugees, and no one seeking to escape desperate poverty. So all the factors that make immigration such a controversial issue for us would be absent in this hypothetical world. One could therefore "solve" the immigration question by prescribing that the world should become stateless or distributively just, but how much practical light would that throw on our own predicament?[36]

The approach I shall take will be realist in another sense as well. I can explain this by saying that this will be a work of political philosophy rather than of ethics. It will ask about the institutions and policies we should adopt in dealing with immigration rather than trying to tell individual people how they ought to behave. To understand the relevance of this point, consider the evidence referred to earlier in the chapter about the effects of immigration and ethnic diversity on support for the welfare state. These effects are usually explained in terms of diminished levels of trust: people are less likely to trust those whom they perceive as "different," and therefore less likely to support services that they believe will be used by these groups. How should we respond to this evidence? One way is to say that it reveals prejudice. People are assuming something negative about those who come from foreign lands or who dress in unfamiliar ways, and this assumption is unwarranted. There is no reason to think that people who look and behave a little differently from us are therefore less trustworthy. Instead we should treat people as equals unless we have specific evidence that they are going to break the terms of the social contract. So any problems that immigration may currently pose for the survival of the welfare state can be resolved by promulgating a norm that people ought to follow, one that follows from basic moral principles. This illustrates what I am calling an ethical approach to immigration. In contrast, a political approach gives greater weight to the evidence about immigration, trust, and support for welfare. It recognizes that the problem is real and needs to be solved collectively, by a policy initiative or an institutional change. That solution could take different forms: it might involve reducing the rate of immigration, cutting back on welfare, or finding practical ways of increasing interpersonal trust in culturally diverse societies. Opting for the third solution, to emphasize the point, cannot mean simply telling people that they should be less prejudiced and more trusting of strangers. It might, for example, require adopting policies in housing or education that put people from different cultural backgrounds, including immigrants, into closer day-to-day contact with each other. It will be a further empirical question whether or not these policies are likely to succeed. Looking at immigration through the lens of political philosophy involves asking how the principles and values we collectively endorse can be pursued consistently with one another in the light of the best available evidence, including evidence about how far it is possible to change individual behavior and the beliefs and attitudes that lie behind it.

The title of my book in one way reflects this approach.[37] Some readers have found it provocative. Why call immigrants "strangers," and why assume a homogeneous "we" in whose midst they are being set down? I believe, though, that it captures how immigration is often experienced, at least on first encounter, in settled societies most of whose members have a sense that they and their ancestors are deeply rooted in a place.[38] Individual people will react to the presence of a stranger in many different ways, including positively embracing the chance of experiencing and understanding a new way of life; others will be disturbed and respond more negatively. In either case, there is going to be some disruption to existing cultural patterns: new cuisines, new forms of dress, new languages, new religious practices, new ways of using public space. The challenges this poses need to be reflected in the way we think about movement across borders. As I have argued in this chapter, immigration is not merely a matter of weighing up economic gains and losses or of protecting human rights. It also raises difficult questions about the way we understand ourselves as members of political communities, with long histories and rich cultures. But to say this is already to take one side in an ongoing debate about the foundations of political morality, which Chapter 2 will attempt to explore.

Cosmopolitanism, Compatriot Partiality, and Human Rights

ON ARRIVING AT IMMIGRATION CONTROL in an international airport, as any seasoned traveler knows, one is likely to confront two lines of human beings: one short and fast-moving, the other much longer and often maddeningly sluggish. The shorter line is for returning citizens who have only to show that their face matches a valid passport in order to pass through; the longer line is for everyone else, those whose claim to enter the country has to be vindicated under one or other heading (tourist, asylum seeker, temporary worker, etc.), by producing visas and other relevant documents, answering unfriendly questions from immigration officials, and possibly undergoing yet more unpleasant scrutiny. Here we see the state exercising its right to discriminate between people; as we dutifully join the appropriate queue, we take for granted that state officials can treat human beings quite differently simply because some are citizens and others are not. But the tedium of being caught in the aliens line is merely symptomatic of a much wider practice in which states treat their own members far better than they treat foreigners, not merely as they pass through border control but by bestowing upon them a plethora of rights and opportunities that are denied to outsiders. This again, we normally take for granted. But how can it be justified? We can't think properly about the specific issue of immigration without knowing where we stand on the wider issue that this chapter addresses, which is whether and to what extent states are justified in showing what I shall call "compatriot partiality"—treating their own citizens more favorably than outsiders.

We need to ask this rather basic question because until we have an answer we have no way of assessing the claims that someone who wants to immigrate can make against the state she wishes to join. Consider a person who applies to enter a country because she sees some advantage in moving there: a new job, a better climate, a different range of cultural possibilities. Once admitted she will have access to economic opportunities she would not have elsewhere and also typically to various welfare benefits such as housing and health care; later on she may apply to become a full citizen. So her interests are considerably affected by the decision to admit her or to refuse her entry. But how much weight should the host state attach to those interests? If it is a democracy it will operate on the understanding that it should pay equal regard to the interests of each of its citizens. Must it do the same in the case of the immigrant, or is it permitted to discount her claims merely because she is not yet a member? Might it attach no weight to her claims at all and make its admission decision simply by considering whether allowing her to immigrate is likely to benefit or harm *existing* members? Furthermore, what about the effects of emigration on the countries from which the immigrants are moving: what weight, if any, should be attached to those? In Chapter 1, I referred to the "brain drain" issue—the possibility that migration might be starving some poor countries of the educated talent that they need in order to develop economically or to staff a health care system. But why should this be of concern to the states that benefit from the migration? Again we can't answer this without taking a stand on the wider issue of social and global justice: what political communities owe, respectively, to their own members and to those who belong elsewhere.

So in this chapter I will lay out a position on compatriot partiality and the external obligations of states that forms a backdrop to the discussion of immigration in the chapters that follow. Some of the arguments I make have been developed in greater detail elsewhere: here I try to bring together the main ideas in a relatively concise way.[1]

As we have just seen, states routinely act on the assumption that they are entitled to treat their own citizens very differently from foreigners. But many political philosophers are critical of the partiality toward compatriots that this reveals. Such critics often describe themselves as cosmopolitans and appeal to cosmopolitan principles when mounting a case for open borders, as for example in the case of Joseph Carens whom I referred to in Chapter 1. But pinning down exactly what it means to be a cosmopolitan is a difficult task. Indeed some suggest that the term is so amorphous that it no longer serves any useful identifying function in debates about global justice.[2] One source of confusion is that "cosmopolitanism" can refer to an identity, a political proposal, or a moral standpoint: it is the third of these that will concern us here. In the first case, a cosmopolitan is someone who professes to have no loyalties to particular places or cultures but declares himself free to pick and choose the best that is on offer anywhere in the world to which he has access.[3] His only identity is as a human being among other human beings. Political cosmopolitanism, by contrast, can take various forms. One is belief in and advocacy of world government: the idea that supreme political authority should rest with a single body that represents all human beings, albeit that below this there can exist many subsidiary forms of regional and national government. Another is the belief that in their political activities people should regard themselves as "citizens of the world" who pursue just causes regardless of where the targets of their activity happen to be located. Thus if one is campaigning to rid the world of torture, one should pay no more attention to cases of torture in the country where one holds legal citizenship than to torture that is occurring half way across the world—unless it so happens that one can be more effective by targeting what is taking place locally.

Political cosmopolitanism often goes hand in hand with the third conception, moral cosmopolitanism, but they are nonetheless distinct. Moral cosmopolitanism can be defined simply as a belief in the equal worth of all human beings.[4] But this axiom by itself does not convey anything very definite, other than that it is unacceptable to respect and treat people differently simply by virtue of some (morally irrelevant) feature such as their gender or skin color. Since discrimination of this kind has often been routinely practiced, declaring in favor of moral cosmopolitanism is by no means a trivial step. But how far exactly does it take us? According to the strongest interpretation, it implies that the fundamental duties we owe to our fellow human beings are exactly the same regardless of the relationship in which we stand toward them. In concrete terms what we are required to do for them may vary: one person may need my assistance while another does not. But aside from such individual claims stemming from differences in needs, preferences, and so on, I must treat them in precisely the same way. Any form of partiality, which of course includes showing special concern for one's compatriots, on this reading contravenes the cosmopolitan principle of equal moral worth. So that principle immediately puts into question routine state practices such as the one that opened this chapter (the immigration lines), where people receive different treatment merely on account of their nationality.

But how plausible is strong cosmopolitanism? The problem is that it seems to rule out not only partiality toward one's compatriots, but any kind of special concern at all, such as concern for our families, friends, and colleagues. If recognizing the equal worth of human beings excludes showing any sort of preference for those close to us, then our everyday behavior would need to change radically, and few have been willing to embrace that conclusion, since it appears to mean giving up much of what we do that gives value to our lives. Our relationships to families and friends involve giving special consideration to their wishes and their needs when deciding how to use our time and our resources. Can we do that while still being cosmopolitans?

We could abandon the strong version of cosmopolitanism in favor of a much weaker version. This would say, first, that we must always consider the effects of our actions on all those who will bear the consequences, no matter who they are or whether they are in any way connected to us; and, second, that if there are no relevant differences between people, we should afford them equal consideration. Weak cosmopolitanism can be illustrated with the aid of a simple example.[5] Suppose I am out hiking in a remote area, and I come across somebody who has run into serious difficulties: she is dehydrated, whereas I have water to spare. Virtually everyone would agree that I have reason to help her just because she is a human being in need of help. To turn away and say that her plight is of no concern to me would be immoral. Exactly how far I must go in order to meet my obligation may need further discussion, but the basic point is that I owe her some consideration; I cannot just ignore her. That is the first part of the weak cosmopolitan principle. To illustrate the second part, suppose now that I come across two stranded travelers, both in a bad way. I may not devote all of my attention to one of them just on a whim or because I like the way she looks. I must show them equal consideration (which may or may not mean treating them in exactly the same way, if for example one is injured and the other isn't). All of this applies regardless of the identity of the people involved: I may be hiking in some faraway land and have nothing in common beyond humanity itself with the strangers I encounter.

I have illustrated weak cosmopolitanism by referring to an individual person's moral obligations, but the principle can be applied in the same way to the actions of a state, where it requires simply that states must consider the impact of the policies they pursue on those outside of their borders. They cannot simply give zero weight to the effects when those involved are noncitizens. So if burning fossil fuels causes global warming, which in turn makes some regions of the earth less able to support human life, this result cannot simply be dismissed as irrelevant by national policy makers. But weak cosmopolitanism alone tells us nothing about how much weight should be attached to the interests of different groups of people who might be affected by a state's policy, other than that *some* reason must be given if they are going to be assigned unequal weights. It is consistent, therefore, with showing strong partiality for the interests of compatriots.

So cosmopolitanism as a moral outlook seems to be profoundly ambiguous. In its strong form it readily excludes any preference for one's compatriots, but by simultaneously ruling out other forms of partiality that are integral to a worthwhile human life, it becomes hard to accept. In its weak form, by contrast, it reduces to a broad humanitarianism that does not rule out anything much at all beyond repugnant ideologies that regard some human lives as of no value. The interesting question is whether we can find some intermediate view that gives reasons for rejecting strong cosmopolitanism but has more to say about our obligations to people outside our own community than weak cosmopolitanism provides. To answer it, we need to look more closely at how relationships between people generate special obligations, and which relationships matter from this point of view.

There is one way of thinking about the question that is regularly advocated by strong cosmopolitans anxious to deflect that charge that their position even rules out showing special concern for family and friends. This introduces the idea of a division of moral labor. It is consistent with the principle of moral equality, the claim goes, to show special concern toward those you are associated with *provided* that people elsewhere are doing likewise, so that everyone ends up being somebody's particular responsibility to look after. I pay special attention to my own children, and you to yours; my state attends to the welfare of its citizens, and yours does the same. The overall goal of equal treatment is most effectively achieved by giving each agent a particular set of responsibilities, which, as it happens, are those our natural sentiments in any case predispose us to accept.[6]

This idea of a moral division of labor at first appears to be an attractive way of allowing us to focus our moral energies on those who are close to us while at the same time indirectly showing respect for human beings at large. But it faces two problems. First, it seems not to capture the way that we actually understand our special responsibilities. The loyalty we feel toward our families and our friends is unconditional—meaning not that it knows no bounds, but that it isn't conditional on other people also being shown the same loyalty. Of course we hope that they are: we hope that every child will receive at least as much care as we give to ours. But the way that we understand our own responsibility doesn't depend on that being the case. So if the division of labor approach is trying to show that we can act as good cosmopolitans while acknowledging special responsibilities to those who are close to us, it has to go behind our backs, so to speak, focusing on the combined effects of our actions rather than the intentions and motives for which they were performed.[7]

But, second, it is very doubtful whether in any case it can be made to work. Because if the aim is to show that special concern can be consistent with strong cosmopolitanism, then we must assume a world in which each person has a similar opportunity to be afforded special treatment by *someone*. But that is clearly not the case in the actual world, whether we are thinking about intimate relationships or about political communities. Some lucky people have many friends to offer them support when needed; others have few or none at all. Some live in states that are able to provide everyone with a rich array of opportunities, while others are far less fortunate. So the conclusion must be that the division of labor approach can be reconciled with (strong) cosmopolitanism only by assuming that we already inhabit a hypothetical world of far greater material equality than our own. In the world we live in, cosmopolitan responsibilities that require people everywhere to receive similar treatment couldn't be discharged by focusing attention on those who are close to us, whether families or compatriots.

As an alternative to the cosmopolitan division of labor, we should begin with the idea of associative obligations—obligations that we have simply in virtue of the relationships in which we stand to other people rather than as part of some universal scheme—and explore how they arise and where their moral limits are set.[8] Starting again with the example of close personal relationships, two factors are important. First, these relationships have intrinsic value: our lives are simply better by virtue of our involvement in them. Second, the relationships could not exist in the form that they do unless they were understood to give rise to special duties: if I don't believe that I owe more to my friend than I would owe to a passing acquaintance, then my relation to that person is not in fact one of friendship but something else. I take these claims to be relatively uncontroversial. What is much more open to debate is how they apply to relationships that are wider in scope and in particular to the type of relationship that exists between the members of a nation-state. Could associative obligations arise in this case as well?

A major difficulty in answering this question is that the relationship that exists between compatriots is multidimensional, and it is not obvious which of these dimensions are crucial for generating special obligations. We can distinguish at least three broad strands. First, the members are involved in an inclusive scheme of cooperation by which they provide one another with all of the amenities of life, in particular through a division of tasks. There is an economic system that produces goods and services, and ancillary systems that insure people against various risks, including that of being no longer able to contribute to and reciprocally benefit from the productive economy. In principle the scheme works to everyone's advantage: it enables us to enjoy a much higher standard of life than we could achieve in the absence of cooperation. Second, members relate to one another as citizens, participating in an elaborate political/legal scheme that on the one hand requires them to obey a multitude of laws, but on the other gives them an array of legal rights, including a right of political participation that allows them collectively to control and shape the scheme as a whole. Third, they also relate to one another as fellow nationals, people who share a broadly similar set of cultural values and a sense of belonging to a particular place. They think of themselves as a distinct community of people with historical roots that exists as one such community among others.[9]

One question that will need to be answered shortly is whether the third strand is indeed a necessary complement to the other two. In other words, must a modern state also be a nation-state, with members sharing a cultural identity as well as cooperating economically and associating as equal citizens? But setting that aside for the moment, what makes this form of association intrinsically valuable? First, it enables people to coexist on terms of justice. By putting in place a set of rules to govern ownership, employment, taxation, access to education and health care, and so forth, they are able to ensure that the benefits and burdens of economic cooperation are fairly distributed among them. Second, they are able to exercise some degree of control over the future direction of their association: they can decide what its priorities should be; for example, whether to exploit or to conserve natural resources, whether to spend money subsidizing sports or the arts. Each person taken separately only exercises a miniscule amount of control, of course, but even those who lack political office know that by combining together they can reverse the direction of change by removing one government and installing another. In short they can achieve, within practical limits, both distributive justice and collective freedom.[10]

These values are sufficient to create associative obligations: to respect existing laws and policies, while engaging actively through voting and in other ways to change them when they are less than just, and more generally to uphold the terms of the association. It should be clear that unless these obligations are recognized and fulfilled, the features of the modern state I have been describing could not be preserved. They can be described as obligations of reciprocity: each member owes his fellow citizens the duty of maintaining justice between them, so long as she reasonably expects others to perform their duties in turn.

What difference does it make if we add national identity to this picture? Does this bring an additional source of value to the relationship? I believe that it does, though not all of those who want to defend associative obligations between citizens will agree—they will treat shared nationality simply as a widely observed psychological fact without moral significance.[11] With national identity comes a kind of solidarity that is lacking if one looks just at economic and political relationships. People feel emotionally attached to one another because they share this identity. They feel that they belong together and have responsibilities to each other that are not simply the result of existing institutions and practices. Their association becomes deeper because the political community conceives of itself as extended in time, indeed often as reaching back into antiquity. This also means that the obligations it creates stretch backward and forward—they can be inherited from the past, and owed to future generations. No two nations are the same: each contains a unique blend or mixture of cultures as a result of the various groups that have contributed to that long history. Furthermore, national identity attaches the community to a particular homeland whose special features often contribute in an important way to the identity itself, whether these are distinctive landscapes, buildings of historic significance, or sites where key events in the nation's history took place. So where citizens also share a national identity, their association has the further feature that they can explain why they belong together and why they should exercise their citizenship in this particular place.

The difference that national identity makes can first be seen when we face proposals to dismember the state through secession. If relationships within the state are simply those of economic cooperation and citizenship, there is no obvious reason to resist the breakup. The relationships will reform within each unit on a smaller scale (there might be reasons of efficiency that count for or against the split, but there are no reasons of principle to resist it, since the values associated with economic cooperation and citizenship will be preserved in any case). Where people are also related as conationals, in contrast, they will resist dismemberment because they attach value to nation-wide self-determination: they want to form a single unit controlling its own destiny as far as possible.[12] Moreover, a state that is also a nation-state has a more communitarian character by virtue of the way that its members identify with each other, making it easier to adopt policies that favor the less well-off, especially those who are able to make little or no contribution to the productive economy. Admittedly this is not so easy to demonstrate with hard empirical evidence.[13] Nevertheless, it seems true that the states whose citizens have been most ready to promote egalitarian forms of social justice, such as the Scandinavian social democracies, have also been those in which national identity is at its strongest.

The value of national identity is more controversial than the value of citizenship. Its critics lay several charges against it. One is that whereas citizens in one place have no particular reason to claim that their association is superior to other citizen bodies elsewhere, national identity leads more readily to assertions of national superiority and inferiority and therefore indirectly to attempts to dominate or even absorb rival nations. Such outcomes do not seem to be inevitable: many nations coexist peacefully and happily with their neighbors. Nevertheless, the historical record of nationalism is marred by dark episodes of the former kind. A second and connected reason is that the territorial dimension of nationality, which is in one way a source of strength, may also turn into a source of conflict whenever there are disputes about where the boundaries of national homelands should be drawn. Finally, it is often argued that national identities are in an important sense fictitious because they rely on the creation of a single narrative that explains what it means to belong to this or that nation—a national story—which is at the very least highly selective and in the worst case starkly at odds with the historical facts. This myth-laden character, it is argued, shows that national identities have little or no intrinsic value, even if they prove to have instrumental value by enabling the citizens who share them to work together more effectively and by motivating them to support social justice.

So there are reasons that can be advanced on both sides of the argument about the value of national identity. Given that in the existing world, the citizens of viable states seem everywhere to possess such identities, why does it matter whether we acknowledge their value or not? It makes a difference in particular when we are thinking about the issue of immigration. Since immigrants will, typically, not already identify in national terms with the political community they are joining, it must influence our thinking both about the issue of admission and about the issue of immigrant integration. How far is it a legitimate objective of public policy to preserve and possibly strengthen the national identity of existing citizens, and how far must that identity change in order to accommodate the cultural values of migrants who enter? This question is only of significance *if* we assume that national identity is something worth preserving. Were we, in contrast, to believe that economic cooperation and citizenship are together enough to constitute a properly functioning state, then questions of identity could be set aside as essentially private matters that should not be allowed to influence the discussion. All that would matter is that immigrants should be able to integrate economically and politically with existing members of the community, and a rule of neutrality over cultural questions should be observed when public policy is being made.

I shall return to this issue later in the book. The point to notice for now is that associative obligations toward compatriots can be defended in several different ways, depending on which aspect of the relationship between compatriots is highlighted. There is now quite a large literature in political philosophy concerning the scope of distributive justice—contributors to this literature try to identify the particular feature of relationships among citizens in virtue of which they owe one another duties of justice that they do not owe to people elsewhere.[14] It may well prove that the quest to identify any one such feature has been misguided and that a better approach is to recognize the multidimensional character of the relationships in question, indeed, to recognize that social justice is complex—it includes more than one principle—precisely because it is grounded in relationships that are likewise complex.[15] Since the nature of social justice is not our immediate concern here, there is no need to delve into this literature. What is more important is to trace the limits of associative obligations, regardless of how exactly they are derived. Their existence as freestanding moral duties negates strong cosmopolitanism and in particular shows that justice permits us to do less for would-be immigrants than we are required to do for citizens. But less is not nothing. Assuming the weak cosmopolitan premise of the equal moral worth of all human beings, what obligations arise across state boundaries? What must citizens do for those who are not their compatriots?

These international obligations fall into two categories: obligations owed to individual human beings, and obligations owed to other political communities. Obligations in the second category can be described broadly as obligations of fairness. States interact with one another in many ways, sometimes in order to achieve benefits that could not be acquired by acting alone, in other cases sharing costs that have to be paid to solve global problems such as climate change. When they interact in these ways, justice requires them to allocate the costs and benefits fairly. How should the gains arising from trade be shared? How much economic growth must each state sacrifice in order to avert global warming? These are important questions that arise whether or not one adopts the strong cosmopolitan position that I identified at the beginning of this chapter. For present purposes, however, they are less important than the obligations that states owe to individual noncitizens, and these are best understood in the first place as obligations to respect human rights.[16]

To say that states in their external dealings are bound to respect the human rights of outsiders is to say something that will command widespread agreement. Respecting their human rights appears to be a straightforward way of acknowledging the equal moral worth of all human beings. Disagreement may emerge, however, when we ask how human rights are to be identified and what exactly it means to respect them. We cannot assume that there is some definitive list of human rights waiting to be consulted. There are of course important documents such as the Universal Declaration of Human Rights adopted by the United Nations (UN) in 1948 and the later International Covenant on Civil and Political Rights and International Covenant on Economic, Social and Cultural Rights.[17] These are relevant for our understanding of human rights, but they are not decisive, not least because even the rights that are formally announced in these documents need a good deal of interpretation. It is also important to notice that the aim of these documents was primarily to set standards that all states should aim to meet domestically; it is only more recently that human rights have come to play a significant role in foreign policy, and it may be that for this purpose a somewhat different understanding of these rights is needed.

To understand how human rights can be justified, we may begin by observing that there are requirements that people everywhere need to have fulfilled if they are going to lead decent human lives.[18] It is not an embarrassment that the concrete form these requirements take may differ from place to place. One requirement, for example, is for adequate clothing, but this may mean a fur coat in one part of the world and a cotton shirt in another. The underlying need is the same in both cases. A more important contrast is between the conditions necessary for a decent human life anywhere and the conditions necessary for a decent life in one particular society, given the expectations and conventions that are present there. This contrast allows us to distinguish between human rights proper and what are better called societal rights, or rights of citizenship. Human rights are the rights that people must have if they are securely to have the opportunity to meet their basic needs; rights of citizenship provide the conditions under which a person can participate fully in the social and political life of the society to which they belong. The second set of rights builds upon and extends the first, but we need to keep them apart because human rights potentially create *international* obligations whereas citizenship rights do not. Securing rights of citizenship for everyone in a particular society is a matter of domestic politics; other countries must not thwart this process but otherwise need not be involved.

Where human rights are at stake, however, a failure on the part of one state may oblige other states to take action, such as providing aid or intervening more directly to protect rights. How this responsibility should be assigned is a question we will need to return to shortly.

It may not be obvious that we can actually identify "conditions for a decent human life anywhere" or what I shall call basic human needs. I assume that we can do this because there is such a thing as the human form of life that we can recognize as a common thread running through the many different human cultures that have existed now and at earlier historical times.[19] Underneath this diversity there are activities and practices that are present everywhere, unless they have been deliberately suppressed or the material means to engage in them are not available. Human beings work productively, play, raise families, make music, participate in religious rituals, and so forth, and in order to do these things, certain preconditions must be fulfilled. We can then define human needs as the needs that must be met if people are to be able to lead minimally decent lives, engaging, if they so choose, in each of the activities on the list that make up the human form of life. And correspondingly, human rights are the rights whose possession allows people to meet these needs, securing them against various potential threats, whether these arise from natural forces, from other human beings, or from the state itself.

What, more concretely, should be included on the list of human rights if we see them as grounded in this way on basic human needs? Broadly speaking, they will fall into four categories. First, there will be rights whose purpose is to ensure that people have the material means to live a minimally decent life, such as rights to food, shelter, and medicine. Second, there will be rights to specific forms of freedom, such as freedom of speech and freedom of occupation, that allow them to engage in the core human activities according to their own predilections and capacities. Third, there will be rights that enable people to form social relationships with others, such as freedom of association and the right to marry and raise a family. Fourth, there will be other rights that do not correspond so directly to human needs, but whose purpose is to protect people's enjoyment of the rights in the first three categories by providing them with safeguards. The right to equality before the law, the right to a fair trial, and the right to political participation belong here: without them, people would be vulnerable to forms of political oppression that would jeopardize their more fundamental rights.

Much more needs to be said to expand upon the brief sketch of human rights I have offered in the preceding paragraphs. The main point to emphasize is that the purpose of human rights is to identify a threshold that must not be crossed rather than to describe a social ideal. Much of what human beings aspire to reaches far beyond the realm of basic rights: a society that secured these rights and did nothing else for its members would be a drab and unexciting place. Why set the threshold so low? In fact it is not so low when set against the actual conditions under which millions of human beings are living today: not only those who live under repressive regimes but also those who live in conditions of material poverty, with inadequate nutrition and access to medical care, are having their human rights infringed. But the key point is that human rights should be understood and defined in such a way that they can create obligations toward the right-holder, even on the part of those who have no preexisting relationship to her. Recall that throughout this chapter I am taking for granted what I called the weak cosmopolitan premise, which says that we are required to treat people with equal concern, understood first to mean that we cannot simply ignore their interests when we are deciding how to act. Important though this premise is, it does not in general mean that we have *obligations* toward them, and especially not obligations of justice that in principle third parties can force us to discharge. If we abstract from all the specific relationships in which we stand toward other human beings, such obligations arise only when their claims against us become urgent—when failing to meet them is likely to cause significant harm.[20] Human rights, understood in the way I have proposed, are urgent claims in that sense, precisely because they serve to meet needs that all human beings share regardless of their cultural or social affiliation. They are not luxury items; they form a moral bedrock. To fulfil that role, they must be understood minimally, as providing the condition for a decent human life, but not more than that.

What obligations do we bear, individually and collectively, in response to the human rights of others? On this question, philosophical opinion is divided. On one side stand those who maintain that the obligations in question should be interpreted simply as negative duties, that is as duties not to violate other people's human rights through active interference. I breach a negative duty when I attack others (violating the right to bodily security), when I prevent them from practicing their faith (violating the right to freedom of religion), or when I pollute the water source that they depend on (violating their right to subsistence). On this view, I have no obligation to take positive steps to provide people with the resources they need to exercise their rights—I am of course permitted to do so, but positive provision is not required. Conversely, other philosophers believe that (depending on the case) the duties imposed by human rights may be either positive or negative, or both together. They will argue that there is something perverse in maintaining that while I may not deprive a fellow human being of water by destroying her well, I am not obliged to help dig the well when it has yet to be dug and its water is needed—since the same right to subsistence is involved in both cases.

The main argument offered in favor of the "negative duties only" position is that human rights, like rights of other kinds, must correspond to clear obligations assigned to particular agents, and negative duties meet this condition because they fall on everyone without exception, while what they require is simply that we should not interfere with other people's enjoyment and exercise of their rights.[21] The duties can be fulfilled, metaphorically speaking, if everyone sits at home and leaves others alone. But with positive duties, their assignment is much less clear: where human rights are not fulfilled because of inadequate provision, who bears the corresponding obligations, and how much must be done to discharge them? Whose well am I required to dig, and after that how many more wells?

There are cases in which the obligation to protect a human right falls directly on an individual person, but much more commonly responsibility it is borne collectively, by states in particular. And the first obligation that each state bears is to protect and fulfill the human rights of its own citizens. A state that fails to do this, despite having the necessary resources, is to that extent an illegitimate state. Here, then, there is no ambiguity about who bears the duties, both negative and positive, that correspond to human rights. But what if one state either cannot or will not protect these rights internally? Responsibility then falls upon all those agencies, primarily other states, that have the capacity to do so. Discharging that responsibility can take various forms, depending on the case. It might require sending material aid, say in circumstances where human rights are threatened by famine; it might mean applying pressure or imposing sanctions on the state whose policies are violating its citizens' rights; it might, in extreme cases, require forcible humanitarian intervention and regime change; and finally it might mean allowing those whose rights are under threat to migrate across state borders to a place of safety. All of these measures are likely to carry significant costs. So the question that arises is which state or states should be asked to undertake them? We are starting from the assumption that every state capable of doing so shares in the responsibility to protect human rights. But how can that be translated into specific obligations that accrue to individual states?

Here we need to distinguish between situations in which the responsibility is indivisible, so that a single agent needs to act on it, and cases where it can be distributed among several. In the former case, we can try to identify a state that has some special connection to the country where the human rights shortfalls are occurring.[22] This connection may take different forms. It might arise from geographical proximity, from historical ties (such as the tie between a colonial power and its former colonies), from cultural links (of language or religion, for example), or from special capacity on the part of the state in question. These links may in themselves be largely devoid of moral significance. But the problem is that one state needs to take responsibility, and so we need to find some special factor that makes discharging the responsibility salient for a particular state. On the other hand, precisely because the connections at stake may be weak and somewhat debatable, it will be hard to justify imposing an enforceable obligation to protect human rights in circumstances of this kind.

Perhaps more commonly, responsibility can be shared more widely, and then we need to discover principles for distributing it fairly. One such principle is equal cost sharing; each state should contribute to the costs of rights protection in proportion to the size of its population, or perhaps in proportion to its GDP, to reflect the fact that the real costs of contributing diminish as states become richer (this principle can be seen at work in the current norm that states should contribute 0.7 percent of GDP as foreign aid). Or a more complex formula may be adopted, perhaps to reflect states' unequal capacity to contribute to particular human rights–related operations, or their greater or lesser degrees of responsibility for creating the situation in which human rights violations are occurring. Later in the book we shall need to explore these possibilities more carefully, particularly with respect to states' responsibility to admit refugees. Here I want simply to contrast two broad positions one may hold concerning states' obligations to protect the human rights of those outside their own borders.

The first position holds that the obligation is unconditional and open-ended. Although it may be better for practical purposes for responsibility to be shared along the lines sketched in the previous paragraph, ultimately any state that has the capacity to protect human rights has the obligation to do so, single-handedly if need be. And this is a matter of justice. One way of putting the position is that justice for the victims of human rights violations must always trump fairness between states. A state that has to shoulder more of the burden than it would do under a fair distribution of responsibility certainly has a complaint against noncompliant states, but it is nonetheless required to act.

The second position, by contrast, holds that the obligation to protect human rights extends only to doing what a fair distribution of responsibility demands; or at least that is all that a state can be required to do as a matter of justice. It may choose to do more, but this would be a matter of humanitarian concern, not something mandated by justice.[23] Why is the contrast important? It matters if, instead of adopting strong cosmopolitanism, we allow that there can be legitimate partiality for compatriots. As agents of their citizens, states will then have a special obligation to promote their particular interests. That obligation is limited by a contrary obligation to respect and protect the human rights of outsiders. Most obviously, no state may pursue the interests of its members regardless of the harm that it inflicts on foreigners. But if the obligation to protect human rights has the restricted form that position two suggests, then a state that intends to do more than fairness demands would need to gain the explicit consent of its citizens. For it is proposing to devote resources that could otherwise be used to promote social justice at home to the cause of human rights protection abroad, despite having already contributed its fair share toward that cause.

It is time to take stock. What I have been exploring in this chapter are the limits to cosmopolitanism as a moral perspective. Assuming as a premise the equal moral worth of all human beings, how far are political communities nonetheless permitted to show special concern for their own members? I have indicated how the relationships that exist among compatriots can be used to ground associative obligations that are internal to such communities. But political communities also have external responsibilities, most notably the responsibility to respect and help protect the human rights of outsiders. I have been exploring how this responsibility should best be understood. But now finally I want to ask whether respect for their human rights is all that those outside the state can ask from its citizens, given the weak cosmopolitan premise I am taking for granted.

Return for a moment to the stranded hiker in the desert who urgently needs water. Since her condition places her human rights in jeopardy, and I am the only available source of remedy, I have an obligation to give her the water she needs, assuming I have a surplus. But now, her need to drink satisfied, she asks whether I could give her one of the books I am carrying in my pack, since she's run out of reading matter. No human right is at issue in this case, and there is no obligation on my part to hand over a book. But I think I must at least consider her request, and if I decide that I have no book I can really spare, I should explain why. In other words, I owe her some consideration: it's a perfectly reasonable request, and I should respond to it with reasons of my own. I don't exactly have to *justify* myself to her if I refuse, but I need to say something.

If this sounds plausible, we can draw a wider conclusion. What weak cosmopolitanism demands, in cases where human rights are *not* at stake, is that if people make claims on us—claims for something that serves their interests—we should always consider them seriously and be ready if necessary to provide reasons for refusal. Indeed if granting the request is virtually costless, we should always accept it. Cicero gave the example of someone asking if he can take a light from the fire that I have made.[24] More generally, to fail to consider such a request amounts to a failure of respect; it treats the person who makes it as though they were of no significance at all.

This conclusion will turn out to matter when we begin to address the specific issue of immigrant admissions. For the immigrant is plainly someone who sees considerable benefit in being allowed to enter. So if we are going to refuse her request, we must give it due consideration and provide reasons for the refusal. But what sort of reasons could these be? Is letting someone enter like allowing them to take a light from your fire—a costless conferral of benefit? Or can we sometimes offer the applicant adequate grounds for refusing? These are questions to be pursued in the chapters that follow.

THREE

Open Borders

AT THE BEGINNING OF CHAPTER 1, I cited some evidence about public hostility to uncontrolled migration. People may welcome some immigration, and they may have quite positive views about individual immigrants, but they tend to be alarmed at the prospect of their state losing control over its borders. For example, in the UK poll I referred to there, and against the background of European Union legislation mandating free movement of people between member states, 80 percent of respondents agreed that the UK government should have the final say over who should be allowed into Britain, and 64 percent said that the government should ignore the threat of legal action and fines if it failed to follow EU rules. The idea, then, that movement across state boundaries should as a matter of principle be unrestricted finds few friends among the general public. Yet many political philosophers are drawn toward this view. They would not say that borders should be completely open under all circumstances: they would concede that if the scale of immigration threatened to create a breakdown in social order, or if the particular immigrants seeking to enter were dangerous people (e.g., they were potential terrorists), some restrictions might be imposed. But the onus would lie on the receiving state to show why such restrictions were justified. The default position is one of free movement, which, these philosophers claim, can be justified by appeal to fundamental moral principles.

In this chapter I explore the main arguments that have been used to justify the open borders view. I shall not aim to be fully comprehensive—for example, I shall not discuss arguments that appeal to economic efficiency (such as the claim that free movement creates a larger and therefore more perfectly competitive market in labor and capital). Applying the general framework set out in the last chapter, I move from arguments that rely on strong cosmopolitan premises to those that appeal only to weak cosmopolitanism. Specifically, I shall consider (1) arguments for open borders that rest on the idea of the common ownership of the earth; (2) arguments that appeal to global equality of opportunity; (3) arguments that postulate a human right to immigrate.

I begin, then, with the idea that the earth as a whole is the common property of all the human beings who inhabit it, from which some draw the corollary that it is wrong to refuse anyone access to part of what they own. If border controls prevent a resident of Niger from entering France, for example, this is unjust, because although the Nigerien may own individual property somewhere in his home society, he also has a claim, in common with everyone else, to the land that is now designated as French territory. This common ownership idea has a long history. It can be found in classical sources, but it is particularly prominent in early modern political philosophy, especially in the work of Hugo Grotius and those who were influenced by him, including Immanuel Kant.[1] But what exactly does it mean to say that human beings are common owners of the planet they inhabit?

There are several possible interpretations. If we examine Grotius's work, he begins from the premise that God has given the world to mankind as a common inheritance, which means that each person is entitled to take the natural resources that he needs to sustain himself on the assumption that this is not to the detriment of anyone else.[2] In a loose sense this arrangement can be described as common ownership, but Grotius makes it clear that it is not common property as we would normally understand it, for the latter would imply that human beings collectively had the right to control access by any of their number to the fruits of the earth, and this is what Grotius explicitly denies. He then explains how private or shared property emerged as people began to develop agriculture and create goods that could be stored up, but the original common right always imposes certain limits on these holdings. The first and most important limit is the right of necessity—that is, a person's right to take whatever is needed to preserve her life even if this means using someone else's property.[3] Initially, Grotius uses examples concerning food, water, and survival at sea, but he adds to these a right of entry to a society and at least temporary residence on the part of those who are endangered through participating in a just war. Other rights are also retained: what Grotius calls "the right of innocent profit," or the right to take and use things when this causes no detriment at all to their owner, such as drinking the water from a stream or Cicero's example of taking a light from someone's fire; the right of passage across territory for peaceful purposes; and the right to occupy land that is currently lying waste.[4] So according to Grotius, when land comes into private ownership or falls under the jurisdiction of a state, the rights that are acquired in this way are always subject to certain limitations stemming from the original common possession: non-owners who qualify under one of the conditions just specified have rights of access.

What bearing does Grotius's doctrine have on the issue of immigration? It plainly does not deliver an unqualified right to immigrate, that is, a right possessed by everyone to move across state borders at will. Instead it grants a limited right of entry to people who fulfill one or more of the relevant criteria. Someone who is driven by necessity can claim the right to enter territory to satisfy his needs, for example a person who is shipwrecked on a foreign shore or a person who crosses a border from a land where he would face starvation. The same applies to a person whose life is threatened by the violence or oppression of other human beings—someone we would now describe as a refugee, a term whose meaning I shall explore more fully in Chapter 5. But necessity also sets limits to the extent of these rights—they are not in most cases rights to permanent residence. The shipwrecked sailors can be asked to take passage back to their home country when they have recovered from their ordeal; once the famine is over, the starving migrants can be asked to return. There may be other reasons to grant them the right to reside permanently, as we shall see in Chapter 5, but here we are just looking at what follows directly from the Grotian idea of common ownership.

Its very title makes it clear that the right of passage cannot yield a full-blown right to immigrate, which would include remaining permanently on the territory that you are passing through. But what about "the right of innocent profit"? It might seem that giving an individual migrant permission to enter is relevantly similar to allowing someone to take a light from your candle, assuming that the migrant intends no harm: so the weak residual claim that he has, stemming from original common ownership, is sufficient. But here there may be a fallacy of composition at work: when thinking about immigration, we cannot think just about the effect of allowing one person to enter. Because the right of innocent profit belongs to everyone, we must contemplate the results of at least a substantial number of people exercising it. This might be beneficial or harmful to the society that they exercise it against, depending on the case (as I argued in Chapter 1), but it cannot be treated as having no effect at all. Again it seems that no general right to immigrate can be derived in this way, since the receiving society may be able to claim, justifiably, that the interests of its members are being adversely affected by the presence of strangers.

Finally, there is the case of land that is lying waste. Grotius recognizes that such land will always remain under the jurisdiction of the state whose sovereign has claimed it, but he maintains that if strangers request to settle there in order to make use of it, their request should be granted. (Similar arguments have been put forward by later philosophers, including Sidgwick and Walzer.[5]) The question, though, is when land should be counted as "waste or barren." What about land that has been kept free of human habitation for environmental or recreational reasons, such as a national park? Or for aesthetic reasons, such as a mountain landscape? These are questions about territorial jurisdiction whose justification we shall shortly be addressing. If, however, we follow Grotius in assuming that jurisdiction can be established "in the Lump," as he puts it, to include "Rivers, Lakes, Ponds, Forests, and uncultivated Mountains,"[6] then it seems that those who hold the territory have the right to decide whether any part of it should be treated as waste. So immigration in order to occupy seemingly barren land would be at the discretion of the receiving state.

There are, however, other ways of understanding the common ownership of the world than Grotius's. Matthias Risse has helpfully distinguished between "Common Ownership," "Joint Ownership," and "Equal Division," with Grotius's view corresponding to the first of these.[7] What then does joint ownership of the earth mean? Here human beings are conceived as a collective body exercising rights of ownership in the same way as commoners exercise rights over a common: they are entitled jointly to decide on the use to be made of the common, in particular how far any member is permitted to extract resources that may become scarce. Before we examine how plausible this conception is when applied to the world as a whole, we should establish what it would entail in the case of immigration. The argument from joint ownership to open borders would be that just as a subgroup of commoners cannot fence off a section of the common and prevent the rest from having access, so a territorial state cannot claim jurisdiction over a portion of the earth if it then proceeds to exclude those who are not citizens—unless the state has been authorized to do so by the whole of humanity. Since we can presume that would-be immigrants will object to their exclusion, borders must remain open if any limited jurisdiction is to be legitimate.

Traces of this view can be found in the writings of Kant, whose claim that "all nations stand *originally* in a community of land" entails that a state can only vindicate its right of jurisdiction over a particular territory if it complies with the principles of "cosmopolitan right."[8] This does not require it to gain the actual consent of the citizens of other states. It does, nevertheless, imply granting them certain rights, in particular the right to enter into commercial relations and to travel for that purpose. As I noted in Chapter 1, however, this by no means entails a permanent right to residence; nor does it even entail a strict right of entry since Kant grants the citizens of the receiving society permission to turn the stranger away so long as they do not treat him with hostility. So on this view jurisdiction is only conditional on a general willingness to allow outsiders to establish contact for commercial purposes. In Kant's hands at least, joint ownership of the world translates into something far less than a demand that borders should remain fully open.

We may also wonder how intelligible this second reading of world ownership is on closer inspection.[9] The analogy with ownership of the commons suggests that there must be some collective means of establishing what use each individual member is entitled to make of the resources of the commons—otherwise we will indeed witness a "tragedy of the commons" where overuse devastates the object that is jointly owned. Without a mechanism to decide upon legitimate use and to enforce the decision made, joint ownership collapses back into common ownership, where each person is allowed to judge what she is reasonably entitled to take. And currently no such mechanism—

no global body regulating territorial jurisdiction and movement across borders—actually exists.

This leaves one further possible way of cashing out the idea that the world is the common possession of humankind, namely the view that Risse labels "Equal Division." This is the claim that each of the n human beings alive at any moment can claim a $1/n$ share of the earth's resources as their private property.[10] Before delving into this view, it is again worth asking where it might lead us with respect to immigration. The relevant corollary is that a state that wishes to close its borders, wholly or partly, must show that it is not excluding any individuals who currently possess less than their $1/n$ share, and who, therefore, have a prima facie claim to some of the resources that fall under the jurisdiction of that state. The complicating factor here is going to be that, within the state, it is very likely that some citizens will enjoy much more than their $1/n$ share, while others will enjoy much less, even if *taken together*, the m citizens hold more than m/n of the global total. So the claim of the prospective incomer is specifically against those who hold more, as indeed is also the claim of those current citizens who hold less than the $1/n$ quota. It is an interesting question for cosmopolitans to resolve whether the latter may resist the entry of the former in order to improve their own chances of winning a fair share of global resources. I shall not address it, however, for reasons given in the next paragraph.

Even if one thinks that "equality of global resources" is the best way of understanding the strong cosmopolitan claim that human beings must be treated as equals, there is a serious problem in giving it a concrete meaning. A physical division of the earth's surface into similar-sized plots makes no sense, given the heterogeneous nature of land itself and the extent to which it can be put to human use. So philosophers who favor equal division quickly switch to the view that everyone is entitled to resources of equal *value:* a square meter in Manhattan may be as valuable as an acre in the Australian outback.[11] But two difficulties immediately follow. One is to find a "neutral" or "objective" way of measuring value.[12] In the example just given, our intuitions are likely to be driven by thinking about the purchase price or rental value of the two sites in question. But can we assume that land values as determined by economic markets are those that should count? Why not, for example, use a biodiversity index instead? Different people and different cultures will be drawn toward one or other of the various alternative ways of measuring land values. The second difficulty is that even if we limit ourselves to conventional economic measures of value, it is impossible to disentangle the "unimproved" value of land from the value it has acquired as a result of past and present human activity. Manhattan contains not only skyscrapers but also throngs of human beings eager to engage in complex financial transactions, which is above all what explains the high economic value of property there. World ownership, in contrast, is meant to refer to *original* ownership—ownership of the earth itself, in advance of the improvements historically wrought upon it by human beings or their present willingness to use it in certain ways.

At this juncture someone favorably disposed to open borders might point out that even if the economic value of land in the metropolis is almost entirely a product of human activity, it is still the case that citizens living in that area have immediate access to resources of far greater value than the natives of Mali, say, and this arbitrary "accident of birth" can be corrected by allowing the Malians who so choose to move to New York or somewhere equivalent. However, this argument no longer makes any direct appeal to common ownership and is better understood as a claim about equality of opportunity, the next principle to be considered. To finish on the first, I have not taken issue with the idea that the earth is *in some sense* the common possession of human beings. Instead I have examined whether there is a way of understanding this idea that is practically intelligible while at the same time providing a justification for open borders. My conclusion is that the best reading is actually the one originally proposed by Grotius, but this generates only residual rights to make use of the earth's resources (implying in certain cases rights to move in search of these resources), but nothing so strong as a general right to move across territorial borders.

So let us move on now to the argument about equality of opportunity, which draws no distinction between opportunities that arise from human practices and those that arise from possession of natural resources. It is concerned simply with the fact that people born into wealthy societies standardly have opportunities—to get education, to enter the job market, and to make money—that people born into poor societies do not have. This inequality is unfair, it is claimed, and opening borders is at least a partial remedy because, although there may still be other barriers preventing people from poor societies from taking advantage of the opportunities available elsewhere, at least one obstacle—immigration control—has been removed.

This argument has appeared persuasive to many.[13] It often obtains its emotive force, however, by starting with examples of severe deprivation—cases involving people who receive very little by way of education or health care, whose opportunities for employment of any kind are limited, and whose life expectancy is correspondingly low. These cases are real enough, but what moves us about them is the absolute lack of opportunity they describe, not lack of opportunity relative to people living in other societies. There are strong reasons to think that people everywhere are entitled to the conditions for a minimally decent life, and that where these are persistently unobtainable in the places where they live, they should be allowed to migrate. But the equality of opportunity argument goes much further. It is about people's comparative prospects no matter how absolutely rich or poor their society is. It should apply as much to people currently living in Slovenia as to people currently living in Bangladesh. It takes a principle that has gained widespread currency when applied within liberal democracies and extends it globally. That principle states that a person's opportunity to obtain education, employment, and other valued positions should depend only on their talent, motivation, and choice, and not on factors such as their family background or their gender that have no intrinsic relevance to the position being sought. Its global extension states that a person's being raised in one society rather than another should also make no difference to their opportunities.

The principle when applied domestically rests on two assumptions. One is that we have some way of measuring the opportunities open to a person. Since the concrete choices that people make in life will be different, we can only detect whether opportunities are equal or unequal if we can calibrate them. Let me illustrate with a simple example. Suppose a white student whose ability and motivation we can measure applies to the University of Sheffield, and is accepted, while a black student with similar motivation and ability who applies to the University of Manchester is turned down. Does this suggest that equal opportunity has failed? It does, if we can show that these two universities enjoy broadly the same academic standing and popularity among prospective students, so that a place at either of them is of roughly equal value. Without using such a measuring rod we cannot apply the principle. The second assumption is that the factors that determine opportunity are susceptible to political control—in other words, that the government can legislate and enact policies that, for instance, outlaw discrimination in the job market and ensure that high school standards in different parts of the country are comparable. No state achieves these goals completely, but equality of opportunity makes sense as a regulative ideal because it is at least possible to move toward them by political action.

It seems to me doubtful whether either assumption holds good at global level. Cultural differences between societies make accurate comparison difficult; if the opportunity sets provided by two states differ in such a way that neither set includes the other, we cannot judge whether a randomly selected citizen of the first state has greater or lesser opportunities than her counterpart in the second. There is no agreed metric that can be applied to rank the sets because how particular opportunities are to be valued relative to one another will depend upon the local culture. If one state provides ample opportunities for its citizens to hold religious office, but relatively few opportunities to direct a large business, while the reverse is true in the second, how can we judge which provides greater opportunities overall?[14]

It has been said in reply that we can at least make comparative judgments at a more basic level, for example, by using Sen's idea of basic capabilities—opportunities to achieve human functionings that are regarded as valuable in all societies, such as enjoying good health and working productively.[15] By combining these capabilities into a common index, we could compare the general standard of living in any two societies and conclude that opportunities were greater in the society where the standard of living was higher. Sen, however, has always maintained that the idea of capabilities cannot by itself solve the indexing problem.[16] If opportunities to be healthy are greater in the first society but opportunities for productive work are greater in the second, we cannot make judgments about their relative standards of living except by introducing a value judgment.[17] Sen envisages this evaluation being made through political deliberation. But why expect that the outcome must be the same in political communities whose public cultures are quite different?

Admittedly, we can still say that by the proposed criterion a state that provides all of its members with the full set of basic capabilities provides a greater range of opportunity than one that leaves some of its members deprived. But this brings us back to the point made previously about the difference between demanding *adequate* opportunities for all and demanding *equal* opportunities. The equal opportunity principle needs to apply to states that have all crossed the basic capability threshold as well as to states that remain below it, or else it is not in fact a principle of equality but what is now often called a principle of *sufficiency*. In this revised form, the principle implies only that people living in subthreshold states can make a claim to migrate to places where opportunities are greater.

So one problem with "global equality of opportunity" is how to measure opportunity sets comparatively. The other problem is whether the principle has practical relevance, given that the opportunities that are available in any particular place will depend to a large extent on decisions taken locally about, for example, rates of economic growth and the provision of public services. In the absence of an overarching authority that could ensure that comparable sets of opportunities were available to everyone, equality of opportunity could only be maintained in the fortunate case that equally resourced states made similar decisions about their future priorities.

But this, it might be said, simply reveals the strength of the case for open borders. Assume that in a multicultural world states will indeed provide different, and incommensurable, opportunity sets to their members. Then by opening all borders and allowing people to take advantage of opportunities everywhere, equality is achieved—or at least the inequality that results simply from the fact of belonging to one society rather than another is removed. So now we must ask why global equality of that kind should matter to us, keeping the distinction between having adequate opportunities and having equal opportunities firmly in mind. In domestic contexts, equality of opportunity matters because opportunities will depend upon public policy decisions (e.g., concerning the provision of education) that the state makes for all of its citizens. If it allows opportunities to become significantly unequal despite having the resources to correct for this, it treats them unjustly. Internationally, however, there is no single agent responsible for creating opportunities, but instead a multiplicity of independent states (things would be different if a world government came into being). So although a citizen of Slovenia might have lesser opportunities in some respects than a citizen of Norway (setting aside the measurement problem just discussed), this is not because they are being treated unequally by any institution. The Slovenian state treats its citizens equally, let us suppose, and so does the Norwegian state. The resulting inequality of opportunity between the two representative people is simply a by-product of their countries' independence from each other. Norway has no obligation to reduce its citizens' living standards so that Slovenian citizens have opportunities that are equivalent to theirs, but neither does it have an obligation to enhance the Slovenians' opportunities by opening its borders to them.

So it is far from clear that justice at global level requires that people brought up in different states should always have the same set of opportunities. But even if it did, it is also far from clear that opening borders is the best way to achieve this. It will depend on who is able to take advantage of the additional opportunities that are created in this way. We can reasonably assume that far more people will try to move from poor countries to rich countries than in the opposite direction. But the ones who have the resources—the savings and the education—that enable them to do this will be the ones who are already relatively advantaged in their societies of origin. Broadly speaking, they will be the members of the local elite or their off-spring. So although the opportunity gap that separates these migrants from people raised in the developed societies will be narrowed, the opportunity gap that separates them from their erstwhile compatriots will be widened. It may even turn out that the opportunities of those left behind are reduced in absolute terms, if those leaving are skilled professionals who would otherwise provide education, health services, or competent administration in their home country (later in the book I shall discuss the contested issue of "brain drain"). It is a mistake, in other words, to judge equal opportunities by focusing attention simply on those who are able to migrate. One needs to consider the impact of migration in broader terms in order to judge whether opening borders would take us toward or away from this goal, either domestically or globally.

So a global version of the equal opportunity principle fails to give us a good reason for abandoning controls on immigration. On the one hand, it may be impossible to apply because of culturally based disagreement about the value of opportunity sets; on the other hand, the reasons why justice requires equality of opportunity at domestic level cease to hold when we move beyond that sphere. Of course people nearly always benefit from having greater opportunities, so if border controls are to be justified, some grounds for imposing them must be given—people who are refused entry are entitled to be told why. Providing those grounds is the task of the following chapter. The final question for this one is whether there is a human right to immigrate: if there is, then in the absence of some overwhelming contrary reason, borders must remain open.[18]

A human rights argument makes no appeal to *inequalities* in the way that people are treated by virtue of living in different states. It claims instead that all human beings are entitled to a range of freedoms, opportunities, and resources that are sufficient for them to live decent lives. Many of the specific rights that meet this condition have been codified in official documents such as the original Universal Declaration of Human Rights of 1948 or the International Covenant on Civil and Political Rights of 1966. These documents explicitly recognize the right to *leave* any country and the right to *reenter* one's own country, but make no mention of a general right to immigrate. So an argument for such a right must be philosophical in form: it cannot appeal to current international law, but must instead attempt to show that the kinds of reasons that justify other human rights also ground a right to cross borders.

Before beginning to examine these reasons, we should note what a human right to immigrate must mean if it is going to justify open borders. It must be understood as a right of all human beings, whatever their circumstances, held against all states to enter and settle on their territory. It attaches as much to the rich Canadian wishing to settle in Germany as it does to the desperate Somali trying to cross the border into Kenya. Later in the book, we shall examine the special case of the rights of refugees (the right to seek asylum from persecution *is* recognized in the Universal Declaration). It should, however, be understood as a right not to be prevented from entering by border controls, rather than as a right to be assisted in moving from one state to another. Even if a human right to immigrate were recognized, many people would face material and other costs that would deter them from moving to the country they would most like to join.

There are broadly three strategies we might use in an attempt to justify such a right. First, there is the *direct* strategy where we examine the grounds that justify human rights generally and then try to show that these same grounds support a right to immigrate. Second, there is the *instrumental* strategy, where we try to prove that other human rights we already accept, such as the right to subsistence, will not be securely protected unless this additional right is also recognized. Third, there is what I call the *cantilever* strategy, where we try to show that the new right is a logical extension of an existing right, such that it would be arbitrary to recognize the latter without also recognizing a right to immigrate.[19] In the case that concerns us, the cantilever strategy begins from the human right of free movement *within* a society and argues that having accepted this premise, consistency requires us to recognize a wider right of free movement *between* societies.

Let us consider these in turn. To implement the direct strategy, we must first know what grounds human rights in general. In the previous chapter, I outlined an account of human rights that connected them to basic human needs. Other popular theories identify different features of human beings as the basis on which human rights are ascribed to them—for example, "fundamental human interests" or "normative agency."[20] What these theories have in common, however, is the thought that people cannot live lives that we would recognize as decent or fully human unless they are protected from various forms of oppression and deprivation, and this necessary protection is what a set of human rights provides. It is important that the rights that make up the set are broadly consistent with one another in order that we do not include rights whose exercise would interfere with *other* rights we wish to recognize; thus we sometimes have to limit the scope of one right to safeguard another (as we do when we limit the right to free expression in order to protect the right to privacy). Therefore, if we are to justify a human right to immigrate directly, we have both to show that having such a right is necessary if people are going to lead decent lives and that recognizing it would not conflict with other rights we might regard as equally or more important.

How could immigration have such significance for human beings that it deserves to be called a human right? There are admittedly ways of life in which crossing borders becomes a necessity, ranging from traditional nomadic forms of life to the kind of cosmopolitan restlessness that leads some young people in liberal societies to envisage a life of constant movement between different cultural milieux. But these ways of life are quite specific: justifying a human right involves showing that it responds to an interest or need that human beings standardly share, and nomadism, or its modern equivalent, has no such basis. If valuing a particular lifestyle were sufficient to generate the human rights necessary to undertake it, the roster of rights would proliferate uncontrollably. We need instead to look for interests that are important, widely shared, and difficult to satisfy without migrating internationally if we wish to defend a human right to immigrate.

Direct arguments for a human right to immigrate do indeed begin from such interests. Freedom of movement in general is obviously valuable because of the numerous activities that are impossible to undertake if a person is confined within a narrow space: finding work, meeting a partner, practicing a religion, enjoying nature, playing sports, and so forth—that explains why there is indeed a human right to free movement. But how should the scope of the right be understood? The case for extending it internationally is that the activities in question may not be accessible within a person's home country, at least not in the particular form that the person in question values. Thus Kieran Oberman, defending a human right to immigrate, points to "life options" in which a person may have a deep interest, such as being together with a lover who resides in another country, practicing a religion that has no adherents in his homeland, or pursuing political aims that require travel abroad for purposes of research or exchange of ideas. Without a human right to immigrate, he argues, these interests are in danger of being frustrated.[21]

Notice, however, that it is only one specific form of a generic interest that is at issue here. Human beings have a general interest in being able to form close, loving relationships, but this can be satisfied so long as someone has sufficient freedom of movement to meet a range of potential partners. It is only the interest in bonding with one particular person that may be blocked by border restrictions (of course that person may be the love of one's life, alas). Notice also that there are other obstacles to the fulfillment of such specific interests: I may not be able to afford the air ticket that would take me to my loved one in New Zealand, and she herself may not want to reciprocate my passion. My wish to participate in Sutrayana practices in Tibet may be stymied by the reluctance of the Tibetan monks to waste their time by indulging an ignorant Westerner. The lesson to be learned is that human beings have a range of generic interests that they are entitled to pursue, but when it comes to deciding on the specific form that these interests should take, they must take account of what is feasible. Practicing a religion, for example, means finding a faith one can believe in, but also finding a community of believers—a church, a mosque, and so forth—that one can actually join given practical constraints of time, money, and distance. The purpose of human rights is to protect the generic interests, not the specific form that these may take for a given individual.[22]

The upshot is that a person's human rights are fulfilled when they live in a society that provides a range of life options sufficient to allow them to satisfy the needs and interests that we recognize as components of a decent human life. They may well have particular preferences that can only be satisfied by moving to another country, but that is not sufficient to justify a general human right to immigrate. But what if their society cannot or will not provide them with an adequate range of opportunities—for example, they cannot receive proper education or health care so long as they remain where they are? This question brings us to the instrumental argument for a human right to immigrate: it is needed as means of protecting other, more basic rights, in the same way as the right to legal representation in court, for instance, is needed to protect various rights to personal freedom. For many people, it is argued, the only realistic way in which they can ensure that their other rights are protected is by having a general right to move to a different society where their freedom will be guaranteed or their other basic needs will be met.

As I noted earlier, international law already recognizes a human right to *exit* one's country of residence, and the moral justification for this right is precisely that it provides a means of escape from persecution and suffering. It may appear that a right of exit and a right of entry are simply two sides of the same coin, but they are not.[23] If a right of exit is to be made effective, its bearer must be able to enter some other country (since there is no habitable unclaimed territory left on Earth), but this requires much less than a right to enter any country of one's choice. What is needed is an international regime that gives everyone who wishes to exercise her human right of exit at least one other place she can move to. This could take different forms: a series of bilateral agreements between states who agree to admit one another's citizens, or an international body charged with monitoring and coordinating migration as the United Nations' high commissioner on refugees does now in the particular case of refugees. Although having an unrestricted right to immigrate might be seen as providing the best protection possible for other human rights, what matters here is ensuring an *adequate* level of protection. This limitation is a feature of human rights generally: the right to legal representation in court does not mean being provided with the services of the highest-paid or most eloquent barrister in the country, but simply having access to someone who is competent to defend you.

A further question about the instrumental argument needs also to be raised: if the justification for an unrestricted right to migrate is that it serves to protect people from having to remain in places where their other human rights are put at risk, then we must consider the position of people who for other reasons (e.g., lack of resources) are unable to move. Even under the existing migration regime, where borders generally are far from open, some very poor countries have lost a high proportion of their professionally trained members, including doctors and nurses, through emigration. (Haiti, an extreme case, is said to have lost about 85 percent of its trained people in this way.)[24] The costs of this out-migration, in the form of reduced access to medical and other services, are borne by those who have no choice but to remain. I shall explore these brain-drain cases in more detail in Chapter 6, but the point to make here is that an unrestricted right to immigrate would make things worse because it would no longer be permissible for rich states to close their borders to professionals exiting from poor countries where their services are badly needed. In other words, taking everyone's human rights into account, recognizing a human right to immigrate does *not* provide optimal protection for other human rights if one of its effects is to encourage more brain drain from poor states.

If neither the direct argument nor the instrumental argument for a human right to immigrate is convincing, what about the cantilever argument? As I noted earlier, this begins from the premise that there is a human right of free movement *within* the borders of each state and argues that the international right of free movement is simply a logical extension of that right. As Carens puts it, "if it is so important for people to have the right to move freely within a state, isn't it equally important for them to have the right to move across state borders?"[25] Now we should notice that freedom of movement within state borders is far from unlimited: it is restricted most obviously by extensive rights of private property, but also by general rules governing movement in public space, such as the traffic laws. Although there can be argument about whether the existing laws are too restrictive (e.g., should there be a right to walk on uncultivated land even when it is privately owned?), few would claim that they violate human rights. So the question that arises is why the domestic right of free movement is as extensive in scope as we normally take it to be. Why, for example, would the United States violate that right if it prohibited people moving from one American state to another, given that the options available in each state are easily sufficient for living a decent human life? So the cantilever argument tries to impale its opponents on a fork: either they have to concede that there is no violation of the right to free movement when people are prevented from moving to Washington state from Oregon, say, or they have to explain why the right is compatible with international border controls between Washington state and British Columbia but not with national border controls between Washington state and Oregon.

There are two reasons to reject the cantilever argument—two reasons why the analogy between domestic freedom of movement and international freedom of movement fails to hold. First, the costs that unrestricted freedom of movement may bring with it are smaller and easier to contain in the domestic case.[26] Recall that human rights have to be defined so that they form a consistent set, which means that any candidate right has to be inspected to make sure that recognizing it would not predictably infringe other human rights. In other words, the costs of implementing a proposed human right must be considered whenever these costs bear on other human rights. When people move and settle, they occupy space, houses, jobs, hospital beds, and so forth, potentially displacing other people or pushing up the price they must pay for access to these goods. In the case of domestic freedom of movement, states have means at their disposal either to encourage or to damp down internal migration without infringing on the right itself. On the one hand, they can implement a uniform system of taxation and social service provision at national level, so that there is no positive incentive to move within the country in order to lower one's taxes or to get access to better schools or hospitals. On the other hand, when too much movement in a particular direction is already occurring, they can reverse the flow by creating employment opportunities in the areas that people are leaving—they can move government offices to regional cities or provide tax breaks to companies who want to set up in business there. In other words, because they are in control of both ends of the migration route, states are able without legal restrictions to offset any unwanted effects of internal movement.

Things look very different at the international level. Here the incentives to move from one state to another may be very great, and there is little that one state can do, in the short term at least, to change conditions in the sending states. A state that is experiencing high levels of inward migration can take certain steps to make itself a less attractive destination for migrants—for example, it can restrict access to some welfare benefits for a period of time after the immigrant has arrived—but if it is a liberal state, it cannot move far in this direction without violating its own basic principles (as I argued in Chapter 1, liberal states are now committed to upholding quite demanding standards of equal treatment for all who reside within their borders). Discouraging messages broadcast in the country of origin are un-likely to have much effect.[27] So border controls may be the only weapon that a state has to prevent unwanted migration impacting on the rights of its own citizens.

The second reason to reject the cantilever argument is that the human right to domestic free movement performs an important protective function over and above the opportunities it creates for citizens to exercise their other human rights.[28] Return to the hypothetical case in which the U.S. govern-ment prohibits people from moving between American states. Why might we find this objectionable? The power to limit internal freedom of move-ment allows the state to control and target individuals and groups that it dislikes or wishes to discriminate against. We can see this by examining his-torical cases in which certain groups were geographically confined—for instance, the apartheid regime in South Africa created separate residential areas for whites and nonwhites, which also meant that those confined to black or colored neighborhoods received lower quality education, medical services, recreational facilities, and so forth. Much earlier, Jewish ghettos were created within European cities that not only enforced religious segre-gation but also exposed the confined group to economic exploitation and social stigmatization.[29] Or consider the program of forced resettlement, mainly in Siberia, carried out by the Soviet Union in the 1930s and 1940s where several million people judged to be politically unreliable by reason of their nationality or social class were required live either in labor camps (gu-lags) or in special settlements which they could leave only by permission of the commandant.[30] These examples show why a right to free movement serves as a significant check on state domination of minorities, helping to safeguard their other human rights.[31]

Can the same be said of international freedom of movement? The state's power to control borders does not allow it to dominate any group in particular. It can of course discriminate against groups it dislikes by refusing them entry, and this refusal may constitute an injustice, as we shall see later. But by doing so, it does not prevent the group in question from seeking to exercise their human rights elsewhere; the group is not trapped in the way that an internal minority may be. So again the analogy between domestic and international freedom of movement fails to hold. We have special reasons for insisting on a right to domestic free movement, understood as a right not to be prevented from entering any particular region within the state, that do not apply to its international counterpart.

That concludes my discussion of the positive case for open borders. I have looked at three arguments offered in support of the claim that as a matter of justice border controls must be removed. Common ownership of the earth, I suggested, might give us a right to cross borders in cases of necessity, but not a general right to immigrate. I challenged the relevance of global equality of opportunity, arguing not only that problems of measurement would make the principle impossible to apply, but also that the reasons that mandate applying the principle within a political community no longer hold at global level. And finally I claimed that none of the three strategies that might be used to defend a human right to immigrate was successful. Having said all that, it remains true that there will always be *some* case for keeping borders open. More freedom is always better than less, including the freedom to migrate between countries. So to show that states should nevertheless have wide discretion in deciding upon their immigration policies, we need to reverse the direction of the argument and ask what makes immigration controls legitimate. What gives states the right to choose who to let in and who to exclude?

FOUR

Closed Borders

WHEN STATES CLOSE THEIR BORDERS to immigrants, serious consequences often follow. Those who are excluded may be desperate to enter, and so there occur human tragedies, such as the Mexicans who die of hypothermia while trying to cross the southern desert of Arizona or the refugees from the conflicts of North Africa and Syria who drown when their overcrowded boats founder en route to southern Europe. The death of illegal migrants is the most extreme case, but since states go to great lengths to ensure that such people do not reach their territories, the human rights of many others are unavoidably infringed.[1] People with humane values may ask whether the cost of keeping immigrants out can be justified, even if they have no human right to enter, as Chapter 3 maintained. The state's right to close its borders needs a strong defense, therefore, and the aim of this chapter is to see how far it is possible to give one.

My intention is not to lay down any particular immigration policy as the correct one for democratic states to pursue, and certainly not to argue that borders should always be kept closed. These are matters to be decided by democratic means within each state. Instead my aim here is to show that policies that involve selecting some migrants and excluding others are legitimate, by outlining some of the reasons that can justify them, as well as responding to some objections that open-borders advocates may raise. I do not here consider cases in which immigrants have urgent claims to be admitted that may override the state's right to exclude them, nor at this stage do I distinguish between just and unjust grounds for choosing between immigrants—these issues are postponed until later chapters. I want simply to show that there may be reasons for restricting immigration that are substantial enough to outweigh the undoubted costs of enforcing the restrictions.

In popular political discourse, it is often asserted that control over borders is straightforwardly a matter of state sovereignty. States are sovereign, it is said: they have an absolute right to decide what goes on within the territories that they legitimately control, and supervising border crossing is simply one aspect of this. People who make this argument imply that the choice is either to have states, together with the range of powers that they are normally understood to possess, or else to invent some new (and untried) form of political organization. Assuming the first alternative, there is no need to justify the right to control borders specifically, any more than there is to justify, say, the state's right to have an army or issue its own currency.

This appeal to sovereignty, however, is too quick. It first takes for granted the sovereign state, by which is meant an institution that has final and absolute authority over a territory,[2] as the best form of government, thus preempting any debate over the merits of possible alternatives that involve dispersing power between higher and lower level institutions (such as in federal systems or in the EU). It further assumes that there is no problem in extending the arguments that are made in favor of sovereignty vis-à-vis domestic society to authority that is directed toward people who are not yet members of the society in question. Even if you agree with Hobbes that social order will break down unless sovereigns are given unlimited rights to rule over those who have covenanted to create them, it does not follow that they can exercise the same rights toward outsiders—or at least not without further argument. So even though the political conventions of our day do treat the right to control borders as simply one incident of sovereignty, we need to dig deeper to see whether this practice is justified or not.

A more promising approach appeals not to sovereignty but to the idea of territorial jurisdiction. The claim here is that having rights of jurisdiction over a given territory implies having the right to control the movement of people in and out of that territory, so that where a state can legitimately exercise jurisdiction it is also entitled to exclude immigrants if it so wishes. This claim needs some unpacking: first we need to establish what jurisdiction means and how it originates, and then we must examine the implied connection with border controls.

Having jurisdiction over a territory means possessing and exercising the right to make and enforce laws throughout that area of land, laws that apply to everyone who is physically present on the territory. As normally understood, this means that the main corpus of law is applied uniformly throughout the area, though there may be local bylaws made by subsidiary bodies set up under the authority of the state that exercises jurisdiction. The effect is that whenever people interact on the territory, whether person to person or by virtue of the property they own, they do so in the knowledge that their transactions will be governed by a body of rules that apply in the same way to all, a necessary though not sufficient condition of justice. The advantages to the inhabitants of being subject to jurisdiction in this sense should be too obvious to need spelling out.[3] But under what conditions can a state rightfully claim territorial jurisdiction? After all, the total amount of land in the world is finite, and by asserting such a claim, the state prevents other possible contenders from establishing a political community in the same place. Most notably, those who are attracted by the idea of the common ownership of the earth, as discussed in the last chapter, might wonder how a particular institution can claim a monopoly right to govern a particular portion of that space—especially if it then proceeds to control entry to the portion it has appropriated.

I believe that for a state rightfully to claim jurisdiction over a territory, three conditions must be met. First, it must maintain social order and protect the human rights of the inhabitants to a sufficiently high degree.[4] Exactly where the bar should be set in applying this condition is difficult to determine, since among other things no state has succeeded in eliminating all criminal activity on its territory, but intuitively we can distinguish between cases in which a well-functioning legal system provides an environment in which most residents are able to go about their lives without the threat of personal violence, theft, destitution, and so on and cases where the opposite is true. Second, the state must represent the inhabitants of the territory. This requirement needs a little more discussion. The underlying idea is that the populace should regard the state as having legitimate authority over them, and this is meant to exclude cases in which social order is established simply through cowing them into submission, whether at the hands of a military dictator or an invading force that has failed to obtain the consent of the inhabitants. One way in which this condition can be met is through having a democratically elected government, which is thereby representative of the population in a strong sense. But democracy is not always necessary. Legitimacy can be conferred in other ways, for example, by inherited allegiance to a ruling family or by recognizing the supreme authority of religious leaders. The third and final condition is that the people whom the state represents should themselves have the right to occupy the territory in question. This means in particular that a state cannot establish territorial rights by expelling most of the rightful occupants of a region and replacing them with its own subjects, even though after the population transfer it can then claim to represent the majority of current inhabitants.

How is legitimate occupancy to be established? The simplest case will be where a group of people settle on unoccupied land and then reside on it continuously: their title appears to be unchallengeable.[5] But more often the movement and mingling of populations over the course of history gives rise to disputes over the identity of "the people" who are entitled to establish jurisdiction in any area (we see this happening especially when secessionist movements arise). Here political philosophers disagree about the basis on which claims to territory can be advanced, some theories invoking individual rights to property, others treating occupancy as a collective right, but differing over the features that qualify a group to make justified occupancy claims.[6] Elsewhere I have defended a nationalist account that vests rights of occupation primarily in groups with shared national identities that over time have transformed the land at stake, typically endowing it with both material and symbolic value.[7] I shall return shortly to discuss the role that national identity may play in thinking about immigration, but for present purposes the debate about the source of occupancy rights matters less than the connection between occupancy and jurisdiction. Where a group has the right to occupy an area, a state that represents the group and that meets the first condition for jurisdiction—maintaining social order and protecting human rights—is entitled to exercise it.

As conventionally understood, the right to territorial jurisdiction brings with it at least two further rights: the right to control and use the resources that the territory contains, and the right to control the movement of goods and people across its borders. These three rights are bundled up together as "territorial rights" and ascribed to states. But the reasons for this bundling may not be obvious: there is no logical necessity why the three rights must be held together by a single institution. There is, for example, nothing self-evidently wrong with the idea that resource management within a territory should be handed over to an international body while legal jurisdiction remains with the relevant state. Such a proposal may face serious practical difficulties, but these need to be spelt out. The same applies to border restrictions: it is not self-evident that jurisdiction also requires control over entry to the territory. A public park can have a set of rules governing behavior in the park, and the park wardens can enforce these without also being able to exercise any control over who enters the park and who doesn't. So how is territorial jurisdiction different?

It is at least arguable that any legal system worthy of the name requires a degree of stability in the population that it serves. In order for offenders to be charged, witnesses summoned, juries commissioned, and so forth, most people have to be living in known places of residence. However, this requirement only imposes a weak constraint on the level of migration, one that is not likely to be exceeded in practice. To discover a stronger constraint, we have to move beyond the bare idea of a legal system and consider the full range of social responsibilities carried by a modern democratic state. We have, in other words, to think about employment, housing, education, health care, social security, and the like. These are all matters that fall within the jurisdiction of the state, which creates legal rights to ensure that their bearers have access to the services in question. Some of these rights also qualify as human rights.[8] Because, as noted earlier, the state's very legitimacy depends upon its ability to protect the human rights of all those who are present on its territory, this responsibility must extend to the rights of immigrants.[9] It may be permissible to withhold *some* rights to employment, health care, and other benefits from recently arrived immigrants—this is an issue to be explored in detail later in the book—but not the rights that are basic enough to count as human rights. Thus, if an immigrant is seriously injured in a road accident or set upon by thugs, the public health service (or its equivalent) must treat her. Equally, the state, as an aspect of its jurisdiction, must produce sufficient opportunities for employment, education, and so forth to protect the rights of the immigrants it admits. As I noted in Chapter 1, this is one of the main features that distinguishes modern liberal societies from their nineteenth-century predecessors, in which over and above the basic protection afforded by the law, immigrants were left to fend for themselves.

Does it follow that jurisdiction must include the right to control inflows? Not in the strictest sense because a state might choose to precommit the resources to cover the rights of all the people who might wish to enter—potentially, let us note, a very demanding decision. So the argument about jurisdiction needs to be complemented by an argument about self-determination in order fully to justify the right to close borders.[10] By self-determination here, I mean the right of a democratic public to make a wide range of policy choices within the limits set by human rights. Among the most important choices are precisely those that concern levels of public expenditure on housing, schools, hospitals, and so forth (I come back later to consider cultural choices). Since, for the reasons just given, both the rate of immigration and the personal characteristics of the immigrants (such as their likely education and health needs) will affect all of these measures, immigration control is an essential lever in the hands of the demos. Deprived of that lever, it loses control of those expenditures, unless it decides to abandon liberal principles and deprive the incomers of these essential services.[11] The argument here, to avoid misunderstanding, is not that a self-determining political community *must* close its borders, but that it must have the *right* to control its borders in order to preserve a meaningful range of policy choices without detriment to the human rights of those it chooses to admit.

A critic might argue at this point that self-determination is not of sufficient value to justify closing borders, given the human costs of doing so. I shall examine this claim in the second part of this chapter when I consider challenges to the case for closed borders. For the time being, I will assume that self-determination, especially when it takes a democratic form, is something of considerable value, and consider some further ways in which it may require border controls to be put in place. Notice next that when immigrants are admitted, their presence will over time change the composition of the citizen body or, in other words, the "self" in "self-determination." I assume here, as before, that all immigrants who become permanent residents should be eligible to apply for citizenship after a suitable period of time has elapsed unless disqualified by virtue of serious criminality. It is also reasonable to assume that their participation will significantly change the decisions that the demos takes, because immigrants will not simply replicate the indigenous population with respect to their beliefs, values, interests, cultural preferences, and so forth. Now self-determination is usually understood to include the right to control membership of the body that decides, subject to the usual human rights provisos. One way to see this is to think of a state that wishes to amalgamate with its neighbor: the second state, we would normally assume, has the right to refuse—this is what self-determination demands. It cannot be required to fuse its citizen body with that of its neighbor. But why does self-determination matter in the first place? A large part of its value is that it gives us, as citizens, some degree of control over what happens to our political community in the future. We can make long-term plans, such as creating protected areas for endangered species of plants or animals or investing in infrastructure whose benefits will mainly be reaped by our children. But this planning will be thwarted if changes in the composition of the citizen body mean that these decisions are later reversed.

A critic might again object here that no self-determining group of citizens can wholly protect itself from changes that might lead to its present decisions being revoked. Some members of the current majority may simply change their minds. More likely, generational replacement will produce a new demos whose values and priorities are different from its predecessor. Since we cannot disenfranchise our children, we cannot guarantee that they will not undo what we have done.[12] But note that, as a matter of observable fact, normal processes of education and socialization will mean that there is a good deal of continuity between our thinking and theirs, unless traumatic events (such as the Holocaust and the defeat of Nazism) cause a generational rupture in the public culture.[13] Immigrants present a different case. Of course they will be subject to cultural pressure to adopt some of the norms of the receiving society, and this process can be helped along by formal citizenship education as a prelude to acquiring citizenship itself. But as I noted in Chapter 1, in modern liberal societies there is a presumption that this will not extend to all areas of culture. On the contrary, immigrants are encouraged not only to retain but to celebrate some of the cultural traits that they bring with them—their styles of dress, their music, their religious festivals, their languages, and so on. The citizen body now contains minorities who can quite rightly ask for policy shifts that will accommodate their cultural needs, such as public subsidies or changes in the pattern of the working week. From the perspective of the indigenous majority, these demands may be welcome or unwelcome—it depends on the case. Immigration can often add spice to a previously dull national culture. What is clear is that scope of free choice has been limited by adding new members to the citizen body with demands that must be accommodated if basic liberal principles of equal treatment and respect for minority interests are to be observed. The larger the volume of immigration and the more diverse the background cultures of the immigrants, the tighter these limits will be.

There is a second, rather different, way in which admitting immigrants may affect democratic self-determination. There is evidence that cultural divisions among the members of a political community may reduce both interpersonal trust and trust in political institutions This reduction by no means entails the end of democracy, but it may change the way in which democratic institutions function.[14] It will become less likely that these institutions can operate in a deliberative manner, in which participants try to reach a consensus on what is to be done, guided by general considerations of fairness to all affected parties. Deliberation requires confidence that the concessions you are willing to make in the search for an agreement will be reciprocated by other participants, that participants are sincere in the reasons they give in support of their demands, and so forth. Where trust is lacking, deliberation is likely to be replaced by self-interested bargaining on the part of each group, where the outcome reflects the balance of power between them. This has a number of side effects. One is that it becomes less likely that *public goods* will be provided, since suspicious group representatives would rather bargain for goods that only their own members can enjoy.[15] Another is that it becomes harder to gain support for policies that involve economic redistribution in favor of the poor, again for the reason that general considerations of social justice are displaced by group-specific demands.

So trust is important to a well-functioning democracy, but how does this relate to immigration? The effect of immigration is normally to increase ethnic and religious diversity in the host society, and as we saw in Chapter 1, most social scientists believe that a further effect is to reduce interpersonal trust.[16] However, the relationship is not straightforward. One variable factor is the degree to which the society becomes segregated, with incoming minority groups clustering in urban ghettos—or on the other hand, integrated through participation in voluntary associations and political movements that cut across ethnic and religious divisions.[17] Another is the presence or absence of an inclusive national identity which can provide a bond that overrides sectional identities. Public policy, therefore, can be used to offset the potentially damaging effects of immigration on trust by encouraging integration and promoting a shared identity (I discuss this at much greater length in Chapter 8). The conclusion we should draw is not that immigration should be stopped forthwith, but that we should include among its possible costs a decline in trust and the ensuing political consequences—or else the cost of the measures needed to ensure that integration is successful. As I suggested in Chapter 1, economic assessments of immigration tend to leave these factors out of the equation when calculating costs and benefits. A democratic policy decision on the size and composition of the immigrant cohort needs to include them.

Let me end this part of the discussion with one further reason that states may have for controlling immigration flows: the overall size of their populations.[18] Population size properly looms large as a public policy issue to be decided democratically, whether the receiving nation is an underpopulated state wanting to develop its agricultural base by bringing new land into cultivation or an overpopulated state trying to limit pressure on its housing stock or its transport system. So far this is just a matter of domestic political priorities that will either welcome or discourage immigration as the case may be. But a bigger issue is the size of the global population. It now seems clear that preventing this from rising far beyond the seven billion people who currently exist is one of the main tasks of the present, alongside other measures to curb global warming and resource depletion. Indeed there are grounds for thinking that the environmentally sustainable population size for the planet is a good deal less than seven billion, so the aim ought to be gradually to reduce existing numbers until that point is reached. Migration does not of course affect the size of the global population directly. But just as global warming can only be combatted effectively by each state agreeing to limit its domestic carbon emissions under the terms of an international treaty, so population growth can only be halted if each state sets a target for its own population (since some states will find it hard to prevent further increases, other states should aim to shrink theirs). Such a policy cannot realistically be pursued if borders are open, particularly were a society to attempt to adopt tough measures such as the (now abandoned) Chinese one-child policy in order to restrict its numbers: even a much less draconian version of this policy would inevitably be rejected by citizens if at the same time immigrants are free to enter at will.

It is sometimes argued in response to these points that if people migrate from poor to rich countries, they are likely to have fewer children because they will adjust to the social norms of their new milieu (this may not happen immediately, but let's assume that over time it will). However, if population growth matters mainly because of its implications for global warming and resource depletion, immigrants who adopt Western lifestyles will consume more and induce more carbon emissions through their demand for energy: so the net environmental effect of migrating may be negative even if family sizes are smaller as a result. Of course one can argue that the real solution is to transform *everyone's* lifestyle so that it no longer has the catastrophic global effects of present-day rich world patterns, but until that happens migration is likely to be bad news for the planet overall even if it does reduce the incentive, on the part of migrants, to have large families. As I argued earlier, policies to restrict population growth, policies to reduce greenhouse gas emissions, and policies to ensure that natural resources are used sustainably are not alternatives to each other but essential complements. States need to pursue all three in tandem, and immigration control is one of the tools they must have at their disposal if they are to do so effectively.

So far in this chapter, I have been setting out the main positive reasons for granting states the right to control their borders; in the remainder of it, I want to extend the argument further by considering three challenges to the case I have just outlined. The first challenge holds that the argument about the cultural composition of the demos mistakenly assumes that without immigration we would have a culturally homogenous body of citizens— whereas in fact liberal societies already exhibit a high level of cultural diversity.[19] The second challenge maintains that, even if immigration limits the scope for self-determination (as argued earlier), political self-determination is simply not an important enough value to outweigh the pressing claims to enter that immigrants may make.[20] And the third challenge says that excluding immigrants is a form of coercion, and no state can be justified in coercing outsiders without their agreement.[21] In responding to these challenges, I hope to buttress the case for adopting potentially restrictive immigration policies on grounds of national self-determination.

The first challenge points to the fact that liberal democracies are almost without exception plural societies, which are not only divided historically into subregions (or even in some cases subnations), but have managed to absorb significant numbers of immigrants from a wide range of cultural backgrounds without either falling apart or losing their democratic credentials. So even if there were a case to be made in favor of cultural homogeneity, there is no chance of achieving it. Moreover, why should diversity be a problem, so long as almost everyone is willing to play by the rules of the democratic game and accept the decisions of the majority when either/or choices have to be made?

To respond to this challenge, we need to look more closely at what "culture" means for purposes of the immigration debate: the term itself is multiply ambiguous. One relevant distinction is between private and public culture. By "private culture" I mean a person's beliefs about what is valuable in her own life: how she should dress, what food she should eat, how she should conduct her personal relationships, what religion she should espouse, what forms of art or music are worth experiencing, and so on. In contrast, by "public culture" I mean a shared (overlapping rather than identical) set of beliefs about the values the wider society should embody and pursue: how people should conduct themselves in public space, what the society should be proud of and what it should be ashamed of, what kind of political system it should have, what the future goals of the society should be, and so on. Obviously, these two forms of culture are not sealed off from one another. A person's private values are likely to influence her public attitudes. But the distinction matters because different forms of private culture can usually coexist peacefully, whereas in the case of public culture there needs to be a considerable degree of convergence if the society is going to function without serious conflict. To put it simply, one can have a state made up of meat eaters and vegetarians in roughly equal numbers,[22] but not one similarly composed of democrats and theocrats. The issue, therefore, is not just the extent of cultural diversity but the kind of diversity that is involved.

A second distinction is also worth drawing. One can look at a culture in terms of its content, as I have done in the previous paragraph. But one can also look on culture as a source of identity. Where a private culture is shared among a large number of people, as often happens, it is important whether the cultural group that is formed in this way becomes exclusive and separated from other groups. The concern here is the formation of what are often described as "parallel societies" where minorities retreat into enclaves with rather little contact with those from outside of their own community.[23] This might happen, for example, on the basis of linguistic or religious differences. Then two consequences may follow. One is that such groups may cease to participate in the shared public culture of their society simply because they have little contact with it. Their sources of information and of value are different; they don't feel the need to engage in any kind of political interaction with those outside of their own circle. The other is that levels of intergroup trust decline, because when people don't have much contact with those who are seen as belonging to an enclosed cultural group, it is easy for negative stereotypes of that group to be formed.

What are the implications for immigration? The key issue is the kind and the scale of cultural diversity that immigration will introduce. How likely is it that immigrants will form themselves into self-contained groups standing apart from the rest of the society, and if they do, what are the implications for public culture? The volume of immigration matters here because the larger it is, the greater chance there is for cultural enclaves to form, and the more work the institutions that are set up to integrate immigrants into the public culture will have to do. The concern, then, is not with diversity itself. We can agree that having a greater diversity of private cultures in a society may be positively a good thing, and certainly not harmful. The real issue is about areas in which private culture and public culture intersect— in which it becomes harder to reach agreement on public matters because people approach them on the basis of conflicting and privately held beliefs and values—and with the possible alienating effect of separate and exclusive cultural identities.

Behind these concerns lie some assumptions about how a democratic society should function, which can be brought out into the open by considering the second challenge to closed borders, which questions the value of political self-determination.

What does "self-determination" mean in the present context? We should not confuse it with democracy as an institutional mechanism for making political decisions, even though democracy understood in this way will normally be the best vehicle for achieving self-determination. Self-determination assumes that there exists a group—the "self"—that is sufficiently cohesive that one can attribute to it a range of aims and values that the members recognize as part of their collective identity, even though no individual member is likely to subscribe to all of them. The group is self-determining to the extent that it is able to order its activities and shape its surroundings in the light of these common aims and values: its members can feel that they are in control of their own destiny. There is no mystery about why in general self-determination is valuable. Think of a theater company whose members want to develop a particular kind of experimental drama. To the extent that they are able to decide which plays to perform, where to perform them, who gets which parts, and so on, they can feel that they are pursuing the values they believe in. If these matters are decided by an impresario who holds the purse strings but doesn't understand the group's aims in the same way, their ambitions will be frustrated. The real question is whether something similar applies when we move to national level and consider why self-determination should matter to the citizens of a modern state, especially when as individuals the opportunity they have to influence the future direction of their society is much smaller than the opportunity each actor has to decide how the theater company should develop.

The first thing to notice is that it clearly does matter in fact. John Stuart Mill once remarked that "the sole evidence it is possible to produce that anything is desirable, is that people do actually desire it."[24] This may be an overstatement, but it is surely relevant when considering the value of national self-determination to observe what people are willing to do to obtain it. Consider the phenomenon of decolonization: why have people been so eager to throw off colonial rule and be governed by those they regard as their compatriots even when there was little evidence that the quality of their governance would actually improve as a result? Such eagerness makes sense if you think that it is better to be governed by somebody who shares your aims and values even if they are not particularly effective at implementing them. At least you can identify with the decisions that are taken whatever the results turn out to be. Or consider secessionist movements within states that are already democratic: the claims for self-government made by the Catalans, the Scots, and the Quebecois, for instance. We might not regard these claims as fully justified, but we have no difficulty in understanding them. When Quebec nationalists assert that they wish to be "Maîtres Chez Nous," that wish is perfectly comprehensible: we are our own people, and we want the right to decide what goes on around here. If we decide after all that these nations do not have a justified claim to full independence, this is not because their desire for self-determination is irrational: it is because they have taken too narrow a view of the self in that expression, failing to acknowledge their deep historical bonds with a larger nation that also has valid self-determination claims.

Despite this impressive body of evidence about the subjective importance of self-determination, critics may argue that at national level it is largely illusory. Even if the political system is democratic, they will say, the decisions taken at best reflect the views of the majority, rather than of the nation as a whole. But this underestimates what a well-functioning democracy can achieve. As I have suggested, it can aim to be deliberative, where minority views are listened to and taken into account, and decisions are based on common ground wherever possible. For this, of course, the area of common ground needs to be quite extensive, which is why deliberative forms of democracy depend upon a large measure of agreement in the background public culture. Democracy in the modern age must primarily be practiced through representative institutions (although there are increasing opportunities to supplement this by direct participation, through citizen juries, deliberative opinion polls, and other means of eliciting an informed public opinion). What is important for self-determination under these circumstances is that the reasons behind the decisions that are taken should be made public, so that they can be understood, and in the best case accepted, by those who are not directly involved in making them.

In arguing that people have an important interest in belonging to a self-governing political community, I have not argued that there is actually a *right* to self-determination. I refrain from taking this further step because the extent to which any particular person is able to enjoy the collective self-determination she seeks is going to depend on circumstances—including whether the group she identifies with recognizes her as a member, and whether, assuming it does, it is actually in a position to make self-determination a feasible option (it might lack the necessary resources, or unavoidably fall under the dominion of some larger group). Talk of rights suggests more determinacy than is possible here. But if self-determination is an interest rather than a right, why must it outweigh the competing interests of would-be immigrants in cases of conflict (i.e., where a self-governing community wishes to exclude some immigrants, for reasons of the sort that I canvassed above)? However much value existing citizens attach to controlling the future shape and size of their community, why must this count for more than the strong interest an immigrant might have in moving to a place where he can enjoy the opportunities that matter to him most?[25]

Notice, however, the perspective from which this question is being asked. It implicitly assumes a strong cosmopolitan commitment where interests are being given equal weight when they come into conflict regardless of whose interests they are. In contrast, if we assume that we owe special obligations to our compatriots, then all we are required to do is to give due consideration to the claim of the prospective immigrant, in accordance with the weak cosmopolitan principle defended in Chapter 2. We do not have to give her claim the same weight as we give to the claims of compatriots (she of course will have special claims against her own compatriots).[26] The strength of her claim will undoubtedly vary. At one extreme, she might merely have an interest in moving to a more congenial cultural environment. At the other extreme, she might be facing a threat to her human rights that can only be met by migrating; or, a different case, she might be entitled to enter under a policy that has already been agreed. In these latter cases, her claim may well be strong enough to outweigh the more routine interests of current citizens, for example, their wish to avoid overcrowding. This is a matter for debate and decision inside the political community. What justice requires is that the interest a particular immigrant (or group of immigrants) has in entering should be properly assessed and weighed against the interests of citizens in self-determination, but in the weighing process a degree of compatriot partiality is permissible.

In reaching this conclusion, I have been assuming that a state that refuses to admit an immigrant is simply withholding a benefit that it might otherwise have granted. But this way of describing the situation has been challenged by Arash Abizadeh, who argues that when a state implements border controls it *coerces* all those who might have been admitted—not only those who are actually trying to enter, but even those who have no particular wish to do so.[27] Because border controls are coercive, he argues, they must be subject to democratic ratification by a body that includes both those inside the state and those outside, on the grounds that coercion can only be legitimate when it is justified in this way. The upshot is that no state is entitled to close its borders unilaterally. As Abizadeh puts it, "the regime of control must ultimately be justified to foreigners as well as citizens. As a consequence, a state's regime of border control could only acquire legitimacy if there were cosmopolitan democratic institutions in which borders received actual justifications addressed to both citizens and foreigners."[28]

Abizadeh's argument here relies on two main premises: that for coercion to be legitimate it must be justified in a democratic forum that includes all of the people toward whom it is exercised; and that the state coerces potential immigrants when it refuses their request to enter. Most of what I have to say relates to the second premise, but it is worth spending a little time on the first. Assuming for the moment an intuitive understanding of what it means to coerce someone, it does not seem that coercion always requires democratic justification. In fact it seems clear that it does not: coercion is often justified simply in terms of its consequences. If I come across someone beating up a small child and I use coercive force to make him stop, there is no need to justify my action to anyone in particular, least of all the child beater. The same applies if my friend is rolling drunk at the end of the evening and proposing to drive home. When I confiscate his car keys and bundle him into the back of my car, I do not have to obtain even *his* agreement, let alone the consent of some democratic body.[29]

So why then do we think that the coercion that the state exercises when it imposes its regime of law upon us needs to be legitimated by democratic means?[30] The two key aspects here are, first, that the threat of coercion is pervasive because the state orders our whole existence by the constraints and requirements it imposes. The state, then, threatens to dominate us: to make us live according to its, rather than our, vision of how life should be led. Second, it is very often controversial whether any particular regulation is needed at all, or if it is what form it should take. My examples in the previous paragraph were straightforward. No one could doubt that the use of coercion was justified in the cases I described. But when the state requires us to pay taxes, or to be educated, or to fight in its wars, the position is much less clear. Even those who accept that these general aims are legitimate ones may disagree strongly about the way they are being pursued in a particular case. Democracy, assuming it is effective, limits the use of coercive force to those cases where it is really needed to ensure justice and promote the welfare of citizens, by requiring that the citizens themselves should signal their approval.

So the thesis that coercion requires democratic legitimation holds only under specific circumstances, paradigmatically in the interaction between the state and its citizens. What about the relationship between the state and foreigners? If it coerces them, must it grant them access to a democratic forum? There seems to be no such general requirement. When the state repels an invading army by force, which must surely involve numerous acts of coercion, it does not have to engage in democratic deliberation with the invaders to justify what it is doing. If the current inhabitants are entitled to be on the territory, and the state is their authorized representative, then the invaders have no business to be disrupting the established political order, and that ends the matter. The same applies when the state excludes an individual person whom it justifiably regards as a threat to its citizens. But perhaps the case is different with immigrants, who in general don't pose any threat of that kind. I have said already that if their claim to enter is turned down, they are owed an explanation for the refusal. Must that involve creating a democratic forum in which the state's immigration policy can be discussed?

Here we need to examine the second premise relied on by Abizadeh, that immigration controls are necessarily coercive.[31] It is easy to jump to this conclusion by focusing attention on the means that states use to enforce their immigration rules against those who try to evade them, because these very often do involve coercion. When people are handcuffed and put on planes to be deported back to where they came from, or the boats they are traveling on are forced to turn around and head back to a home port, these are rightly described as coercive measures. But the question is whether the act of exclusion itself, as opposed to the means used to enforce it, is coercive. Here it can be helpful to think of a largely hypothetical case in which a state has simply erected an impenetrable barrier along its borders, so that people trying to enter without permission find their path blocked. Are they being coerced when they are obliged to turn back? To answer this question we need to understand what coercion means and why using it calls for special justification.

The central case of coercion is one in which agent A forces agent B to do something that he would not otherwise have done by threatening B with some bad consequence if he does not comply; and the something in question is something that A wishes to be done.[32] Thus a mugger coerces his victim to hand over her purse, which she would not otherwise have been willing to do, by threatening her with a knife. When coercion succeeds, A imposes his will upon B; B's action is no longer her own, but something done at A's behest. Since we believe in general that people should be autonomous, and coercion removes their autonomy for as long as it lasts, there is a strong presumption against it—which can, however, sometimes be overridden, as my examples of the child beater and the drunken friend showed.

Coercion needs to be distinguished from prevention. When I coerce someone, I narrow down her options to the one thing that I want her to do—hand over the purse, for example. When I prevent someone, I remove one option from the existing set, but leave many others available to be selected. If I prevent a stranger from entering my house, he still has plenty of alternative places in which to seek accommodation. So prevention needs much less justification than coercion, in general. How much it needs may depend on the value to the agent of the action that is being prevented. Notice too that pure cases of coercion and prevention stand at opposite ends of a spectrum, and in between will lie instances in which an intervention rules out many options for the person concerned but leaves a similar number available. How we classify these cases may depend on how valuable, respectively, are the options that are ruled out and those that are left open.

With that conceptual apparatus in place, we can now tackle the question of whether immigration controls are necessarily coercive. I argue that they are not. The immigrant is being prevented from doing something—entering the United States, for example—that he may very much want to do, but he is not being forced to do anything else in particular. He is left with all the options that are available to him in his home country, together with the options that are open in other countries that will take him in.[33] The U.S. authorities are not trying to direct his life, even though they may be frustrating his wishes by excluding him. If the immigrant enters illegally, he may become subject to coercive means to remove him, just as I may have to call the police to get rid of an unwelcome intruder in my house—but that does not imply that initially refusing entry was *itself* coercive, in either case.

If border controls really were coercive, in the proper sense of that term, they would be hard to justify. The reasons I gave in the earlier part of the chapter for restricting immigration—concerns about self-determination, the functioning of democracy, and population size—although weighty enough, would hardly seem sufficient to exclude immigrants who posed no direct threat to the inhabitants if exclusion was a form of coercion. Perhaps it would be necessary to follow Abizadeh's lead and invent democratic forums in which potential immigrants were represented, although Abizadeh himself admits that turning principle into practice would be a complicated matter.[34] Once we see that closing borders is properly understood as preventative, by contrast, we can then direct our attention more fruitfully to two other questions: how strong, relatively speaking, are the claims that different categories of immigrants can make to enter? And what forms of coercion may and may not justifiably be used against those who enter in defiance of the state's laws? Another way of putting this is to ask what responsibilities states have toward prospective immigrants once we grant that states have the right to close their borders. This question is taken up in the chapters that follow.

FIVE

Refugees

WHEN PROSPECTIVE IMMIGRANTS FILE their application forms, or turn up unannounced at an international border, they are making a claim to enter and to join the political community behind the border. But what kind of claim do they have? I have argued so far that states are not obliged to keep their borders open to everyone who might like to enter (so there is no *right* to enter); but also that if someone *does* apply to come in, their reasons for seeking entry must be considered seriously. There are then two issues that need to be addressed. The first is the extent of the immigrant's claim. Is it to enter permanently, and in due course become a full citizen of the receiving society? Or is it to enter for a period, and then to return home once training has been completed or conditions in the home society have sufficiently improved to make going back a reasonable option? The second is the basis on which the claim is made. What grounds can the applicant produce to show why she should be admitted, in circumstances where not everyone will automatically be allowed in?

There two issues seem likely to be connected: the reasons someone gives for being admitted will help determine what their terms of admission should be. In looking at these reasons, however, we soon discover that they have two separate dimensions: first, the type of need or interest that has impelled the immigrant to make his claim; second, the prior relationship (if any) that exists between immigrant and the receiving state. On one dimension, we have the familiar distinction between refugees and economic migrants, where refugees are those whose claim is based on the threat to their human rights created by remaining in their current state of residence,[1] and economic migrants are all those who have an interest in moving to a new society, whether to study, to find work, or to pursue some personal project, but who cannot cite a threat to their human rights as grounds for admission.[2] On the second dimension, there are those who qualify as what I shall call "particularity claimants" and those who do not. Particularity claimants are people who assert that one particular state owes them admission by virtue of what has happened in the past. A clear case would be one in which a group of people have been led to believe that they had a right to immigrate should their circumstances require it.[3] Another example would be people who have performed some service for the state and claim now that being allowed to immigrate is the appropriate form of recompense.[4] Particularity claimants might also be refugees or economic migrants, but what distinguishes them (and justifies the rather awkward label I am applying to them) is that their claim is held against *one particular state,* whereas refugees and economic migrants, although they have chosen to apply in one place, might in many cases find that their needs or interests were equally well served by being admitted elsewhere.

This chapter explores the basis on which refugees can make their claims to be admitted and the extent of the obligations incurred by the state in which asylum is sought. Must all the refugees who apply be accepted, and must they be given permanent residence, or can they be asked to return when the danger they are fleeing from has passed? When is it acceptable to transfer refugees to a third country that is willing to accept them? The first step in answering these questions is to pin down more precisely what it means to be a refugee. This may sound like a pedantic issue, but in fact we can't understand the nature of the claim that the refugee is making until we understand what entitles her to make it—in other words, what her situation must be in order to justify describing herself as a refugee. Politically, too, the skepticism we frequently hear expressed about refugees stems from the belief that many who claim this status are "bogus"—they are simply economic migrants seeking to improve their chances of being admitted. To combat such skepticism, a clear definition is essential.[5] As we will see, however, providing one has proved to be somewhat controversial.

What is not in dispute is that refugees are people toward whom states have more stringent obligations than toward immigrants in general. Without saying that refugees have an automatic entitlement to be admitted to the state they first approach—this is a question to be addressed in due course—we can at least say that the state has duty of care toward them that includes not sending them back to the place of danger they have escaped from, under the principle of *non-refoulement*.[6] The definition we give should reflect this special status, for that is precisely the point in having a separate category of refugees. So in moving toward it we need to think both about the objective situation of the refugees themselves—the manner in which their human rights are threatened—and about the level of obligation it is reasonable to impose on receiving states.[7] There is a parallel here with the duty of rescue born by individuals in emergencies. For this to come into effect, there must on one side be a potential victim or victims facing a threat of death or serious injury, but on the other side the rescuer must be able to intervene without incurring serious risk himself and is entitled to look for an alternative course of action, such as contacting the relevant authorities if there is time to do this. There is not, in other words, an unlimited and unconditional obligation to carry out rescues: the duty that is imposed aims to safeguard the urgent interests of the victim without placing an unacceptable burden on the rescuer.

Most discussion of refugee status starts with the wording of the 1951 Geneva Convention, according to which a refugee is a person who

> owing to a well-founded fear of being persecuted for reasons of race, religion, nationality, membership of a particular social group or political opinion, is outside the country of his nationality and is unable or, owing to such fear, is unwilling to avail himself of the protection of that country.[8]

This fairly narrow definition stands in stark contrast to the much wider definition favored by some authors, according to whom what matters is whether a person's human rights are put at serious risk by remaining in his country of origin, regardless of whether this is due to persecution on the grounds laid down in the Convention, or whether he has already left that country. Michael Dummett, for example, claims that "the qualification laid down by the Convention for being entitled to claim asylum is too restrictive: all conditions that deny someone the ability to live where he is in minimal conditions for a decent human life ought to be grounds for claiming refuge somewhere."[9] What, then, can be said in favor of the narrower definition set out in the Geneva Convention?[10]

Note first that a good deal hinges on what is meant by "persecution." This immediately conjures up cases in which a state threatens an individual or group of individuals with death, or imprisonment, or banishment to some remote region of the country. But it can be given a broader interpretation, such that it covers, for example, discriminatory employment practices whereby members of the oppressed group are denied any opportunity to find paid work, and this is indeed the way in which "persecution" has increasingly been interpreted by courts in democratic societies who have been asked to adjudicate refugee claims. A similar interpretation has sometimes been applied in cases of unequal access to health care and education. Thus active denial of those social and economic rights that count as human rights, as well as of civil and political rights, can be brought under the heading of persecution.[11]

Another respect in which the Convention definition is wider than it may initially appear is that it does not require that the persecution that is feared should be persecution instigated directly by the state.[12] Refugee status could be granted to someone who came under threat by rogue police officers or by local militias, so long as the state had the capacity to offer protection but failed to do so, thereby openly or tacitly colluding in the persecution. The key point is that the person who is claiming refugee status is not in a position to turn to her own state to protect her human rights, either because the state is actively hostile to people like her or because it is willing to allow violations of her human rights by other agents to take place under its auspices.

Even so, it may still seem arbitrary to distinguish between cases in which a person's human rights are put at risk by persecution, however broadly construed, and cases where his rights are unfulfilled because of natural disasters or of continuing poverty that the state he is living in cannot remedy.[13] This thought has motivated Andrew Shacknove's influential definition of refugees as "persons whose basic needs are unprotected by their country of origin, who have no remaining recourse other than to seek international restitution of their needs, and who are so situated that international assistance is possible."[14] As in the case of Dummett's comment on the Convention definition, this broader definition may seem to put the emphasis where it ought to be put, morally speaking, namely on the vulnerable situation of the refugee rather than on the particular cause of his vulnerability. As Carens remarks, "from a moral perspective, what is most important is the severity of the threat to basic human rights and the degree of risk rather than the source or character of the threat."[15]

Accepting Shacknove's definition, or one like it, would certainly increase the number of people worldwide who qualify for refugee status far beyond the nearly 20 million who are currently recognized as having it[16] because it would embrace many, if not all, of those who are living below the UN's $2 per day poverty line, estimated to be in excess of two billion people. But this by itself is not a good reason to reject it. A more relevant reason is that it fails to explain why *refuge*—moving to another society—is the right response to the predicament it describes, rather than intervention aimed at improving the situation of the people it applies to. There is nothing in Shacknove's definition to suggest that the state in question must intend, or be complicit in, its failure to satisfy basic needs. It may simply be unable to deliver sufficient food, water, or medical aid as the case may be, in which case it may welcome external assistance to provide these resources. The Convention definition, by contrast, makes it clear that leaving the society is the only way to escape vulnerability because the state itself is the problem: it is the breakdown of the relationship between the refugee and the government of his country, whereby the state is either the direct agent of persecution or stands aside to allow others to inflict it, and not merely the state's failure as a provider of goods or services, that generates a claim to refuge, and an obligation on other states to provide it.

We may reasonably assume that states that take their obligations toward human rights seriously would normally prefer to discharge those obligations by providing aid externally than by admitting people whose rights are at risk. This, then, is a reason for restricting refugee status to those who cannot be helped except by taking them in. But that does not fully resolve the issue of where the line should be drawn. What should we say, for example, about a firmly entrenched but corrupt government that prevents aid or development funding from reaching the people who need it, not out of malice or hostility, but simply out of greed? Those who try to leave are not fleeing persecution, but they can argue that their human rights are put equally at risk by remaining and that this state of affairs will not change in the foreseeable future. More radically still, we can consider the position of those whose territory becomes uninhabitable, whether temporarily as a result of a natural disaster[17] or permanently as a result of climate change—people in these categories are often now referred to as "environmental refugees." Should we adopt this wider use of the concept, so that it applies to everyone driven by necessity to leave their country of origin?

Those who argue that we should stick to the narrower, Convention-based definition point out that it singles out a class of people for whom the normal bond between a person and her political community has been shattered. Matthew Price puts it this way:

> When people are persecuted . . . they not only face a threat to their bodily integrity or liberty; they are also effectively expelled from their political communities. They are not only victims, but also exiles. Asylum responds not only to victims' need for protection, but also to their need for political standing, by extending membership in a new political community.[18]

Price's argument is that people who are granted asylum—refugees in the strict sense—should also rapidly be granted full and permanent membership in the receiving society, whereas those who are forced to leave for other reasons can be granted temporary residence rights, periodically renewable on the basis of evidence about conditions in the home country. But this rests on the assumption that the causes that gave rise to persecution are such that the refugee will never be in a position to return in safety, whether because these causes themselves persist or because he has been mentally scarred by the experience and would experience psychological hardship if forced to return. Although this may be true in some cases, there will be other cases in which a change of regime means that those who have fled are more than willing to go back and pick up the threads of their previous lives.[19] As I shall argue in Chapter 7, there are strong reasons for granting rights of permanent residence and access to citizenship to all immigrants who have been present in their new society for long enough. But it seems wrong to single out those who are escaping persecution and grant them permanent residence immediately on the grounds that having arrived they will all choose to identify politically with the society that takes them in.

To sum up, we need to distinguish between three categories of people whose human rights go unprotected in their current place of residence:

(a) Those who suffer from actual or anticipated persecution on one of the grounds mentioned in the Geneva Convention that they cannot avoid without leaving the state, whether the state engages actively in the persecution or merely condones it.

(b) Those whose human rights are under threat either from natural calamities or from private acts of violence that the state is unable to prevent, and who can only avoid this threat by migrating.

(c) Those whose human rights are presently under threat, but who could be helped *either* by migrating *or* by outside intervention of one kind or another (aid, investment, the creation of safe havens, etc.).

I suggest that when thinking about immigration we should not count as refugees those who fall into category (c), even though outside states will often have obligations to protect their human rights, and discharging these may take the form of temporary or longer-term admission. In practice, states who decide to admit people in this category describe them not as refugees but use different terms, for example as persons having "temporary protected status" (United States),[20] or "discretionary leave to remain" (United Kingdom). What is more moot is whether we should reserve the term only for those in category (a) or extend it also to those in category (b), perhaps using "Convention refugees" to designate the narrower group. Lawyers tend to prefer the first option (while also arguing for a wide interpretation of "persecution") on the grounds that it is easier for tribunals to establish whether somebody has "a well-founded fear of persecution" than to judge whether their overall situation is such that a serious human rights violation will occur unless they are allowed to migrate.[21] They also express a practical concern that any attempt to widen the Convention itself might backfire by making states even more reluctant than they presently are to carry out their obligations under international law.[22] Philosophers, as we have seen, tend to argue that the morally relevant line falls between (b) and (c) and therefore prefer a wider definition that includes those who fall under (b); the key issue for them is whether migration is *necessary* to ensure that basic rights are fulfilled.[23] Although I see force in the arguments of both sides in this debate and recognize that the definition of "refugee" in international law ought probably be limited to those in category (a), in a book that aims to set out the underlying principles that should guide the treatment of immigrants by states (including in their domestic policies), the wider interpretation is the one to use. In what follows, therefore, I shall understand refugees to be people whose human rights cannot be protected except by moving across a border, whether the reason is state persecution, state incapacity, or prolonged natural disasters.

Our next question is how to understand the obligations that outside states bear to refugees so defined. The source of their obligation plainly lies in the unprotected human rights of the people concerned. This follows from the general position set out in Chapter 2 about the obligations imposed by human rights in cases where a person's own state is unable to provide the necessary protection. It is also clear, to use the distinction made there, that in most cases the responsibility is shared among all those states who are able to help the refugee by admitting her—I discuss some possible exceptions to this principle later on. The question that arises, therefore, is how this collective responsibility can be distributed between states, such that it becomes particular state S's responsibility to look after refugee R.

In practice this issue is resolved by R applying to S for asylum—either by making a visa application at a distance, by turning up at the border, or by entering illegally and then asking for asylum. The assignment of responsibility issue is solved, but in a way that seems arbitrary because there is no reason to assume that the many people who qualify for refugee status will spread their applications in such a way that the cost of processing and admitting them is shared fairly between host states. On the contrary, there are likely to be destinations that are favored by most refugees for reasons having little to do with their quest for asylum itself. So why should the state that the refugee approaches acquire a special responsibility by virtue of this choice?

Notice first that we are quite familiar with the idea of responsibilities that are acquired in seemingly arbitrary ways, having no connection with any specific feature or voluntary choice of the agent who bears them. It is just a matter of chance that I should be passing by when someone collapses in the street. Here a responsibility that in principle could fall to anyone is attributed to a particular person by establishing a salient connection between that person and the individual in need to help. The relevant connections—here a matter simply of physical proximity—may be of different kinds, some having independent moral weight and others not.[24] In every such case, sufficient weight is supplied by the plight of the individual—the threat to his human rights—and the need to find someone to take remedial responsibility. The same logic applies when the responsibility-bearing agent is a collective body such as a state. By the act of applying for asylum, the refugee establishes such a connection, and the state he has approached is obliged to respond, in the first place by carrying out a proper check to see whether he does indeed qualify for refugee status.

There is more to be said, however, because in many cases the refugee by applying to S makes herself *vulnerable* to S, so that what S decides cannot but help to determine her eventual fate. Consider the person who arrives at a land or sea border. If her application is valid but the state nevertheless turns it down, then by effectively forcing her back to the state from which she came, or back out into the open sea, it is actively exposing her to the risk of harm.[25] So it has a duty of care toward her that arises from such vulnerability. This may not be so apparent in the case of someone who applies for a refugee visa from a distance. Here it may seem that a state that refuses the application is not actively exposing the refugee to risk, but simply failing to remove it (and I assume, along with many others, that there is a morally relevant difference between imposing risk and failing to protect against it). But this may overlook the urgency of the refugee's situation. Given limited resources and limited time before the threat to her human rights materializes, she may only be able to approach one possible place of sanctuary. So there is again a sense in which by applying to move to that country, she makes herself vulnerable to the state's decision.

Besides explaining why international law places an obligation on the state that the refugee first reaches to respond to her plight—initially the obligation of *non-refoulement*—the account I have sketched also explains why states have a special responsibility toward *refugees* as such, as opposed to other people whose human rights are at risk and who could readily be assisted. For some commentators, it seems hard to explain why states should give priority to admitting refugees, as opposed, for example, to sending aid to poverty-stricken people who can be helped in situ. The latter policy might well be a more efficient way of protecting human rights in general, and thus will appeal both to utilitarians and to those who want more specifically to minimize violations of such rights.[26] The explanation, as we can now see, is that the refugee has not only a general human rights claim that can be met by admitting her but also a *specific* claim against the state she has approached by virtue, first, of having established a physical connection to that state and, second, of having become vulnerable to the decision it takes regarding her. Someone living in poverty in sub-Saharan Africa, by contrast, who has no effective claim against his own state, has only an undirected claim against all those states that might be able to send aid or intervene in some other way (which is, of course, another misfortune for him).[27]

We might balk at the idea that one person's claim against another is enhanced to the extent that the first becomes vulnerable to the second. But this is perhaps because we are thinking of cases in which the first person intentionally makes himself more vulnerable. Some refugees appear to be behaving like that—for example, people who deliberately choose to travel on unseaworthy boats or people who destroy their identity papers so that it's difficult or impossible to establish their nationality and therefore to return them to their country of origin. These are clearly desperate men and women, and we may find it hard to blame them for using these strategies, but at the same time we should not want their claims to be enhanced by such means. But simply lodging a claim for asylum does not usually make the claimant more vulnerable to having her human rights abused; rather what it does is make her vulnerable (in a different sense) to the decision that the state she has applied to will take. Her claim that was previously indeterminate now has a specific target, and that is why the state where asylum is sought now has a special obligation to her.

So far I have been explaining how states acquire specific obligations to refugees. But what exactly are they obliged to do in response to the latter's claims? Must they admit all who apply, and must they admit them as permanent residents, or may they give them temporary status with the possibility of renewal? Not all refugees are unwelcome or impose net costs on the receiving state, but in aggregate they are likely to be regarded as a burden—not least because the state may have an overall target for net immigration and accepting them will take spaces away from others whom the state may positively wish to attract.[28] Since the pattern of applications is somewhat random, there seems to be a case for burden sharing—for distributing refugees between states in a way that roughly matches each state's capacity to receive them. So this suggests that the state in which asylum is initially sought is entitled to pass them on once their claim has been properly checked, so long as it complies with the spirit of *non-refoulement* and does not return them either to their country of origin or to anywhere else where their human rights would be similarly under threat.

Of course this denies the refugee her choice of abode. But assuming as I am that there is no human right to immigrate as such, the refugee's claim is to reside somewhere where her human rights are secure, and this need not be the place that she most prefers. (I shall later examine whether there might be some other objection to the involuntary transfer of refugees between states, such as that it demeans them.) How is this human rights standard to be applied? This will depend to some extent on how long the period of refugeehood is likely to last. If it is short term (as sometimes in the case of escape from a civil war), it may be sufficient for the refugee to be housed in a purpose-built camp so long as this provides physical security, adequate food, medical care, and so forth. But as the time period extends, it becomes essential that the refugee should be in a place where he has opportunities for work and recreation, can have his children educated, can practice his religion—in other words, is able to engage in all of the activities that make up a decent human life. This would not necessarily imply being in an advanced Western society, but it might well mean being in a place where conditions of life were considerably better than in the society he was escaping. Is it a paradox that the refugee can insist on a higher standard of living than his compatriot who is living in poverty but was not forced to flee? Not if we think through the logic of his claim. He applies for asylum because his human rights are under threat in his country of origin and the only way that he can avoid this threat is to migrate. The state he applies to has a provisional responsibility to admit him, but is permitted to transfer him to a third country so long as his human rights are secure there; but to meet this condition the destination chosen may have to be one where general living standards are higher than they were in the place of departure.

How might it be possible to manage the distribution of refugees in a less arbitrary way than by simply attributing responsibility to the state of first application? There are three broad alternatives. The first is to establish an international system whereby refugees are assigned to states by criteria that are agreed to be fair, taking account of the numbers involved; this would need to be managed by an international agency responsible for directing the movement of refugees. The second is to continue with the system whereby states are obliged to respond to asylum claims lodged at their door, but to permit and indeed encourage transfers between states by means of side payments from sending to receiving countries, so that states could avoid having to take in more refugees than they would wish to admit. The third, which is closest to the current situation, is to allow states to control refugee flows by making it more or less difficult for asylum seekers to reach their territory—in other words, permit each state to assess its fair share of the refugee burden, and then to limit access by using the kinds of methods that states now use to deter migrants from arriving.[29]

The first proposal faces two main difficulties. The first is the practical one of getting states to agree to the creation of an international authority with sufficient power to organize the scheme, given their general wish to retain control over their borders. For that reason, schemes of this kind that have been proposed in the literature on refugee protection tend to be less ambitious and to recommend the formation of consortia of states with shared interests and cultural connections to exercise "common but differentiated responsibility."[30] In practice this would mean the bulk of refugees being housed in developing countries neighboring the territory they have fled, with financial contributions to support them from richer states within the consortium. Evidently the success of this watered-down proposal depends on enough states being willing to join responsibility-sharing groups and also on the belief that most refugees only require short-term protection rather than permanent resettlement. There is also a more principled difficulty for any scheme that requires states to accept a designated quota of refugees. This is to find criteria for distributing refugees fairly that would command widespread assent. The general aim must be to equalize the burden between states. But should the numbers be calculated on the basis of population size, population density, GDP, or some other indicator of the state's capacity to receive and accommodate refugees?[31] This is further complicated by uncertainty at the point of admission about whether what is required is short-term sanctuary or permanent settlement. If it is the latter, states may differ in the ease with which they are able to accommodate refugees whose cultural background is markedly different from that of their own citizens—for example, East Asian states have proved particularly reluctant to take in people who fall under this heading. In such cases, presumably, integration costs will be higher. Taking these various factors together, it is hard to imagine a weighting being agreed by all participating states.[32]

Consider next the proposal that states that are unwilling to accommodate as many refugees as apply to them should be able to make financial payments to third countries to take them in instead. This does not eliminate arbitrariness over which countries are approached by asylum seekers, with "popular" countries having either to accept greater numbers or to pay more in transfer fees, though it can be argued that once such schemes are in place there will be less incentive to apply to a particular state. Alternatively, the transfer scheme could be combined with a quota system, such that states would be able to pass on without payment refugees in excess of their quota.[33] This of course depends on being able to achieve agreement on quotas in the first place, in face of the difficulties raised in the previous paragraph.[34] But is it acceptable to pass on refugees in this way, not on the grounds that it was impossible to accommodate them, but simply because the state preferred to pay for them to be transferred? Critics argue that this "commodifies" refugees in an unacceptable way.[35] But this charge is very rarely spelled out in any detail. According to Michael Sandel, for example,

> A market in refugees changes our view of who refugees are and how they should be treated. It encourages the participants—the buyers, the sellers, and also those whose asylum is being haggled over—to think of refugees as burdens to be unloaded or as revenue sources, rather than as human beings in peril.[36]

But consider by way of analogy the case where it becomes difficult for a family to cope with an elderly relative who has been living with them, and who therefore shop around for a suitable retirement home that they will pay for. From the family's point of view, this is paying to avoid a burden, and from the home's point of view, the elderly person is a revenue source. This surely does not mean, from either perspective, that Granddad is no longer regarded as a human being in need of help. His humanity is fully respected provided

(a) that the family chooses a place where he can be looked after properly rather than simply opting for whichever is cheapest; and (b) that the staff in the home treat their new resident with dignity. Similarly, under a refugee-trading scheme, the sending state needs to verify that the human rights of the people it passes on will be adequately protected in its partner states, and the latter need to put in place a program that responds to refugees' needs, distinguishing in particular between those in need of temporary protection and those requiring permanent resettlement. If these conditions are met, their human dignity is not put in question.

Matthew Gibney raises a more specific concern, namely, that a market in refugees will attach a price to *particular* refugees, and "there is something uniquely dubious about a market that registers in price terms how much states *don't want* particular groups of refugees. It is as if refugees are now not only being rejected by states, but, to add insult to injury, they are also being provided with a monetary measure of how unwanted they are."[37] However, this objection assumes that under a transfer system states will vary the amount they pay to pass refugees on according to the specific characteristics of the refugees themselves, and there is no reason why this should happen. The payments made are meant to reflect the material costs borne by the receiving states in accommodating the refugees who are transferred, and these will be uniform costs (if a *receiving* state is reluctant to accept particular groups of refugees for cultural reasons, then this can be handled by making the scheme multilateral rather than bilateral; there is no reason for the price paid to vary).

Gibney's objection to refugee trading does, however, raise a further question, about the criteria that states can legitimately use when deciding which refugees to take in and which to pass on. I shall have more to say in Chapter 6 about criteria for selecting immigrants generally, but the question here is whether (reasoned) selection is permissible *at all,* or whether states must use some randomized procedure if they are only going to take in a fixed proportion of those who apply for asylum. Consider four possible grounds for selection: (1) The refugee's need for permanent settlement; (2) The causal role played by the receiving state in creating the situation from which the refugee is escaping; (3) The likely economic contribution of the refugee to the receiving society; (4) The degree of cultural affinity between refugee and host political community.

(1) This seems a relevant consideration. I have argued that the places to which refugees are transferred must be human rights compliant, and this means that they provide all the opportunities that are needed to live a decent human life and not just food, shelter, and the other immediate necessities. Nevertheless, under the kind of arrangement we are envisaging (realistically one in which rich developed states pass on a proportion of those who apply for asylum to less developed countries, where the vast majority of refugees already live), there will inevitably be less assurance that the same opportunities will continue to be available far into the future. This matters less if the stay is only going to be temporary. Moreover, the refugee has chosen to apply to state S, and although I have argued that this does not confer an entitlement to enter and remain in S, this adds weight to his claim when the chances that he can return safely to his country of origin are remote. In contrast, for someone who needs only short-term protection, an expression of preference for a particular state counts for less.

(2) Consider next situations in which the state to which the asylum seeker applies is at least in part responsible for making her into a refugee. These will typically be cases in which it has intervened in her country of origin, creating conflict between national or ethnic groups that expose her to threats of persecution—for example, the position of some Iraqi Kurds after the Iraq War. The granting of asylum may then be viewed as a form of reparation.[38] This makes the refugee into what I have called a "particularity claimant" and provides grounds for admitting her to the intervening state rather than to some other place; her reparative claim is a claim against that state in particular and may not be satisfied by a promise of refuge somewhere else (this will depend on the extent of her loss). As Souter argues, refugees' choices about where to claim asylum gain additional significance in these circumstances: "after causing or contributing to their displacement, heeding refugees' wishes is the least that responsible states can do."[39] Indeed they may be able to claim not just temporary asylum but permanent residence on reparative grounds.

(3) Many states choose which immigrants to accept by examining whether they bring special skills that will contribute to the economy. But can this criterion also be used, legitimately, when deciding which asylum seekers to admit? Keeping in mind that the refugee's claim is based on the threat to his human rights, not on his potential contribution, it might seem

arbitrary to give him any kind of priority on this basis. Certainly it would be unacceptable if the asylum claim itself were to be assessed more generously in the case of those who were seen as having valuable skills. But assume that the claim is assessed strictly on the grounds set out earlier in this chapter (namely, the necessity of escaping a serious threat to human rights), could productive skill nevertheless count at the second stage, when deciding whether asylum is offered in the state of first entry or somewhere else? I believe such a practice would be legitimate only in cases where the state is offering something more than asylum to the refugee, for example when it is offering permanent settlement to someone who does not otherwise qualify for it. States are surely permitted to do this, just as they can offer resettlement to refugees who have been granted asylum elsewhere, and in these circumstances it is reasonable to take account of the refugee's prospective contribution. Could those who are moved elsewhere under a burden-sharing arrangement complain about the unequal treatment they are receiving? I do not think so. The important point is that they are treated equally at the point at which their claim to asylum is assessed and thereafter in ways that respect their human rights. That the state does more than it is obliged to do for some refugees is not an injustice to the others.

(4) Can states select in favor of their cultural kin when deciding whom to admit as refugees? The rationale for doing so is set out clearly by Carens, though it is not so clear whether he accepts it himself:

> As an empirical matter, it is almost certainly the case that a state's willingness to take in refugees will depend in part on the extent to which the current population identifies with the refugees and their plight. Moreover, other things being equal, it will be easier for the refugees themselves to adapt to the new society and for the receiving society to include them, the more the refugees resemble the existing population with respect to language, culture, religion, history, and so on.[40]

To take a concrete example, the wars in Syria and Iraq that broke out in 2014 led to calls in some quarters for traditionally Christian countries such as the United Kingdom to give priority to Christian refugees escaping from these countries. This was justified in part on the grounds that Christian families were undergoing particularly severe persecution, but also on the grounds that

Christian states had special obligations to people who shared their national religion. The first ground is clearly relevant, but what about the second?

Such an argument from common culture seems hard to defend, unless it can be presented as a way of dividing responsibilities between states. In the Iraq/Syria case it was claimed that Muslim refugees would be more likely to be offered sanctuary by neighboring Islamic states such as Jordan. Assuming this is true, and that in general states are disposed to give precedence to those who share their citizens' cultural or religious values, then any one state in formulating its policy can justifiably take this into account. But without such a background, and considering the nature of the obligation toward refugees, cultural selection does not seem defensible (whether it might be in the case of economic migrants is an issue to be considered at length in Chapter 6).

I have been discussing refugee selection in the context of arrangements whereby countries of first asylum can pass asylum seekers on to other places willing to take them in; the state's obligation to the refugees can be discharged in this way so long as human rights are safeguarded. But what if it proves impossible to create adequate burden-sharing schemes, and states are unwilling to admit all those who apply for asylum? In practice, as noted earlier, receiving states have taken measures to prevent refugees from reaching their shores, thereby evading having to discharge their duty of *non-refoulement*. Such behavior is widely condemned as a breach of human rights. On the other hand, defenders will argue that this is self-defense in a situation in which other countries are unwilling to carry their fair share of the refugee burden.

To resolve this dispute, we need first to be clear about the nature of the obligation to admit refugees. It is a remedial obligation in the sense that there would be no refugees in the first place unless other states were either actively violating or passively failing to protect the human rights of people living on their territory.[41] Obligations of this kind are limited by considerations of cost. So the general reasons that can justify limiting immigration given in Chapter 4 come into play here. A state that has set an overall immigration target, on grounds that are publicly justified, can also take steps to ensure that the number of refugees it admits does not exceed that target. What it cannot do is use indefensible means to prevent refugees arriving while continuing to take in significant numbers of "desirable" immigrants—this would simply be hypocrisy on its part. If it is going to deter physical arrival, it must allow refugees to apply remotely, through consular offices abroad, for example.[42]

The net effect, nonetheless, may be that there are some refugees for whom no state is willing to take responsibility: each receiving state sincerely and reasonably believes it has done enough, taking into account the cost of accepting refugees, to discharge its fair share of the burden.[43] Here we are confronted with a tragic conflict of values: on the one side, people who are liable to be severely harmed as a result of the persecution they are undergoing; on the other, bounded political communities that are able to sustain democracy and achieve a modicum of social justice but need closure to do this. I shall return to reflect further on this conflict of values at the end of Chapter 9. We can hope, of course, that it does not arise because the number of people entitled to claim asylum remains small enough that a fair system of burden sharing can accommodate them all. But supposing this hope is unfounded: then it is better to say honestly that not everyone can be rescued, just as in the other cases where human rights are at stake—such as conflicts that require humanitarian intervention—we may have to acknowledge a gap between the rights of the vulnerable and the obligations of those who might protect them.[44]

I have focused in this chapter on refugees' claims to be admitted and the corresponding responsibilities of receiving states. I have not so far discussed in any detail how a state must treat those who arrive on its shores claiming asylum, and what rights it must grant them. These questions will be addressed in Chapter 7, after a discussion of the claims of immigrants who are not applying as refugees in Chapter 6.

SIX

Economic Migrants

IF WE EXAMINE THE PROFILE of those who migrate into (and sometimes between) the liberal democracies, we quickly discover that by far the larger number count as economic migrants rather than as refugees, to use the distinction introduced in Chapter 5.[1] They are not driven out by a fear of persecution or some other immediate threat to their human rights, but drawn in by the advantages that their new society has to offer. Often the incentive to move is strictly economic. Those who move from poor countries to developed countries without changing the kind of work they do can typically expect their wages to rise by between four and twelve times.[2] Not everyone who migrates does so for economic reasons, of course. But because of the immigration policies that the receiving societies have come to adopt (which very often require immigrants to prove that they have jobs waiting for them on arrival), migration on narrowly economic grounds is the only kind of migration available to most.[3]

In this chapter my focus will be on the *admission* of economic migrants, by which I mean both the way in which they are selected and the general terms on which they are admitted (e.g., whether permanently or temporarily). I postpone till Chapter 7 most questions about the rights that should be given to resident immigrants who are not (yet) full citizens. I shall also focus, in line with the general aims of the book, on immigrants who apply to enter the developed liberal democracies. This means setting aside other large-scale migration schemes that may raise serious ethical and political issues, such as the temporary labor programs sponsored by the oil-rich Gulf states; some of the conclusions that I reach may apply to these too, though I shall not pursue the point.

I have already argued at length, in Chapter 3, that economic migrants cannot claim admission as a matter of justice: neither common ownership of the earth, nor global equality of opportunity, nor the human right to free movement can be appealed to in support of such a claim. Broadly speaking, what can justify their admission is mutual advantage: the migrant has an interest in improving her condition, and the members of the receiving state can expect to benefit from her presence. But this doesn't mean that no questions of justice arise when admission decisions are made. The gain that is created should be distributed fairly between the two parties, which means that the terms of admission cannot merely be the least that the migrant would be willing to accept to induce her to move. Furthermore, the criteria used to decide who to accept and who to reject must also be fair. Although I shall elaborate on this later in the chapter, the underlying point is that even when it is matter of discretion that some benefit is provided, the distribution of that benefit between possible recipients may still be subject to constraints of justice—so, to take the most obvious case, racially selective admissions policies must be ruled out. And finally, some attention must be given to obligations of justice between receiving and sending states. Migration can be a boon when it results in immigrants sending home remittances or returning after some period with enhanced physical or human capital; it can be a curse when it drains poor countries of their most highly trained professionals. Assuming that rich democracies are required at the very least not to hinder, if not positively to help, development in countries where people cannot yet enjoy all of their human rights, the effects of migration on sending countries must be factored into a just immigration policy. So the task of this chapter is to spell out what justice requires of us, citizens of liberal democracies, when responding to the claims of prospective immigrants who are not refugees.

I begin by considering the terms of admission. Admissions policies in the real world come in many different shapes and sizes, but to simplify matters it is worth dividing them into three broad categories:[4]

1. Unconditional and permanent admission. The immigrant may be required to meet certain preconditions in advance of being admitted, but once these are satisfied he is then accepted on a permanent basis and need do nothing more to remain legally in the receiving country (becoming a *citizen* may, however, require taking extra steps, such as passing a test).

2. Conditional admission. The immigrant is issued with a visa that allows her to remain for a period of time and may also include a requirement to remain in paid work. At the end of that period, the visa may be renewed upon meeting provisos such as continuing to hold a qualifying job. After a number of years in this status, a permanent right of residence may be granted.

3. Temporary admission. The immigrant is admitted for a strictly limited period of time and required to return home when that period ends. During the period of residence he is required to work either for a particular employer or within a particular sector (such as agricultural work or nursing). Admission on the same basis can be renewed on future occasions, but there is no transfer route to permanent residence.

Our first question must be: Is each of these in principle acceptable as an admissions policy, so long as appropriate safeguards to protect the immigrant (to be discussed later) are put in place? Or must immigrants always be admitted under a policy of type 1, as permanent residents with access to full citizenship at some later point? This more restrictive view was defended by Michael Walzer, initially by considering the position of noncitizen metics in ancient Athens. Walzer claimed that by living among the Athenians but having no political rights, they were subject to a form of tyranny.[5] Something similar, he suggested, was true of the guest workers who had been encouraged to migrate to European states such as West Germany from the mid-1950s onward, but who were then disbarred from acquiring citizenship and as a result suffered from economic vulnerability and social exclusion.[6] Reflecting on these experiences, Walzer maintained that all immigrants must be allowed to become full members of the political community, with the opportunity to gain rights of citizenship in due course. As he put it,

Men and women are either subject to the state's authority, or they are not; and if they are subject, they must be given a say, and ultimately an equal say, in what that authority does. Democratic citizens, then, have a choice: if they want to bring in new workers, they must be prepared to enlarge their own membership; if they are unwilling to accept new members, they must find ways within the limits of the domestic market to get socially necessary work done. And those are their only choices.[7]

According to Walzer, therefore, type 3 admission policies would be categorically ruled out, and type 2 policies would be inadmissible unless they were so constructed that progression to full citizenship was swift and more or less automatic (in which case they would barely differ from type 1). Such a view would outlaw most of what democratic states currently do to regulate immigration, but might it nonetheless be the correct view to hold?

I believe there are two ways in which to read Walzer's argument. The first is to focus on the position of the migrants themselves and to claim that only unconditional admission policies of type 1 sufficiently protect their substantive rights—for example, give them sufficient security against being exploited economically by their employers or forced to work in unsafe conditions. The second is to appeal to the character of the political community as a whole and to claim that it cannot be a genuine democracy so long as it makes and applies laws to an internal minority who are less than equal by virtue of their provisional status and lack of political rights. These two arguments don't contradict one another, and Walzer includes elements of both in his discussion, but they are worth separating, because while the second appears to condemn policies of types 2 and 3 *categorically*, whatever their precise form, the first leaves it an open question whether some conditional or temporary migration programs might be sufficiently well regulated that participants' rights are properly protected.

Historically that has certainly not been the case with "guest-worker" programs.[8] Because admission and continued residence were often dependent on remaining with a particular employer or at least working in a particular occupation, and because guest workers were unable to join unions, they had little bargaining power and were largely at the mercy of their employers. And even if they were not required to return home after a fixed period, there was generally no opportunity to move beyond guest-worker status. Receiving governments saw them primarily as a source of cheap labor, and sending governments were reluctant to insist on greater protection since they benefited indirectly from remittances and were anxious that their own people might be substituted by workers from elsewhere. These political incentives still exist and pose a danger to any temporary or conditional migration policy that aims to comply with human rights and social justice. But it is nonetheless possible to set out the rudiments of such a policy.

The first is that the government of the host society should fully protect the human rights of the migrants to the extent that their temporary status requires. The last clause is needed because there are rights that belong to permanent residents that are not essential to temporary migrants, given their actual needs while living abroad—for example, because guest-worker programs often do not include the right to bring family members in, the human right to family life doesn't have to be protected in the usual way in the host society.[9] It is reasonable to assume that in many cases migrants will have families in their home societies waiting for them to return. In view of their relatively short period of residence, temporary migrants cannot demand political rights (though they ought to continue to hold these in their home societies). On the other hand, such migrants should enjoy a complete set of civil rights—rights to security of the person, to privacy, to freedoms of expression and movement, and so forth—and these rights should receive the same level of protection (through legal representation, etc.) as for other residents and citizens. At work, they are entitled to be protected against dangerous and oppressive working conditions in the same way as everyone else. They should also enjoy some social rights, rights to housing and to medical care, for example. It would not in principle be wrong for temporary migrants to be required to insure themselves to cover the costs of providing these rights, but the underlying point is that by virtue of their presence on its territory, the state becomes ultimately responsible for ensuring that basic rights such as these are safeguarded.

Temporary migrants cannot then claim to be treated as citizens are in all respects (the position of those who are admitted on a longer term basis will be discussed in Chapter 7).[10] They are not full members of the receiving society: the underlying assumption is that they are citizens of another society and will continue to enjoy a complete set of rights in that place when they return. Their primary purpose in migrating is to work and earn money that they can send or bring back home.[11] Although they are properly awarded fewer rights, they are also protected against some of the burdens that citizens have to carry: for example, they cannot be conscripted, called on to perform jury service, or required to vote where voting is compulsory (though they are usually liable to pay taxes). To insist on complete equality would run contrary to the purpose of guest-worker programs, which on the one hand is to make guest workers attractive to employers and to the receiving society, and on the other to allow the workers themselves to derive maximum financial benefit from the program. Employers must pay guest workers at least the minimum wage that has been fixed for the society as a whole, but the level at which their wage is set above that minimum, and the terms and conditions of employment more generally, provided they are agreed in advance under conditions of full information, need not correspond exactly to what other workers receive. Equally, temporary workers should be relieved of having to pay into social insurance and pension schemes from which they cannot expect to benefit.[12]

The underlying idea is that temporary migrants should be offered a fair deal, given the reason for their migration. They should not be burdened with unnecessary expenses or obligations; nor should they expect to receive all of the benefits that citizens standardly receive. The resentment that is sometimes felt by the locals against temporary migrants is often driven by a perception, usually a false one, that the deal being provided is not fair but rather is weighted in their favor. So it is important that its terms should be publicly aired. It is also important that these programs should have a definite termination point for each participant, and that their duration should be short—one or two years at most. A large part of the objection to twentieth-century guest-worker programs in countries such as Germany and Switzerland was that guest-worker status could be prolonged indefinitely with no prospect of moving beyond it toward citizenship. A receiving society might of course choose to allow temporary migrants to transfer to permanent resident status (and thereafter to citizenship) when the period of the program comes to an end, though this is not required and might be seen as anomalous given the program's aim.[13] What is objectionable is to leave people initially admitted on a temporary basis in limbo thereafter.

Let me now consider two objections that might be made to such programs from the perspective of the migrants' own interests (recall that I am considering two readings of Walzer's argument against temporary migration; we are still looking at the first). One is that the justification for allowing wages and conditions of work to be set (within the limits noted above) by agreement between migrants and their employers assumes that such an agreement is indeed voluntary. But in many cases, it will be argued, migration is *not* voluntary: the migrant moves abroad on a temporary basis out of desperation, hoping to earn enough to keep his family out of extreme poverty. At the same time, he may know very little about what awaits him in the society that he is joining.

This objection has some force, even though it is probably true that most people who migrate on a temporary basis are not in such desperate straits as the argument supposes.[14] Since we cannot assume that migrants will always be in a position to offer their consent, it is important to ensure that the programs in question are properly regulated by the receiving state and also that sending states provide accurate information to those about to embark on them. As a matter of general principle, if an arrangement is fair, in the sense that it would be agreed to by people who are in a position to consent freely, then it is also fair to apply it to those whose consent cannot be assumed.[15] An acceptable program must pass that test, and the state must ensure that its rules are applied to everyone who participates, even if they would be willing, because they are desperate, to settle for less.[16]

The second objection holds that temporary migrants will not be adequately protected against exploitation by their employers unless they are given the option of becoming permanent residents (and eventually citizens) at the end of the program.[17] Lenard and Straehle offer two reasons in support of this objection:

> First, the knowledge that these workers are entitled (in time) to citizenship will decrease the receiving society's willingness to permit them to work under abusive and exploitative conditions (since doing so will reflect their failure to protect their citizens and future citizens), and second, it will give temporary workers the authority they need to demand that their rights are respected by their employers, since they no longer need to fear automatic deportation.[18]

The latter argument, as presented by Lenard and Straehle, assumes that temporary workers will be tied to a single employer who is authorized to determine their legal residency status. However, this need not be the case, and indeed there are good reasons to grant migrants the right to change their employer and to join trade unions to ensure that this right is protected, as well as for other reasons. This is consistent with requiring that they work in a particular branch of the economy, for example, as nurses or caregivers. Such flexibility provides protection against abusive employers even if the overall duration of the migrants' residence is time limited.

What now of the claim that where temporary workers have the right to progress to citizenship in the future, this policy will induce existing citizens to ensure that they are safeguarded against exploitation? Because the migrants presently have no share in (formal) political power, this could only be a psychological claim about the way that voters will think. As such, it does not seem intuitively compelling. There seems to be no psychological inconsistency in citizens valuing guest-worker programs because of the benefits they bring to both parties, and accepting that these programs need to be properly regulated to ensure that the migrants are fairly treated, yet not wishing to enlarge their community permanently by granting the migrants residency rights.

We come finally to Walzer's argument that guest-worker programs are inconsistent with the democratic idea that everyone who is subject to the state's authority must be given a say in what the authority does; the objection to such programs is that they corrupt the political community as a whole by creating a subjugated class toward whom the citizens act as "tyrants."[19] This argument must be qualified somewhat, since democracies routinely exclude some of those subject to their authority from political rights—the young, the insane, some prisoners.[20] More relevant perhaps is the fact that short-term visitors such as tourists and students are awarded no such rights despite being subject to the country's law during their time of stay. In these cases we assume that the visitors implicitly consent to the imposition and that they are being offered a fair deal since they also benefit from the law's protection while they remain. So how are temporary migrants different? The crucial issue, plainly, is the length of their stay, together with the fact that they are more vulnerable to exploitation by virtue of being employed. This means that both consent and legal protection take on additional significance. But provided those two pillars are in place—the migrants are properly informed about the conditions they will enjoy in the host society, and there are mechanisms in place to ensure the protection of their legal rights—it is not clear why being deprived of political rights should amount to "tyranny."[21] It is relevant here to reflect that many decisions a political community might make will have consequences that extend far beyond the end of a temporary worker's stay. So there would also be something anomalous, on democratic grounds, in granting her the same political rights as permanent residents.

I concede nonetheless that there is something troubling about the image of a two-caste society that temporary migration on a large scale without accompanying political rights creates. We feel this particularly when the immigrants are taking on menial work that the natives are unwilling to perform. And so we may be faced with a value conflict where we have to set the benefit to the migrants themselves, and even more to the societies from which they come, against the cost to the host society in (egalitarian) solidarity.[22] This makes it particularly important that the programs should be designed in a way that maximizes these benefits. I will return to this later when discussing the brain-drain problem (which suggests that sometimes migration may be a net loss to the sending societies). My conclusion now is that (genuine) temporary migration programs should not be regarded as unjust so long as the safeguards I have outlined are put in place and that the greater problem lies with type 2 conditional admission schemes, which create greater uncertainty on the part of those who join them about what the future holds and which may potentially condemn them to permanent second-class status.[23] This is partly a matter of how the schemes are designed, and I will return to this question in Chapter 7. Here I want to move to the equally contentious issue of selection criteria, whether for temporary or permanent admission. On what basis is it permissible to choose among economic migrants, in circumstances when only a fraction of those who apply are going to be accepted?[24]

The last hundred years or so have seen liberal democracies engaging in a major shift in policy on this question.[25] At the beginning of that period, it was routinely accepted that immigration policy should be heavily biased in favor of immigrants from particular national or ethnic backgrounds: United States policy, for example, initially favored northern Europeans, while Australia's was even more narrowly focused on immigrants of British origin. Today, with few exceptions, it is regarded as impermissible to select migrants (leaving aside refugees) on any grounds other than their possession of relevant qualifications and skills, especially work-related skills. But this creates a puzzle. Why, if states have discretion to decide whether to take in migrants at all, are they obliged to select the ones they do admit on such a narrow basis? Why exactly was it unjust for Australia to pursue a "White Australia" policy in the 1920s and 1930s or for Britain as late as 1981 to pass an Immigration Act specifically designed to discourage migration from countries other than the white Dominions?

As I remarked earlier, there are circumstances in which justice does not require that a benefit be provided, but does nonetheless place constraints on how the benefit is distributed if it *is* provided. In particular, certain forms of discrimination may be outlawed. An example of Michael Blake's makes the point well: a state is not required as a matter of justice to supply each citizen with a car, but if it decides to go into the business of providing cars, it cannot then offer them to white people but not to blacks.[26] However, we might think that this stems from a general principle of equal treatment that a state is required to follow in dealing with its own citizens, whereas there is no reason to assume that the same principle will apply to the state's interactions with outsiders.[27] So why exactly should an equality rule that excludes "selecting by origin" apply to inward migration?

One possible reason is that there is a human right against discrimination, and this applies to all policies that discriminate between people on the grounds referred to in the relevant international documents, such as the International Covenant on Civil and Political Rights, which prohibits (in Article 26) discrimination on grounds such as "race, colour, sex, language, religion, political or other opinion, national or social origin, property, birth or other status,"[28] But this right clearly stands in need of interpretation. Its scope cannot be deduced from the formal statement in Article 26. There are presumably many contexts in which one or other of these criteria may properly be used for purposes of selection. It would not, for example, be considered a breach of human rights if a political party decides to draw up an all-women short list to select its candidate in a particular constituency, if a public broadcaster chooses only among those able to read the news in Welsh, or if a church confines membership to those who belong to its own faith. But these are examples of discrimination on the grounds of sex, language, and religion, respectively. So the human right against discrimination must be interpreted as prohibiting discrimination on grounds *that are irrelevant to the right or benefit being allocated*—and, as the examples just given show, the grounds that are listed in Article 26 are not always irrelevant. Those who in the past defended selecting immigrants by race or national origin thought that they could justify using these criteria by appeal to the "character" or "moral health" of their societies. To defeat these arguments requires giving substantive grounds for thinking that such claims are either false or irrelevant to the good that is being provided, namely, admission. Appealing simply to the human right against discrimination will not settle the matter.[29]

An initially more promising avenue is to argue that selecting immigrants on grounds such as race or religion is an injustice to some existing citizens, namely, those who belong to the group or groups that the immigration policy disfavors.[30] By discriminating in this way, the state appears to be labeling these people as second-class citizens. As Michael Blake has put the point, "the state making a statement of racial preference in immigration necessarily makes a statement of racial preference domestically as well."[31] This will often provide states with strong reasons not to pursue discriminatory admissions policies, but a limitation of this approach is that it would not apply to a state that was already religiously or ethnically homogeneous and whose members wished it to remain so.[32] Notice also that the argument hinges upon the injustice that is done to existing citizens whose status is lowered by the discriminatory policy, not on any wrong that is done specifically to the excluded candidates for admission. We might therefore think that the focus is in the wrong place: the primary injustice of a wrongfully discriminatory immigration policy is the one done to those whom it excludes, whereas the signal it sends out to existing citizens is a secondary (though still important) matter. But given the assumption that no economic migrant has a prior right to be admitted, what explains that injustice?

We need to consider the kind of claim that an economic migrant can make against the political community that she is seeking to enter. At this point the weak cosmopolitan position that I defended in Chapter 2 comes into play. The economic migrant cannot claim that she has a human right to enter, such that the state is obliged to admit her. But typically she will have a strong interest-based claim to lodge: given the degree of personal dislocation that migration involves, she must anticipate gaining considerably by moving to the new society—for example, by working in a different kind of job, or for a much higher wage, than she could hope to obtain in her own society. According to the weak cosmopolitan premise, to turn down such a claim without giving relevant reasons for the refusal is to show disrespect for the person making it. It is to treat her as though she were of no moral significance. This extends also to the selection of immigrants from the pool of applicants. It is not sufficient merely to put forward the general reasons in favor of immigration controls. If John is going to be granted entry while Jaime is turned away, the latter must be offered relevant reasons for his unequal treatment.[33]

This appeal to weak cosmopolitanism explains why the state is not entitled to use merely arbitrary methods in choosing which immigrants to admit, but it does not yet settle which reasons should count in making the selection, and so far, therefore, does not explain what is wrong with using race, ethnicity, and other such criteria. One way to narrow down the list is to say that the reasons must be ones that the immigrants themselves can accept. We can assume that no immigrant will regard her own skin color as legitimate grounds for exclusion. But a problem then arises in cases where the receiving state and the prospective immigrant hold different views about what should count as relevant. Suppose, for example, that a state decides to admit only high-skilled immigrants on the grounds that it has a greater economic need for these than for low-skilled workers. An immigrant without the relevant skills might reject this reasoning on the grounds that he (and others like him) deserves a chance to improve his condition, and that both he and the receiving state will gain something by admitting him. So it is asking too much to say that the reasons the state gives must also be ones that the immigrants can accept (if "can accept" means "will in fact accept once these reasons are explained"). Instead the relevant condition is that the reasons the state gives for its selective admissions policy must be good reasons, reasons that the immigrants *ought* to accept given that the general aims of the policy are legitimate ones.[34]

Here we need to revert to a point that I made at the beginning of the chapter, namely, that the admission of economic migrants should be understood in terms of mutual advantage—both parties must expect to gain from the decision to admit. The receiving state has certain policy goals—for example, it is aiming for economic growth or to provide its citizens with generous welfare services—and it is entitled to use immigration policy as one of the means to achieve such goals. This explains why selecting immigrants

according to the particular skills that they can deploy is a justifiable criterion. Moreover, it is also a criterion that prospective immigrants ought to
accept, given the relationship that they wish to establish with the state they
are trying to enter, which depends upon mutual advantage. In contrast, selection by race or national background is unjustifiable, since these attributes
cannot be linked (except by wholly spurious reasoning) to any goals that a
democratic state might legitimately wish to pursue.[35]

More difficult issues arise in relation to selection on the basis of immigrants' political or cultural background. The question is whether it can be
justifiable to select in favor of those who already have the political or cultural attributes that will enable them to fit more easily into the society they
are joining. Consider political attributes first: Can liberal democracies choose
immigrants who have already demonstrated their democratic credentials as
opposed to those who espouse other political values, assuming that this can
be reliably established? Most commentators, including strong liberals such
as Joseph Carens, agree that states may exclude people who pose a threat to
national security by virtue of the beliefs that they hold, such as those liable
to engage in terrorist acts.[36] But in such cases it is the disposition to act,
rather than the beliefs themselves, that forms the reason for exclusion. What
about those whose political beliefs are such that they do not acknowledge
the authority of the state they wish to join, even though they have no intention of sabotaging it by violent or other means? All states, not least liberal
states, depend on their members complying voluntarily with their laws most
of the time, and presumably a belief in the state's legitimacy is one of the
main sources of compliance. Someone who lacks that belief may keep the
law for other reasons (prudence, respect for the rights of others) but is likely
to be less reliable in carrying out her duties as a citizen. So there is some
reason for favoring committed democrats when choosing immigrants. On
the other hand, liberal democracies do not require all of their existing citizens to sign up personally to their founding principles: they are prepared to
tolerate anarchists, fascists, and others, leaving them free to express their beliefs and to attempt to persuade others of their correctness within the limits
of the law. So what could justify adopting a more restrictive position in the
case of immigrants?[37] Moreover, a migrant's political belief system is unlikely
to be immutable, and there are opportunities to shape it in a democratic direction after she arrives, through citizenship classes and so forth—I will

discuss defensible integration policies in Chapter 8. On balance, then, it seems that selection on political grounds would be justifiable only in cases where immigrants with illiberal or undemocratic views were applying in sufficient numbers that their presence might create violent social conflicts or disrupt the working of democratic institutions.[38]

The argument that can be made for cultural selection raises different questions. We are contemplating here immigrant groups whose cultural affiliations are different from those of the majority of existing citizens—though we should also distinguish between cases where the existing state is already multicultural and has enacted multicultural policies (e.g., Canada) and cases in which it is more culturally homogeneous (e.g., Japan): the issue becomes more pressing in the latter circumstances. Immigrants who speak a different language, practice a different religion, or have a different lifestyle from the majority may pose two kinds of problem. The first is simply the cost of incorporating them into the host society on terms of equality. Exactly what this means—how far the commitment to cultural equality should be taken—is a topic for Chapter 8, but assuming that some accommodation is required as a matter of justice, this will typically impose costs on the receiving community. There will, for example, be the cost of translating public documents into a new language or of providing translators in courts and social service agencies; or if religion is the source of the division, the cost of accommodating religious practices where these impose different requirements on believers outside of the mainstream. Some of these costs can be passed to the immigrants themselves, but others will be borne by the state, and indirectly, therefore, by citizens at large.

There are of course likely to be compensating benefits that come with increasing cultural diversity. The point is simply that if we look at (economic) immigration as a practice that is governed by the logic of mutual advantage, both costs and benefits need to be factored in when considering selection policy. Some of the costs may only be apparent with hindsight, as it becomes clear what a successful immigrant integration policy that nevertheless allows sufficient space for incoming groups to sustain their own cultures actually requires. This also applies to the second potential problem. Culture is not only a matter of belief or of practice, but also of identity. Here we return to the question discussed in Chapter 4 about the way in which culture can come to constitute a line of fracture within a political community, possibly leading to the formation of "parallel societies," whose members have very little contact with those beyond their own community; and the question discussed in Chapter 1 about the effects of cultural diversity on social trust, and through that on people's willingness to support welfare states and other instruments of social justice. These are by no means inevitable consequences of admitting immigrants with cultural backgrounds different from those of the majority, but they are *possible* consequences, and avoiding them may again prove to be somewhat costly, this time in the form of support for programs of language learning, citizenship education, and so forth. This is the point at which the state's existing cultural character becomes important: a state that is already well equipped with multicultural policies can more easily tackle these problems than one that is not. There is, however, no independent requirement that a state should embrace multiculturalism before deciding upon its admission policy. Democracies are entitled to decide how far they wish to protect their inherited national cultures and how far to encourage cultural diversity within their borders.

To sum up, selective immigration requires that states give reasons for the policies they apply, and these reasons must relate to the legitimate purposes of the state itself, as manifested in its other policy decisions. Selection on economic grounds is the least controversial example, but other forms of positive discrimination cannot be ruled out: if a society wants to enhance its sporting reputation, for example, I cannot see why it should not seek to attract immigrants who will later qualify for the national teams. Giving reasons of this kind shows sufficient respect for those who are refused entry, disappointed though they may be (recall once more that we are considering only *economic migrants,* in the broad sense, in this chapter). But to conclude this discussion something needs to be said about the impact that selective immigration may have on the societies that the immigrants are leaving.

Unfortunately, like the question of whether immigration lowers the wages of (some) domestic workers, the question of whether out-migration harms poor societies is much disputed among economists and others.[39] The mechanisms at work—the loss of talent that might otherwise be productively employed in the sending society versus the incentive this creates there for investment in education; the income forgone in the society of origin versus the remittances sent back from the society of destination; and so forth—have been widely studied. But their net effect appears to vary considerably from case to case. That there is indeed a brain-drain issue that should concern us is established by observing that the societies most likely to lose are those that are small and poor, and therefore already prone to exhibit human rights shortfalls.[40] The most urgent cases are those that involve doctors and nurses leaving to take up better-paid jobs in rich societies: countries such as Ghana and Zimbabwe, for example, have been losing up to three-quarters of their trained medical staff, leading to acute shortages in health care coverage in those countries.[41] So even if there is some compensation in the form of remittances flowing to the families of the emigrants, these are unlikely to fill the gaps in health provision that the brain-drain creates.

In such cases, therefore, migration is damaging to the human rights of those left behind, who are deprived of health workers and, looking beyond health, of other professionals such as engineers who might make an important contribution to development goals if they stayed at home. Are the migrants themselves therefore under a duty not to leave but to stay and contribute? The grounds for such a duty are twofold.[42] First, they are likely to have been educated at public expense to equip them with skills which, it is reasonable to assume, were intended to be used for the benefit of the citizens who have paid for their education. Second, even leaving the cost of their education aside, they have special obligations to their compatriots, which they can best discharge by using their skills in a way that ministers to basic needs.[43] Now the duty to contribute only holds within certain limits. If it is a matter of making a fair return for the cost of one's education, then there will come a point at which the investment made in the doctor or nurse will have been repaid. And the wider duty toward compatriots must by qualified by a personal prerogative to pursue goals of one's own. So on the one hand, a trained doctor who loses her vocation and comes to detest medical practice cannot be required to continue working in that field; and on the other hand, if it is simply impossible to lead a decent life within her country of origin, for whatever reason, the doctor is entitled to find a way out. Subject to these qualifications, however, potential emigrants with the requisite skills appear to be under a moral duty to stay and work in the places where their skills are needed, especially when exercising those skills will enable others to enjoy their human rights.

It is a further question, however, whether this duty can be enforced by prohibiting migration. The sending state has a strong interest in holding on to its qualified citizens, but does it have the right to prevent them leaving if this is their choice? To do so would contravene one of the human rights laid down in the UN Universal Declaration, according to which "everyone has the right to leave any country, including his own." But it might be said that all rights come with qualifying clauses attached, and in this case the grounds for limiting the right of exit are the other rights that can be protected by requiring the migrant to stay.[44] However, this argument is unconvincing. The reason for treating the right of exit as unqualified (except perhaps in the case of catastrophe)[45] is that it plays a vital role in protecting human rights generally against oppressive governments. Put simply, so long as people can leave, there is a limit to how far governments will be able to go in limiting their freedoms and other rights; and it is too risky to grant governments the power to prevent exit on the assumption that they will only use it benignly, to retain people with essential skills.[46]

But what of the position of the states to which the emigrants intend to move? By allowing them to immigrate, these states can be accused both of complicity in creating human rights shortfalls—they are enabling the migrants to escape the duties they owe to their needy compatriots—and of exploitation, since they are acquiring the use of expensive skills for which they have not had to pay at the expense of the countries where the skills were developed (training a family doctor in the UK is estimated to cost about £500,000 in total).[47] So in the first place it is clearly wrong for such states actively to recruit medical staff and other professionals from poor countries in response to domestic labor shortages. Although they have obligations of social justice to meet the needs of their own citizens, they cannot fulfil such obligations regardless of the costs they impose on outsiders. Putting human rights at risk by importing doctors and others with essential skills counts as an unacceptable cost. But what if the initiative comes from the immigrants themselves? Must states refuse to let them in when they are badly needed in their own societies?

Consider first a couple of alternatives to barring entry that have been proposed. One is that sending states should be compensated for the losses they incur when their skilled workers leave: this might be done by taxing the emigrants and transferring the resulting revenues back to their home states, or in some other way.[48] The problem here is that general compensation may not address the specific losses that emigration creates: if doctors are leaving in large numbers, then sending money back won't directly elim-inate the shortfall in health care that their departure creates (it might be used to train more medics, but what if they also then leave in large numbers?). A second alternative, therefore, is for rich states to pay to raise the salaries of skilled professionals in poor societies, or to create incentives for reverse migration—for example, paying their own medical staff to spend periods of time in the countries where the health care shortages occur.[49] This, however, is an expensive alternative to exclusion: justice would require it only if turning immigrants away was itself regarded as a breach of some duty.[50] But recall that I am assuming in this chapter and elsewhere that there is no general right to immigrate. Given that it is permissible to admit some immigrants and refuse entry to others, we are considering the grounds on which their selection can properly be based. On these premises, the fact that someone who is ap-plying for admission has skills that would otherwise be employed in her home country to do work that helps to meet the basic needs of her compatriots should be treated as a disqualifying condition, however much her talents are valued by the receiving country. So skilled professionals from developing countries with human rights deficits should only be selected for admission where it can be shown that their skills are not in short supply at home.

The analysis I have given shows that there may well be conflicts of interest over immigration policy between sending countries, receiving countries, and the migrants themselves. Unless, like the Philippines, they have deliberately prepared large numbers of their citizens to work abroad in occupations such as nursing in the expectation of receiving remittances, sending countries will usually prefer that their emigrants should be low-skilled workers. These may be surplus to requirements at home, and a valuable source of foreign exchange through the money they remit. Receiving countries will prefer to take in high-skilled workers on a long-term basis and to admit low-skilled workers only on temporary permits to cover short-term labor shortages (e.g., in agri-culture). The migrants themselves will gain in both cases, but the gains may be greatest for manual laborers who would be unemployed at home.[51] What justice demands, therefore, are selection policies that divide up the costs and benefits of migration in a way that is fair to all three parties, and in this chapter I have tried to sketch what such policies might look like.

SEVEN

The Rights of Immigrants

IN THIS CHAPTER AND CHAPTER 8, my attention shifts to the question of how immigrants are treated once they have been admitted to their new society. I ask what they can claim, as a matter of justice, from the state that now hosts them. Must they be granted all of the rights and opportunities that other citizens enjoy, or only some of these? Conversely, is what they are entitled to strictly equal treatment, or can they ask for special forms of accommodation to reflect their cultural or other needs? What principles should govern the awarding of citizenship to immigrants? And in what ways should they be expected to integrate politically and culturally with the host society? Immigration should be regarded as a two-way street, in which immigrants who are treated fairly by the society they join in turn recognize obligations to contribute to that society and to help it to function effectively as a democracy. But that general assertion leaves a large amount of detail to be filled in. In the present chapter, I examine the claims that immigrants can make, and in Chapter 8, the reasonable expectations of the host society about how far they should adapt to their new surroundings. This will involve some discussion of multiculturalism and national identity, and the pressure points at which these two ideas may appear to collide.

As we saw in Chapter 6, it is important to distinguish between different categories of immigrants if we are going to inquire into the rights they should be awarded. Since I was discussing admissions, I distinguished between those granted permanent residence, those admitted conditionally, and those assigned temporary status. But in this chapter, a fourth category needs to be added: those who have entered without permission with the intention of staying for a period or permanently. These are "illegal immigrants" or "irregular migrants" according to the terminology one prefers.[1] We will need to ask how the state should respond to their anomalous legal status and what steps it should take to rectify this.

Before delving into these matters, however, there is one last set of admissions questions to be resolved. These concern those whom I described in Chapter 6 as "particularity claimants"—essentially people who claim permanent admission to state S on the grounds that they have already established a relationship to S that entitles them to enter. Particularity claimants fall into different categories. One comprises those who have explicitly or implicitly been promised admission under certain circumstances (e.g., as noted in Chapter 5, Ugandan Asians holding British passports). These raise no difficult or interesting questions of principle—their claims should clearly be honored. A second category contains people who apply to enter on grounds of family reunification. I am also going to set this group aside, even though in practice they make up a considerable proportion of those currently being admitted by most democratic states. The reason is that the relevant claim lies with the person who is already entitled to residence (whether a citizen or not) and who wants to bring family members in to join her, and not with the immigrants themselves.[2] Although there is indeed a human right to family life that everyone possesses, to turn this into a right to engage in family life in a specific place (the territory of state S), it needs to be coupled with a right on the part of at least one family member to reside there.[3] There are questions to be asked about how far the right to family reunification should extend beyond a person's partner and their children, but these are matters of policy that cannot be resolved by appeal to general principle.[4]

The more interesting particularity claimants (for purposes of this book) are those who by virtue of past events already stand in some relationship to the state, but without having an agreement that guarantees them a right of entry. There are two main ways in which such claims may arise: as claims to reparation, and as claims of desert. In the first case, a right to immigrate is being asked for as a way of redressing some wrong that the receiving state has inflicted on the prospective immigrant; in the second case, the claim is that the person deserves to join the society by way of reward for some service she has performed on its behalf. The logic of these claims is plainly different, so they need to be treated separately.

Immigration as a form of reparation has been defended by James Souter, who applies it specifically to asylum seekers.[5] His argument is that if a state is responsible for the harm involved in turning somebody into a refugee, then it owes reparation, and granting asylum is often the most fitting way in which this can be done. Refugees are certainly people who have been seriously harmed, and if their situation can be shown to be a by-product of something that the responsible state has done—for instance, it has intervened militarily in such a way as to create civil conflict in the place where the intervention occurred—then reparation may be due. However, our judgment about the form that this reparation should take is liable to be clouded by the fact that we face two intersecting claims: first, the claim that any refugee can make to be provided with sanctuary, and second, the claim that someone who has been wrongfully harmed can make to be restored as nearly as possible to the position she was in before the harmful act occurred. So we need to be clear which is being offered as the reason for admission. If it is the first, then the import of the responsibility claim is to single out state S as the one that ought to provide asylum. This would not necessarily entail permanent admission (as opposed to being housed for a period of time until it was safe to return), but it would give a strong reason for the asylum to be granted by state S itself. If it is the second, then we need to ask whether granting a right to immigrate is necessarily the best form of remedy for actions that lead to people having to flee from their home country.

In general, when states inflict harm on those outside of their borders, they should ideally respond by rectifying the damage in the place where it occurred, rather than merely by offering compensation to the people who have been injured. Suppose that one state damages another's natural environment: a ship from the first state suffers an oil spill that pollutes the second's coastline, or a river that runs through both states whose water is needed for agriculture is diverted. The right course of action is to remedy the damage directly—clean up the oil spill, restore the river, and meanwhile provide short-term relief to the people affected. The principle is to return to a state of affairs that is as close as possible to the status quo ante, assuming that itself was not unjust. A similar logic applies to a chain of events that creates refugees. Ideally, the responsible state should try to engineer conditions that would enable those affected to return to their previous lives rather than move them to entirely new surroundings.[6] Sometimes repair is impossible, in which case granting the refugees the right to remain permanently in S may be an acceptable, albeit second-best, alternative. In these cases, then, admission as a form of reparation is warranted.

What next of desert as a source of particularity claims to immigrate? The problem here will be to show that immigration rights are an appropriate way of recognizing the deserts of noncitizens who have conferred benefits on the receiving state. The most relevant examples seem to be cases of military service.[7] The French Foreign Legion, for example, has a rule whereby anyone who has served in the legion "with honour and fidelity" for three years or more is entitled to apply for French citizenship.[8] Those who cannot wait that long may apply immediately under a law of 1999 if they have been wounded in battle while fighting for France, thereby becoming "Français par le sang versé." Although no doubt incentive considerations also play a part in explaining these measures, they have a clear desert rationale: how better to recognize and reward those who are willing to shed their blood for the country than to give them the right to live there (in the French case as full citizens)?[9]

As I recorded at the beginning of Chapter 5, a similar case was made, successfully, on behalf of Gurkhas who had served in the British army and in retirement wanted to move from Nepal to Britain. But the experience of a number who have since moved has proved to be an unhappy one, and the British Gurkha Welfare Society has been campaigning for enhanced pension rights that would allow retired Gurkhas to live comfortably in Nepal rather than having to rely on meager state-provided pension and housing benefits in the United Kingdom.[10] What this case suggests is that foreigners who have contributed significant military service to the state really deserve something like "the conditions for a comfortable life," rather than the right to immigrate as such. Although immigration might indeed be the only way of providing these conditions in some cases, there does not seem to be an internal link between desert and reward such that the only way in which desert of this kind can properly be recognized is by awarding the ex-soldier rights of residence and/or citizenship.

This brief review of particularity claims reveals that they often carry considerable weight, but do not always translate into rights to immigrate. Although it may be perfectly clear which state is the proper target of the claim, its content—in the sense of what, specifically, is required to meet it—is less determinate. So a just response may involve providing an alternative to immigration. Our conclusion should be that particularity claims are most powerful when combined with other factors that make the granting of admission the only appropriate response—in which case the claimants should be moved to the front of the immigration queue.

We are now ready to return to the main theme of the chapter, the claims that immigrants belonging to different categories can make against the state they have joined. To frame the discussion, I need to reintroduce the distinction drawn in Chapter 2 between human rights and wider questions of social justice. As I argued there, human rights are the rights that people must possess in order to be able to lead a minimally decent life, and no state that fails to protect these rights can be regarded as legitimate. But liberal democracies aspire to provide more than this: they bestow rights of citizenship that are more generous than bare human rights, and they also aim to distribute resources and opportunities in ways that match relevant criteria of distributive justice such as merit and need (depending on the case). So we need to ask, first, whether immigrants can demand that their human rights should be protected, and then second, whether they can also demand to be included along with existing citizens in the practices and policies that deliver social justice.

The answer to the first question may seem obvious because legitimate states are required to protect the human rights of all those present on their territories, whether permanently or temporarily. So this must include immigrants in all categories, including the irregular migrants. And indeed rights to bodily security and to subsistence, to freedoms of speech and movement, and many others besides should have that protected status. But as we saw in Chapter 6 when discussing temporary migrants, there are certain human rights for which the position is not so straightforward. The state that accommodates them does not, for example, have to protect the right to family life directly, by allowing the migrants' families to enter. However, the state should *respond* to the existence of the right, for example by allowing migrants opportunities to return home to visit their families without running into bureaucratic obstacles on reentry, by facilitating remittances, and so forth. Political rights furnish another example. The right to vote, especially the right to vote in national elections, is one of the defining features of citizenship, and it would be anomalous, therefore, to extend it to immigrants who have not yet acquired that status (access to citizenship will be discussed later). In the case of temporary migrants, their strongest interest lies in the exercise of political rights in their homeland, and again the state that accommodates them meanwhile has an indirect responsibility to help facilitate this. In these cases, then, we should regard the responsibility to protect human rights as divided between the home state and the receiving state—though the receiving state by granting entry takes full responsibility for protecting basic rights to subsistence, shelter, health care, bodily integrity, safety at work, and so forth.

What next of the irregular migrants, the people who are present on the state's territory without its permission? It might seem bizarre to claim that the state must take responsibility for their human rights as well because most will have arrived in contravention of its immigration laws. But the logic of territorial jurisdiction continues to hold: a state that claims authority to apply its laws to everyone within its territory must also protect the human rights of all those present, whether legally or not.[11] It may of course remove people without residence rights from the territory so long as the methods employed do not themselves violate human rights by virtue of their brutality. Whether it is justified in doing so, in the case of those who have remained within the country for a substantial amount of time, is a further question to be addressed shortly.

Might it be argued here that irregular migrants have forfeited some or all of their human rights by crossing a border illegally? The idea that human rights can, in certain circumstances, be subject to forfeit is defensible in itself: it is otherwise hard to make sense of the partial loss of human rights that occurs when criminals are imprisoned.[12] But the reasoning that justifies this—essentially that people who show a wanton disregard for the rights of others may forfeit some of their own—does not apply to irregular migrants. Their behavior may be regarded as in certain respects unfair, since by entering without permission they are at the very least engaging in a form of queue-jumping with respect to all those who are attempting to enter through legal channels, with the delays, costs and bureaucratic procedures that this will usually involve. But there are likely to be excusing factors in play, such as the dire economic circumstances they are trying to escape from by migrating, and their presence does not threaten the human rights of citizens or of others who are legally resident on the territory. The unfair behavior may need to be redeemed, as I shall shortly argue, but not by treating irregular migrants in ways that violate their human rights.

How should the state balance its responsibility to protect the human rights of irregulars against its legitimate interest in investigating them so that it can decide whether to require them to leave or grant them permission to stay? Joseph Carens has argued that a "firewall" should be created such that contact with the police and other agencies responsible for rights protection does not lead to immigrants being brought to the attention of the immigration authorities. According to Carens,

> Democratic states can and should build a firewall between the enforcement of immigration law, on the one hand, and the protection of general human rights, on the other. We ought to establish as a firm legal principle that no information gathered by those responsible for protecting general human rights can be used for immigration enforcement purposes. We ought to guarantee that people will be able to pursue their human rights without exposing themselves to arrest and expulsion.[13]

Carens's empirical assumption is that without such a firewall, many irregular migrants would be reluctant to approach the police when they were victims of crime or to contact doctors when they were ill. His normative assumption is that rights are not sufficiently protected if people are unwilling to assert them because of a fear that this might lead to their immigration status being investigated. The empirical assumption is almost certainly correct.[14] What about the normative assumption?

It is not in dispute here that the police have the same duties toward immigrants, whether authorized or unauthorized, as they have toward everyone else, and the same applies to other public officials. Victims of assault or harassment should all be treated with the same respect, and hospital staff should not discriminate when confronted with seriously ill patients. Nor, on the other hand, is it disputed that the immigration authorities may (using legitimate means) gather information in order to discover who has entered the country unlawfully, and if appropriate, take steps to deport them. The issue is about whether a firewall should be built between these two sets of activities.[15] If someone who has been involved in criminal activities approaches the police on some unrelated matter, we would not think it wrong for the police to take further action if in the course of responding to the person's request, evidence of his criminality comes to light. A firewall would not be appropriate here. The case for treating irregular migrants differently rests on two pillars: their likely vulnerability to human rights abuses, and the fact that being present in the country without authorization is not, in itself, a criminal offence.[16]

Carens's claim is that if immigrants are deterred from asserting their rights for fear of deportation, they are in effect being denied those rights: "It makes no moral sense to provide people with purely formal legal rights under conditions that make it impossible for them to exercise those rights effectively."[17] Perhaps, though, Carens overstates the case here. "Impossible" is too strong. What the immigrants we are considering cannot do, in the absence of a firewall, is to exercise their rights without some risk of deportation proceedings being initiated. Whether they actually are initiated must depend on the policy of the state in question and the particular circumstances of the immigrant—for example, she might have entered as an asylum seeker but absconded out of fear that the decision would go against her, whereas in fact her claim is justified and would be accepted. Then there is the issue of what the consequences of deportation would actually be, assuming that the state is sticking consistently to the principle of *non-refoulement.* The immigrant will lose what may be enhanced rights in the society she has moved to and enjoy only more basic rights in the society to which she is deported. This admittedly may give her a strong incentive not to expose herself to the risk of deportation. But how should we judge the situation from a human rights perspective? This person is trading rights of different kinds off against one another, thinking that the various material advantages she enjoys at present make it worthwhile for her to give up some protective human rights, such as the right to go to the police when she is a victim of crime.

We might think, nonetheless, that rights of the latter kind are so important that they need to be safeguarded at all costs, regardless of whether this hinders the state in enforcing its immigration law. Yet we need not say the same about lesser rights or more generally about services that public bodies may provide to residents (Carens concedes this himself in the case of what he calls "administrative and social rights" such as rights of access to libraries or swimming pools, or to social housing.)[18] This reveals a difficulty in the firewall argument: it recommends that the wall be built between institutions—between the immigration authorities and other public bodies such as the police, social services, health services, and so forth—whereas the relevant normative line falls between access to basic rights and access to other benefits. It is not an injustice if irregular migrants decide not to available themselves of rights in the nonbasic category they might otherwise enjoy because of a concern that their immigration status will be exposed, rendering them potentially liable to deportation. The firewall should only apply to interactions between immigrants and public institutions where basic rights are at stake. But this would only reinforce the doubts of those who find the firewall proposal unworkable.

The background assumption here is that the state has discretion in deciding which benefits irregular migrants should be able to receive over and above human rights proper. What justifies this assumption, however? Why is it permissible to exclude irregular migrants from benefits that other immigrants as well as citizens may enjoy, or in other words, not to include them fully within the state's practices of social justice?[19] The point is not that they should be penalized for their unlawful entry (the penalty for that is that they remain liable to deportation until their status is made regular, that is, categorized as permanent, conditional, or temporary by the state). It is rather that the state has not chosen to admit them as members, either on grounds of mutual advantage, as in the case of economic migrants, or on grounds of its responsibility to protect human rights, as in the case of refugees. So they are physically present on the state's territory, but not enlisted members of the political community; furthermore, it is impossible to predict whether they intend to stay permanently or return home after a longer or shorter period. Unlike the temporary migrants discussed in Chapter 6, they have not entered under a formal scheme whose terms have been settled in advance. Nor, on the other hand, have they been admitted like other migrants with rights of residence that are expected to expand in due course to full citizenship rights. The institutions of social justice are set up to apply to people who are assumed to be permanent members of the society in question: as Rawls put it, principles of social justice are designed for "an ongoing society, a self-sufficient association of human beings which, like a nation-state, controls a connected territory . . . a closed system; there are no significant relations to other societies, and no one enters from without, for all are born into it to lead a complete life,"[20] As I argued in Chapter 3, principles such as equality of opportunity can only be applied to a society that approximates Rawls's idealized description.

Yet even though one cannot predict how long irregular migrants will remain in the country they move to, we know that many will in fact want to remain permanently. So now we must ask what difference the passage of time might make to their claims. This issue does not only arise in the case of irregulars. For those admitted conditionally or on short-term visas, there is also a question of what their long-term residence in the society implies for their status. In fact there are two questions. At what point (if any) does continuing residence in a society entail a right to remain permanently? And, at what point (if any) does continuing residence entail full inclusion in the society's scheme of social justice? I shall examine these questions in general terms first before returning to the difference that initial unauthorized entry might make in the case of those who have succeeded in staying for the long term.

There is broad agreement among authors who write about immigration that being present in a society for a considerable period—usually somewhere between five and ten years—creates a very strong if not indefeasible case for permanent inclusion.[21] This view is often linked to the claim that admission to full citizenship should follow automatically, but I set this aside for separate discussion. Beneath the consensus, however, there is some disagreement about exactly why long-term presence should entail permanent inclusion. It is therefore worth disentangling different strands of argument that might be used to support this conclusion—though one should also be alert to the possibility that the case for inclusion might be made up of overlapping arguments all pointing in the same general direction. I begin with the arguments whose limitations seem to me most obvious.

The first holds that the fact of being subjected to the state's authority, over time, itself generates a claim to inclusion on terms of justice.[22] One might derive this from a thesis advanced by Thomas Nagel, in a different context, about coercion and distributive justice: "We are required to accord equal status to anyone with whom we are joined in a strong and coercively imposed political community."[23] Nagel's idea is that when people are subjected to a coercive state that claims to rule in their name, they only have reason to accept its authority if it governs them in a socially just way. Immigrants, it might be thought, are "joined" to the political community in the relevant sense, so they are entitled to socially just (e.g., nondiscriminatory) treatment along with everyone else.

There are general reasons to doubt Nagel's claim about the connection between coercion and distributive justice.[24] But setting these aside, it seems that the relationship between immigrants and the state that they join is relevantly different from that of native-born citizens who have been incorporated into it involuntarily. The state does owe immigrants just treatment—I have emphasized its obligation to protect their human rights in all cases, and in the case of authorized temporary migrants to provide programs that offer them a fair share of the programs' benefits—but their being present in the society by virtue of a voluntary decision sets them apart from the native-born.[25] The fact that once inside they are subject to the coercive authority of the state does not entail that they must be included on equal terms with citizens whose subjection is involuntary. Moreover, Nagel's argument cannot explain why a right of *permanent* residence must be granted. Even if we were to concede that all immigrants are entitled to equal treatment while they remain under its authority, the state could simply cancel its obligations by requiring them to leave.

An argument that might close this gap is offered by Ayelet Shachar when she appeals to the legal concept of "adverse possession" to claim that even illegal migrants gain a right to stay after a sufficient period of time has elapsed.[26] The analogy is with property that has been acquired without the owner's consent and then held without interruption over time. Does the analogy work, however? To acquire a property title by adverse possession, a person must occupy and use land openly, or "notoriously" in the legal phrase, thereby giving the present owner the opportunity to take steps to recover what has been taken from him.[27] That he does not seize the opportunity is presumably evidence that he lacks interest in what he owns. Thus the doctrine of adverse possession brings together the possessor's reasonable expectation that she can continue to hold and use what she has been holding and using over a long stretch of time and the previous owner's indifference toward (or, it might be said, implicit consent to) his loss of property. Now apply this concept to the case of irregular migrants. They do not advertise their presence within the state's borders openly—in most cases they try to remain invisible. Of course, the state does know of their existence en masse, though usually without knowing who in particular has this status. It has procedures in place to deport those it discovers to have entered illegally. Whether it pursues the deportation option wholeheartedly may be open to question.[28] But the fact that it does have policies in place to discourage illegal immigration and to take action against those who nevertheless enter without authorization implies that it is not indifferent toward the presence of irregular migrants. So the conditions laid down for adverse possession—openly displayed taking coupled with inaction on the part of the legal owner—do not really apply here. What remains true, however, is that immigrants who have lived in the country for many years may reasonably have acquired an expectation that they will be allowed to remain. This brings us to what I regard as the more persuasive arguments in favor of permanent inclusion for those who have been immigrants (in whatever status) for a sufficient length of time.

These fall under the heading of "social membership" arguments, whose general form is that people will become integrated into a society and will build their lives around the activities they become involved in simply as a result of living there over time. As Carens explains, "the term 'social membership' evokes the sense that being a member of a society involves a dense network of relationships and associations. What is at stake is a person's ability to maintain and develop a rich and highly particular set of human ties."[29] There are two rather different ways of spelling out the implications of this claim, however. The first invites us to contemplate the costs of removing someone from the society via deportation—the breaking of social ties that occurs when someone is forced to leave the place they have been settled in for a long time and, especially perhaps, the costs to children who have been brought up and educated in that place. These are very real costs and should never be discounted. There is, though, a potential paradox here. Recall that we are thinking about *immigrants*, who by definition were willing to break or at least attenuate the ties that bound them to the places where they themselves had been raised. In some cases this will have been because conditions of life there had become unbearable. But in other cases the motive will have been simply an innocent and perfectly understandable desire for greater opportunities. The point, then, is that anyone who migrates has to make a trade-off between the costs that are borne (by their families as well as by themselves) in moving to a new country and the potential benefits stemming from the opportunities available there. That many people either do or would wish to migrate shows that the costs of moving—including the breaking off of many established social ties—are not so high as to form a decisive obstacle.

Of course there is a great deal of difference between choosing to migrate, despite the cost, and being involuntarily returned to the place from whence you came. I raise the question only to guard against the assumption, which seems sometimes to be implicit in arguments in favor of permanent residence on the grounds of social membership, that the losses involved in removal are so great as always to make it an injustice. It would be better to say that someone's having lived in a place for many years and developed a set of close relationships with colleagues, friends, and neighbors creates a strong presumption in favor of allowing her to stay—but one that can be legitimately set against the other goals that immigration policy is intended to achieve.

Residence over time may also matter for a different reason, however. The immigrant is likely to have entered into a system of social cooperation centered around the workplace, but extending beyond that to include leisure activities and so forth. These interactions are governed by norms of reciprocity: each person contributes and in return receives benefits. The most obvious practical manifestation of this will be the taxes the immigrant has paid through working, consuming, owning property, and so forth. Once somebody belongs to such a scheme, it will be unjust to force them to withdraw from it after having made contributions that have not yet been reciprocated in full. As I argued in Chapter 2, schemes of cooperation of this kind give rise to associative obligations among the participants, and to expel a participant who has played her part would be a breach of these obligations.

This explains why immigrants who are admitted through normal channels, but not explicitly under the auspices of a temporary migration program, are entitled to be included in, and remain within, a society's practices of social justice. They are contributing members and therefore entitled to be beneficiaries of the scheme. Whether they should be entitled immediately to all of the benefits that the scheme provides, or whether there should be a probationary period in which some benefits are withheld, is open to debate.

In favor of full inclusion, it can be argued that people raised in the society and entering the workforce gain full entitlement immediately without having to prove that they are willing contributors—so why should immigrants be treated any differently? Perhaps a short probationary period serves the symbolic purpose of underlining the reciprocal nature of the scheme. But this is a relatively minor issue. The more difficult question concerns immigrants who have entered illegally, because their situation necessarily makes it harder to establish that they are contributing in the way that is required. By definition, they have not been selected on the basis of the economic or other value that they are expected to bring to the receiving society.[30] So the presumption that supports full inclusion for legal immigrants seems not to apply. The issue, then, is whether they can establish membership simply by virtue of residing within the society over time, or whether they have to produce evidence of relevant forms of social participation, such as paying taxes or contributing to the work of civil society associations.

This is again to some extent a matter of policy. Defenders of automatic inclusion, such as Carens, argue that if the decision to grant irregular migrants legal residence were to involve investigating each individual to see what contributions they have made and how well integrated they are into their local community, this process would be likely to lead to discrimination against people from minority ethnic or religious backgrounds.[31] However, the immigration authorities are already entrusted with using impartial selection criteria in the cases of new immigrants applying to enter through legal channels, so automatic inclusion for irregulars would give the latter cast-iron safeguards against discrimination that are not available to new immigrants. It is hard to see how doing so could be justified.[32] This supports the "earned citizenship" view of those such as Shachar who argue that although time of residence should be taken into account when decisions are made, it should be considered alongside concrete factors that indicate attachment, such as employment status and membership in voluntary organizations.[33] Much will depend on whether it is possible to gain reliable evidence about these factors.

A closely related issue, fiercely debated in the United States, is whether the state should declare an amnesty for all irregular migrants, allowing them to acquire legal status without fear of deportation. This would not necessarily mean granting a right of permanent residence immediately, though the expectation would then be that all who wanted to would move in time toward that status and eventually to citizenship. The debate is clouded by ambiguities about what amnesty signifies, as Linda Bosniak has pointed out.[34] Is it a matter of pardoning the original offense of border crossing or overstaying on a visa? Or is it a forward-looking declaration that the past is no longer relevant and should simply be forgotten?[35] This makes a difference, because on the first interpretation it might be reasonable to expect the immigrant whose position was being regularized to perform some act that would express recognition of former wrongdoing. The question therefore turns on the moral standing of the irregular migrant. As noted earlier, it does not seem right to treat such migrants simply as criminals. Equally, however, by evading border controls they have acted unfairly in relation to those who submitted applications either as economic migrants or as asylum seekers, and therefore ran the risk that their applications would be turned down. The integrity of the system would be put in question if amnesties were simply granted unconditionally. This counts against "amnesty as forgetting" and suggests that unauthorized migrants should be made to do something to redeem themselves before being granted permanent residence. One possibility would be to ask them to show that they had already made a significant contribution to the host society—a claim of desert, which would make them into particularity claimants, to use the language introduced in Chapter 5. Failing that, irregulars could be asked to undertake part-time military or civilian service for a suitable period of time. This is sometimes regarded as an unacceptable imposition, but if the claims being made by proponents of the social membership argument hold good, what is being offered—secure residence and access to the full range of opportunities that the society provides—is a benefit that vastly outweighs the cost of redemption.

The underlying principle here is that all those who have been social members for a sufficient period of time and who plan to continue to make their lives in the society should advance toward full membership: the society should not be permanently caste-divided between citizens and strangers, to use Walzer's image.[36] The principle is widely shared: the debate is about how the advance should be regulated, that is, what conditions immigrants in different categories should be expected to meet in order to be fully included. Admission rules and integration rules taken together must be morally cohesive, and visibly so, if the immigration system is to enjoy widespread public support. This is not easy to achieve: some critics argue that there is a deep tension between the proposition that states are entitled to decide whether or not to admit immigrants and the proposition that they are obliged to provide an extensive bundle of rights (including full citizenship) to all long-term entrants.[37] The approach I have sketched emphasizes the reciprocal relationship between immigrant and receiving state, according to which all immigrants are entitled to fair treatment (which in the case of those who stay long-term includes access to the full panoply of civil and social rights) but are expected in return to contribute to society and uphold its legal and social norms. Confronted with the fact of irregular migration, and the ensuing presence of people who remain largely outside the reach of the law and other social institutions, the problem is how best to bring them within the scope of the immigration system without undermining it. Conditional amnesty, as sketched earlier, seems the best solution.

I turn finally in this chapter to citizenship itself, not in the wide Marshallian sense that embraces civil and social as well as political rights,[38] but in the narrower political sense: the right to vote, stand for office, serve on juries, carry a passport, and so forth. This is normally seen as the culmination of the immigration process; the point at which the immigrant is finally granted full recognition as an equal by members of the host community. But why, one might ask, should the granting of political citizenship come later than the other rights, as it normally does: What justifies withholding it for several years in defiance of the standard democratic principle that all those who are subject to the laws are entitled to a say in making them? The answer is that citizenship involves responsibilities as well as rights. Casting a vote is in a small way an exercise of political power, and it matters therefore how that power will be exercised. Liberal democracies educate their own future citizens, formally through civic education and informally through normal processes of socialization in the family and elsewhere, in the hope and expectation that when they come to exercise their voting rights, they will do so in a way that respects the rights and considers the interests of other members. Incoming migrants may have little knowledge of the societies they are entering. They won't yet understand the explicit or implicit norms that govern the political system, the major problems that the society faces, or the range of interests that the system has to accommodate. To learn about these things involves, on the one hand, exposure to the national and local media, and on the other, talking to native-born citizens about political matters. This takes time: how much time will depend on how quickly and effectively integration occurs, the subject of Chapter 8.

Democracies are now increasingly likely to make access to citizenship depend on passing a formal test. Can this be justified? What should the test comprise? It is often argued that such tests are meaningless because they involve providing set answers to set questions—a feat of memory that reveals little about how far the examinee really understands, let alone subscribes to, the principles and values that the test is intended to capture. I will look more closely in Chapter 8 at the content of citizenship tests—what they can and cannot legitimately include—but here I will just give reasons why such tests are valuable. First, they ensure that the person taking the test has learnt the national language (or one of them) sufficiently well to be able to complete it—itself an important precondition for political participation. Second, they help to emphasize that becoming a citizen is a serious matter, and not just a convenience (such as getting a new passport)—especially when the test is accompanied by a citizenship ceremony for successful applicants. Third, where the test involves answering political questions about democracy or freedom of speech, say, then even though there is no guarantee that the person taking it will believe the answers that she gives, she will at least know what the society expects of her politically. She is being told that if she is going to be politically active, there are certain ground rules she will have to observe, such as having to tolerate the expression of views she finds offensive. Many immigrants, of course, will be only too ready to embrace these principles, having experienced the effects of their violation in their home countries.

Suppose, then, that an immigrant with residence rights has spent a number of years in the country and has passed a citizenship test: Are there any further conditions that he needs to meet before the award of citizenship is made? Should there be an integration requirement, which I suggested might be appropriate when irregular migrants are being granted an amnesty? Here I think that the justification for imposing such a requirement is not strong enough to outweigh the possible danger—namely, that applicants are selected or rejected on the basis of how far they look and sound like native citizens. The danger can be illustrated by a study of naturalization (i.e., citizenship) decisions in Switzerland, where municipalities are responsible for deciding who is sufficiently integrated and familiar with Swiss habits and customs and who isn't.[39] The study revealed significant variation between municipalities (rejection rates varied from 0% to 47%), explained chiefly by different understandings of what it meant to be a (good) Swiss citizen held by the most influential political actors in each place. Although one can imagine less politicized ways of testing for integration, none can avoid the fact that ultimately some official or committee will have to make a subjective judgment about an individual on the basis of a limited array of evidence. If one starts from the assumption that access to citizenship should be within the reach of all, subject only to showing a modicum of political competence, then a waiting period plus success in a formal test (which offers no scope for bureaucratic discretion) should be a sufficient qualification.

Immigrant rights are as controversial a topic among the general public as immigrant admissions. For an immigration policy to win widespread acceptance, citizens have to be convinced that it assigns rights and responsibilities fairly. When these conditions are not met, tolerant acceptance of newcomers can rapidly give way to hostile resentment. There is never a shortage of anecdotal evidence about newly arrived immigrants being pushed to the front of the queue for jobs, housing, or school places. To counteract this perception, the policy that is adopted with respect to the rights of immigrants must be demonstrably fair. Although drawing a clear line between temporary and long-term migrants may be difficult, it is necessary to do so because the requirements of fairness are different in the two cases. From this point of view, the presence of irregular migrants is a complicating factor, since it is not clear on which side of the line they fall, and what, therefore, fair treatment means in their case. In handling these difficult questions, I have been guided by three principles: the need to protect the human rights of everyone present on the state's territory; full inclusion and access to citizenship as the final goal for all those who plan to live permanently in the society; and reciprocity between immigrants and citizens, implying obligations to contribute on the part of the immigrants, and obligations to provide equal opportunities and welfare rights on the part of the state. These same principles guide my discussion of immigrant integration in Chapter 8.

EIGHT

Integrating Immigrants

IN THE SUMMER OF 2001, several of Britain's northern cities were convulsed by rioting and violence involving white and Asian youths, members of the British National Party, and the police. In Oldham on the evening of May 26, after police had intervened in a fight between groups of white and Asian men, they were confronted by up to five hundred Asian youths carrying bricks, bottles, and petrol bombs in a riot that lasted until the early hours of the morning. Violence on a lesser scale continued for several weeks and spread to Burnley and then to Bradford, which in early July witnessed several nights of fighting on a large scale between National Front supporters and Asians. Properties were set alight, three hundred police were injured, and in the aftermath two hundred people were convicted of riot and jailed.

Such events involving violent clashes between ethnic minority immigrant groups, indigenous whites, and the police have by no means been confined to the United Kingdom. The autumn of 2005 saw violence on an even larger scale erupt in the deprived *banlieues* surrounding Paris, mainly involving immigrants of North African origin, and spread out from there to many other French cities. Thousands of cars and buildings were set alight, and on November 8 a state of emergency was declared: more than 2,800 arrests were made. Smaller episodes have occurred in more unexpected places, such as Sydney, in December 2005, and Husby, a suburb of Stockholm, in May 2013. Although the triggering events differ in each case, what unites them all are the presence of immigrant communities concentrated in deprived areas of the city, with Islamic backgrounds and visibly different from the natives; strained relations between these communities and the police; and resentful working-class whites, susceptible to incitement by far-right parties. Commentators accordingly can point the finger toward alternative underlying causes, whether heavy-handed policing, racism, economic deprivation, or unwillingness to integrate on the part of the immigrant groups. What interests me more, however, is the widely held view that the immediate problem is one of social segregation between immigrants and natives, whatever its deeper causes may be, and the proposed solution, accordingly, one of promoting integration.[1]

For evidence, return to the case of Oldham. In the widely cited Cantle report on the events of 2001, the following diagnosis was presented:

> Separate educational arrangements, community and voluntary bodies, employment, places of worship, language, social and cultural networks, means that many communities operate on the basis of a series of parallel lives. These lives do not touch at any point, let alone overlap and promote any meaningful interchanges. . . . There is little wonder that the ignorance about each others' communities can easily grow into fear; especially where this is exploited by extremist groups determined to undermine community harmony and foster divisions.[2]

In a separate official report, compiled by David Ritchie, a civil servant from Birmingham, the proposed solution was equally clearly stated:

> We do not argue here for assimilation or absorption of any one group in Oldham by another. That would be a denial of diversity rather than its celebration. But we do argue for an integrated community and by that we mean one in which all citizens of the town, in looking at the things which identify themselves, see being an Oldhamer as high up the list. This will mean that they feel a stake in their community and in the future success of the town, with a common set of values as to what contribution individuals need to make and what it is right in their turn to expect from one another.[3]

Statements such as these raise a series of questions. What does it mean exactly for immigrant groups to form part of an "integrated community"? Is the aim of integration just to forestall future race riots, or does it have a wider purpose?[4] And what steps can governments or local authorities legitimately take to promote integration? Is compulsory integration a feasible and/or desirable goal?

To answer such questions, we must first clarify the concept of integration itself. Despite its widespread use in the literature on immigration, it is rarely given a clear definition. I propose to distinguish between *social* integration, *civic* integration, and *cultural* integration. Social integration describes a pattern of behavior. The people who live in a particular place are socially integrated to the extent that they regularly interact with one another across a range of social contexts: for example, they work alongside each other, join the same clubs and associations, live as neighbors and talk to one another when they meet, and so forth. Within this broad pattern, we could draw further distinctions, as Elizabeth Anderson does, when with the example of black-white relations in the United States in mind, she distinguishes four stages of integration: "(1) formal desegregation, (2) spatial integration, (3) formal social integration, and (4) informal social integration."[5] One key point that Anderson makes is that it is not sufficient for full integration for people to occupy the same physical space if within that space they divide into separate social units (e.g., "a school may be spatially but not socially integrated if students of different races attend different tracked classes, participate in different school clubs, rarely befriend one another, and inhabit different halls or dormitories"[6]). A second point is that even if members of different groups are participating in the same institutions or associations, the way they interact with each other is still important: "informal social integration involves cooperation, ease, welcome, trust, affiliation and intimacy that go beyond the requirements of organizationally defined roles." Using Anderson's helpful categories (which she admits need not always be fulfilled in a linear sequence), we can see that, if we begin from a situation of complete segregation or "parallel societies," then moving to full social integration requires several things to happen, involving not only creating a rich pattern of social interaction but also interaction of the right kind—involving friendly, respectful relationships between equals.

Next consider civic integration. I mean by this people coming to share a set of principles and norms that guide their social and political life. For example, they not only share a commitment to democracy as an abstract principle, but also share an understanding of what "behaving like a democrat" means—how one should use one's vote, how political debate should be conducted, and so forth. It extends from simple behavioral rules like queuing for cinema tickets, to more complex issues such as how to handle a dispute that might arise in a neighborhood about the use of a common facility like a hall or a public park. Civic integration does not involve people having the same substantive goals, whether in politics or in other areas of their lives, but it does involve a shared understanding of how these goals are to be pursued, and within what constraints. Common sense tells us that social integration is likely to lead to civic integration—because when people are in regular contact with one another, they will usually adapt to one another's behavior and find workable rules to govern their interactions, but they are clearly not the same thing, and as we shall see in a moment, may be valuable for different reasons.[7]

Finally, there is cultural integration, which is both more controversial and more ambiguous than the other two forms. People are culturally integrated when they share a common culture, which might mean having the same values and experiences or, on the other hand, having a common cultural identity. Thus we might say that cultural integration occurs when people enjoy the same TV programs or films, read the same books or newspapers, or listen to the same music; or alternatively when they identify with the same religion, with the same city ("being an Oldhamer"), or with the same nation. The value of these different possible forms of cultural integration will be strongly contested: multiculturalism, after all, can be regarded as a defense of cultural pluralism within a society against the demand for across-the-board cultural integration. My purpose at this stage is not to defend cultural integration, but to distinguish it clearly from social and civic integration: there is obviously a danger that those who respectively defend and attack immigrant integration as a policy goal simply understand that objective in different ways.

So let us now consider communities of immigrants, who for various reasons may cluster together in particular localities, and ask why it might be valuable for them to be integrated with their neighbors and with the wider society, taking the various senses of "integration" in order. There are two quite different reasons why we might think social integration was important. One connects it to social justice and draws upon the frequently made observation that communities are never in reality "separate but equal." Immigrant communities are likely to be less well endowed with resources of various kinds—physical, human, and social capital—and so their members' opportunities will be diminished unless they have access to the wider networks that integration would create. Admittedly, there are countervailing arguments pointing to the support that community members can offer each other under conditions of segregation—so it is sometime said that immigrant groups who cluster in ethnically homogenous neighborhoods are behaving rationally because this allows them to benefit from the specific social capital that these milieux create.[8] It seems unlikely, however, that such neighborhoods can provide anything to match the opportunity range available to people in the social mainstream. A society concerned about equal access to education, employment, health care, and so forth will therefore want to encourage social integration.

A second reason to support social integration is that people in poorly integrated societies are less likely to understand, to communicate with, and to trust one another, and these failures become particularly significant when intergroup conflicts arise. That is the lesson many drew from the interethnic riots referred to earlier: once an incident had occurred, rumors rapidly spread and feelings became inflamed, in part because of the lack of cross-community contacts between people who were used to working together and could therefore counteract these developments. Were the communities totally separate from one another, this might be less important, but the reality is that they overlap in public space, and so inevitably misunderstandings and disagreements will arise that trusted intermediaries are needed to resolve. So a society that wishes to be conflict-free, as far as possible, will again have reason to foster social integration.

But is this a goal that the state can legitimately pursue? In his discussion of immigrant integration, Carens draws a distinction between requirements, expectations, and aspirations.[9] Requirements are conditions that can be enforced; thus, to take a banal example, immigrants can be required to keep the law. Expectations are norms, and compliance with them is brought about by informal social sanctions; thus there is likely to be an expectation that immigrants who do not speak the language of the host society will at the very least encourage their children to learn it, and officials and others will show their disapproval of a parent who failed to do so. Aspirations are hopes about the way that immigrants will behave that are not enforceable even informally, and Carens takes social integration as the prime example: "People might think that the process is really going well only if there are high levels of residential and social mixing between immigrants and their descendants on the one hand and the rest of the population on the other without thinking that it would be appropriate to impose particular expectations on people about where they should live and with whom they should socialize."[10] Carens does not say explicitly why integration shouldn't be elevated to the status of an expectation or a requirement, but by implication he thinks that this would interfere unjustifiably with personal liberty. So is the state morally disabled from acting on "the imperative of integration" in the social domain? It appears not, because there are indirect ways in which integration might be encouraged without issuing orders to people about where they should live or with whom they should socialize. One simple method is antidiscrimination legislation that aims to tackle not only obvious cases such as workplaces that are segregated along lines of race or religion, but also practices such as estate agents informally ushering their customers into "appropriate" ethnic neighborhoods or encouraging white flight by the technique of "blockbusting."[11] Housing policy more generally can aim to integrate neighborhoods by requiring builders to mix housing types (and thereby income groups) together. Funding support for community organizations can be directed toward clubs and associations whose membership is drawn both from immigrant and nonimmigrant groups. Such policies may well prove to be controversial because individual people may have preferences to associate only with people from their own religious or ethnic group, but the point is that if social integration is judged to be important, it can be pursued in ways that do not place demands on individual citizens to integrate (though they do place requirements on employers and public officials to follow the relevant guidelines).

A number of European countries, including Austria, Denmark, France, and the Netherlands, have in the last decade introduced the idea of "integration contracts" for newly arrived immigrants that do impose requirements on the immigrants themselves.[12] These, however, relate primarily to civic rather than to social integration. They typically require immigrants to attend language classes if they are not already competent in the language of the host society and also to take classes designed to promote knowledge of the host society and its civic values. They are then asked to take a test or attend an interview, and the outcome may determine whether they qualify for permanent residence. So the contract can be seen as a double-edged sword. On the one hand, it provides the immigrant with skills and knowledge that are likely to be immediately useful for finding a job and getting access to social services, while also preparing him for acquiring citizen status when that becomes available. On the other hand, failure to fulfill the contract may constitute grounds for exclusion from permanent residence, if not outright expulsion.

Countries that have not chosen formally to adopt the integration contract approach, such as Canada, Britain, and the United States, have nevertheless aimed to achieve similar results by making citizenship acquisition depend on passing a test in which candidates are required to show significant knowledge of life in the host country.[13] The test may not be particularly difficult to pass (in the British case about 75% of those who take the test are successful, and failure is most commonly due to lack of language proficiency[14]), but its rationale is presumably that studying for it involves familiarizing oneself with various features of the society one is joining, and in the process becoming attuned to the relevant social and political norms. Of course there can be no guarantee that the immigrant will actually embrace those norms herself. But if she is willing to adapt her behavior, she will at least know what the ground rules are that she is expected to follow in the society she has moved to.

What justification can be given for these policies that aim to promote civic integration? In the eyes of some critics, they are examples of "repressive liberalism" by virtue of their attempt to put pressure on immigrants to abandon their previous beliefs and values and to conform to liberal principles of freedom and equality.[15] That the goal of civic integration is to change people's mind-set, where necessary, is not in doubt. But in defense of the practice, three things can be said. First, part of the aim is to equip immigrants with the linguistic, social, and political skills that will enable them to take full advantage of the society they are joining—so if the society is committed to norms of equal opportunity and political equality, it is hard to fault civic integration programs from that perspective. There is an element of paternalism, certainly, inasmuch as participation is made a requirement of permanent residence and/or naturalization rather than simply being left to the discretion of the immigrant, but paternalism of that kind is not difficult to defend, especially when it serves to counteract pressures within the family in the case of women. Second, there are practices that immigrants may bring with them that liberal societies have a legitimate interest in outlawing: examples would include coerced marriages and the punishment of apostasy. If communicating liberal values through civic education succeeds in convincing immigrants that these practices are unacceptable, that is sufficient justification. Third, liberal societies now routinely include preparation for citizenship as part of the school curriculum;[16] they are not hesitant about promoting liberal and democratic principles among the rising generation, nor should they be. But if they do this for citizens who have been raised at home, it seems reasonable that they should also do it for future citizens who have been raised abroad. In both cases what is being provided is a combination of useful knowledge, such as information about how the electoral system works, and normative guidance, such as about the value and limits of free speech. It's a reasonable assumption that liberal democracies work better when all of their citizens share this basic knowledge and the accompanying principles.

Some have argued that there is a tension, if not a contradiction, between insisting that immigrants should join civic integration programs and/or take citizenship tests and the principle defended in Chapter 7, namely, that all permanent residents are entitled to become citizens after a suitable period of time has elapsed. Whether there is indeed a contradiction here depends on how easy or difficult it is to complete the program or pass the test, which in turn depends on the level of support that is provided, especially in the case of language requirements. The content of the tests themselves are generally not demanding, requiring mainly learning the approved answers to a series of questions. The current U.S. citizenship test, for example, contains 100 questions out of which the candidate must answer 6 out of 10 correctly in the course of an interview. The topics include details of the U.S. Constitution and system of government, significant events in American history, and major symbols such as the flag and the anthem: most questions allow alternative answers to be given. The Canadian test is broadly similar, though it includes a few items that address issues of principle, such as the responsibilities of citizenship and equality between men and women. It is presented in multiple-choice format and requires 15 out of 20 correct answers. The new British test, introduced in 2013, stands out from the others by virtue of the quite detailed knowledge of British history, culture, and political practice that is required to pass it. Although it is effectively a memory test based on a booklet of 143 pages,[17] it is doubtful if many UK-born citizens could achieve the 75 percent passing grade without preparing specifically for the test.

Joseph Carens has objected to such tests on the grounds that, besides violating the principle that all long-term residents are entitled to become citizens in the case of those who fail, they do not track the requirements for being a competent citizen: "The knowledge required for wise political judgement is complex, multifaceted, and often intuitive. It's not something that can be captured on a test of this sort."[18] This is undoubtedly true. But the objection misunderstands the purpose of citizenship tests. They are not meant to select between competent and incompetent future citizens. Instead they serve two purposes. One is to provide an incentive to those preparing for the test to learn something about the political system that governs them, and to understand at least a few things about national history and prominent national icons and symbols. This applies regardless of whether they pass or fail the test. The other is to serve as an implicit statement of the nation's political values at any moment (we should therefore expect the content of citizenship tests to change over time, as indeed they have done).[19] For citizenship tests are one of the few places in which we actually find such a statement being made. As I remarked earlier, preparing for and taking the test doesn't compel an immigrant to adopt those values, but it does force her to recognize that these are the principles under which the society declares it will operate, giving her at least a prudential reason to comply with them.

But what of those who, despite repeated attempts, still manage to fail? Their position, as permanent noncitizens, is clearly anomalous and unenviable, even if their social rights are well protected, as they should be. The issue then becomes one of the balance of gains and losses. Citizenship programs and tests (and the accompanying ceremonies) are created out of a desire that people should think of acquiring citizenship as an important accomplishment. New citizens should feel proud of what they have achieved, even if their original motive for seeking citizenship was instrumental. But this can't happen if the test becomes a mere formality with a 100 percent pass rate. What matters is that the test should be passable by anyone who puts in a modest amount of effort in preparing for it, and that there is support for those who, for example, have reading or comprehension difficulties.

The tests that are currently used in the countries previously referred to seem to me to meet the first of these conditions at least (though, as noted, the new British test requires considerable study beforehand). Despite this, large numbers of permanent residents choose not to follow the path to citizenship.[20] This raises a further question, namely whether it should be made compulsory for people in this position to become citizens—to make citizenship a requirement and not merely an expectation, to use the terminology introduced earlier. This has recently been proposed in a paper by Helder de Schutter and Lea Ypi.[21] Although they recognize the controversial nature of their proposal, they offer several arguments in support. One is that it will make the society more cohesive. Another is that it prevents the creation of a two-caste society, following the democratic arguments of Michael Walzer and others (see Chapter 7). But perhaps the most challenging is that it would remedy the unfairness involved in people enjoying the rights that come with social membership while not taking on the potentially burdensome obligations of citizenship (duties connected to elections, but also jury service, and liability to conscription).[22] This seems to violate the well-known principle that "a person is under an obligation to do his part as specified by the rules of an institution whenever he has voluntarily accepted the benefits of the scheme or has taken advantage of the opportunities it offers to advance his interests, provided that this institution is just or fair,"[23] Most long-term immigrants can plausibly be said to have joined the relevant "scheme" voluntarily, and they clearly benefit from living under a legal system that offers personal protection and a range of goods and services such as education and health care, so might they have a reciprocal obligation to become full citizens, with the burdens attached to that status?

In answer to this question, we can ask, first, whether there is a moral obligation to become a citizen, and second, whether there should also be a legal obligation as De Schutter and Ypi propose. The basis for a moral obligation is fairness, as set out earlier. Suppose, though, that someone claims he has complied with the other requirements of fairness—has conscientiously kept the law, for example, and paid his taxes in full—but has moral objections to becoming a citizen. What might these be? There could be an objection to the oath of allegiance that he is required to take. In Canada, for example, a group of prospective citizens went to court in 2014 to challenge that part of the Oath of Citizenship that required them to pledge allegiance to Elizabeth II as Queen of Canada, citing their antimonarchist beliefs and appealing to their rights of free speech (their challenge was rejected by the court on the grounds that "the reference to the Queen is symbolic of our form of government and the unwritten constitutional principle of democracy").[24] A more substantive reason would be opposition to one of the policies that the state is currently pursuing: by becoming a citizen, the objector could argue, she becomes involved in collective responsibility for, let us say, a foreign war that she regards as fundamentally unjust. But it can be said in response to this that by virtue of being a permanent member of the society, this person is *already* included in collective responsibility, and the morally required course of action is therefore to become a citizen and agitate and vote against the objectionable policy. As to the formal wording of the citizenship oath, the question is whether it forces the oath taker to affirm something that contravenes a requirement of basic justice, not whether the wording corresponds to his own political beliefs. The American citizen required to swear allegiance to the Constitution may well take personal objection to some of its clauses (such as the one asserting the right to bear arms), but taken as a whole that document is an expression of the liberal principles on which the state is founded. Neither formal nor substantive objections therefore seem strong enough to outweigh the argument from fairness that makes becoming a citizen morally obligatory. But there might still be reason to hesitate before making this a legal requirement. First, to do so would clearly be at odds with imposing a citizenship test, a practice I have just defended, since a person would then be legally bound to do what he might be unable to do, namely, pass the relevant test in order to become a citizen.[25] Second, despite what has been said earlier about the moral requirement to obtain citizenship, this might be overridden in certain cases by the demands of conscience. Someone might hold religious views that made it impossible for him to swear allegiance to a secular power. So if there were to be a legal requirement on the part of immigrants to progress to full citizenship, there should at least be a conscientious objection clause to allow people with such beliefs to escape from it.[26]

Citizenship is not just a formal legal status, with accompanying rights and obligations. It is also a social role that encompasses a wide variety of everyday activities, ranging from joining neighborhood associations and conservation groups to protesting against government policies that treat some of your fellow citizens (or indeed foreigners) unfairly. Most people would agree that engaging in these activities is what makes somebody into a "good citizen," but there is disagreement about whether there is a moral obligation to undertake them.[27] It is wrong, therefore, to make access to formal citizenship dependent on evidence that somebody has already been politically active or engaged in other forms of social participation that express a civic commitment on their part. Equally, there is legitimately wide variation in the kinds of activities that people undertake in their capacity as citizens, so immigrants should be not be faulted for having a somewhat different pattern of engagement from others. What matters for civic integration, beyond acceptance of a common set of ground rules, is that people should feel a responsibility to make a social contribution; there is nothing wrong with a civic division of labor.

The value of civic integration is rarely questioned. Cultural integration is another matter, however, and it is very contestable whether states have any business trying to encourage (or force) immigrants to integrate culturally with the native population (which anyway is not a cultural monolith, but is likely to be divided by social class, region, religion, and so forth). The case against cultural integration is essentially twofold. First it is oppressive: it involves forcing or inducing people to abandon their own cultural matrix in order to assimilate to somebody else's. It offends against the basic liberal principle that people should be free to follow their own path (which might also be the path of their ancestral group) in matters of belief, taste, and value, so long as they don't trample on anyone else's equal freedom. Second, it is unnecessary. Provided immigrants integrate civically, and to a sufficient extent socially, that will create the social bonds needed to avoid conflict and enable a democratic state to function effectively. In practice, so the argument goes, the culture of immigrant groups is likely to change over time as they adjust to life in their new surroundings, but there is no need for the state to do anything to steer or hasten the process. Instead, the state's role with respect to culture is to provide an environment in which many different cultures can coexist and flourish; in other words, its basic policy should be one of (liberal) multiculturalism.

That is the case against making cultural integration a political goal. Even defenders of multiculturalism like Will Kymlicka concede, however, that immigration is also inevitably a process of cultural transformation. In Kymlicka's account, immigrants cannot expect to reproduce their own "societal culture" in the country they have joined, where a societal culture is "a culture which provides its members with meaningful ways of life across the full range of human activities, including social, educational, religious, recreational, and economic life, encompassing both public and private spheres."[28] They cannot do this because societal cultures are upheld by common public institutions—social, educational, economic, and political—and when people migrate they remove themselves from one set of institutions and place themselves under another. So multiculturalism for immigrants, at least in Kymlicka's version, is a claim about how the state should respond to the private cultures of different groups—a claim that members of minorities should not be disadvantaged in pursuing economic and other opportunities by virtue of their cultural membership. The rules of the receiving society must adjust in certain ways to accommodate the religious beliefs or ethnic practices of migrants. So here a line is being drawn between private and public culture. On one side stands the culture of the wider society, expressed in its language, its symbols, and its institutions: these must be common property, since there can only be one national flag or national legislature. On the other side, there is room for many different forms of private culture—different religions, different forms of art and literature, different cuisines, and so forth. Multiculturalism is a matter of showing respect for, or perhaps even celebrating, these differences. It is not, at least in Kymlicka's version, an argument against all forms of cultural integration.[29] Indeed, for Kymlicka, multicultural policies and nation-building policies should be seen as complementary:

> It is a mistake to view MCPs [multicultural policies] in isolation from the larger context of public policies that shape people's identities, beliefs and aspirations. Whether or not MCPs encourage trust or solidarity, for example, will heavily depend on whether these MCPs are part of a larger policy package that simultaneously nurtures identification with the larger

political community. In the absence of appropriate nation-building policies, a particular MCP may reduce solidarity and trust, by focusing exclusively on the minority's difference. But in the presence of such nation-building policies, the same MCP may in fact enhance solidarity and trust, by reassuring members of the minority group that the larger identity promoted by nation-building policies is an inclusive one that will fairly accommodate them.[30]

The real issue, then, is about where the line between public and private culture should be drawn: what should or should not be included in the common cultural matrix into which immigrants can legitimately be expected to integrate. Or to put the question in Kymlicka's terms, what kinds of nation-building policies are justifiable?

Those who oppose "cultural integration" will argue that the common public culture must be understood in a thin way, to include only the principles and the political institutions by which the society is governed, and perhaps the official language in which public decisions are debated and promulgated. But the difficulty with this proposal is that it may be impossible even to understand these things without some grasp of the broader cultural context in which they are set.[31] Consider the many countries that include minority nations within their borders and have devised special political arrangements to reflect the identities and practical demands of these communities: Canada, Spain, or the United Kingdom, for instance. No one could understand why Quebec, Catalonia, or Scotland have (and are entitled to have) devolved parliaments with very significant powers of decision without having some sense of the historical process whereby these arrangements came into being and of the national-cultural differences that justify their continuance. Nor could the specific form that democratic institutions take in a particular country—whether it is presidential or parliamentary, what form the second chamber takes, whether it is a constitutional monarchy or a republic, whether there is a separate bill of rights, etc.—be understood without knowledge of the relevant historical background. That, presumably, is why even those citizenship tests that are more narrowly focused on political institutions also require candidates to know something about the past events that have shaped those institutions. Thus candidates for naturalization in the United States are not just required to name the two branches of Congress or explain why some states have more representatives than others but are also expected to be able to identify the authors of *The Federalist Papers* and say what caused the Civil War.

This, however, still falls short of an argument for seeking to integrate immigrants into national culture in a broader sense that includes recognizing cultural landmarks such as feasts and holidays, artistic and literary icons, places of natural beauty, historical artifacts, sporting achievements, popular entertainers, and so forth.[32] So what could justify policies that have this as their objective? We can answer this question, first, from the perspective of the immigrants themselves, and then, second, from the perspective of the host society as a whole. From the immigrants' perspective, although they will probably wish to maintain many aspects of the culture that they bring with them and are entitled to ask that it should be supported in various ways, they also have an interest in learning from the inside about a societal culture that has profoundly shaped the physical space in which they are now going to live. Much of what they see around them will appear mysterious without that background knowledge—and they also risk giving offense, inadvertently or otherwise, if they don't grasp the national significance of some event or institution.[33] Immigrant groups may also want to change that societal culture in certain ways or add to it new elements of their own (think of the St. Patrick's Day Parade in New York or the Notting Hill Carnival in London), but to do that they need to know first what they are aiming to change. Moreover, being integrated culturally will make it easier to be integrated socially, which for reasons set out earlier is going to be important if immigrants want to take full advantage of the opportunities available in the new society. Recall that the final stage of integration, in Anderson's schema, is "informal social integration," which in her example "happens when members of different races share conversations at the lunch table, hobnob over the coffee break, and play together at recess."[34] But what should one hobnob about other than last evening's baseball or football match, or the latest episode in the switchback career of some media celebrity? And that requires a range of taken-for-granted points of reference that familiarity with the societal culture will provide.

From the perspective of the host society, cultural integration matters because it allows immigrants to identity with that society more fully and to adopt its national identity as their own. Certainly that identity must adjust in order to acknowledge their presence: the historical narratives that citizens adopt to explain who they are must now include the fact of immigration and the cultural diversity that results from that. But a shared national identity is a resource that can allow a society to solve collective action problems, pursue policies of social justice, and function more effectively as a democracy. It matters that the identity should be inclusive because part of its raison d'etre is to establish trust between groups who might otherwise be disposed to treat each other with hostility or disdain. My argument here rests on the simple psychological claim that we are disposed to sympathize with, help, trust, and take responsibility for those with whom we feel we have something in common, and a sense of identity creates this feeling of likeness even with people with whom we are not in direct contact. There is ample evidence to bear this claim out—for example, evidence from experiments in which participants are told that they are interacting with people with whom they share some common attribute—and this information influences their willingness to engage in various forms of helping behavior.[35] The nature of the attribute is not so important—it can be a style of dress, a political ideology, or a skin color. The bare knowledge that someone forms part of your identity group is sufficient to trigger the disposition, even though you have never encountered them in person. The disagreement, then, is not over whether a society benefits in multiple ways from its members having a common identity, but between those who believe that a thinner citizen identity is sufficient to the task, and those who think that a thicker national identity is required—though it can also be recast as a debate about national identity itself and the extent to which this needs to include cultural as opposed to more narrowly political elements. As one might expect, the evidence suggests that those who adhere to a richer, and therefore potentially more exclusive, understanding of what it means to belong to nation X are also likely to identify more strongly with X—and therefore are more willing to display solidarity with other members of X, provided they see them as members in good standing.[36]

The cultural components of national identity will naturally reflect the historic culture of the majority of native-born citizens, and this may pose an obstacle to integration. The problem arises most acutely in the case of religion, where the religious beliefs and practices of immigrants may collide with the religious elements embedded in the national culture, such as an established church or the presence of religious symbols in schools or in public ceremonies. Some critics claim that where a state grants precedence to a particular religion such as Christianity in these ways, it violates the liberal requirement that all citizens must be treated with equal respect. Martha Nussbaum, for example, a vociferous critic of religious precedence, argues that it unavoidably "subordinates" or "marginalizes" those who do not belong to the favored religion; it amounts to a public declaration that they are second-class citizens.[37] This extends to purely symbolic forms of recognition that, she claims, convey a message to the minority groups that they do not properly belong to the nation in question. Citing the example of crucifixes displayed in Italian school classrooms, she says that "some religious symbols, set up by government, threaten the equal standing of citizens in the public realm."[38] The difficulty here is to know how to interpret such symbolic displays: Are they intended simply to reflect the country's Catholic heritage, including the traditional appearance of its schools, or do they convey the message that only Catholics can be "real" Italians, as Nussbaum implies? Moreover, any endorsement or support on the part of the state for cultural forms might be faulted in the same way for failing to display equal respect for all citizens. What if the French government decides to subsidize its film industry in order to promote French language films, or the British government chooses to distribute free copies of Shakespeare to children because it wants them to absorb some of the language and imagery of his plays? In either case immigrants might feel that their own native cultures were not being recognized as equally valuable. But would they have any reason to think that their status as equal citizens was being denied?

For the equal standing of minority groups to be preserved, three conditions must be met. First, the state must ensure that opportunities, whether economic, educational or political, are not restricted by virtue of membership in a religious or ethnic group, except of course where the group's own culture is the source of the restriction (we should not expect to find Quakers serving in the Armed Forces, or Jews working as pork butchers). This may require exempting the group from legal restrictions, or accommodating them in other ways. Exactly how far this accommodation must go in order for opportunities to be equalized is likely to be debatable because group practices can also reasonably be expected to change to make it easier for members to comply with existing restrictions: there needs to be dialogue between the two sides, and a willingness to give and take.[39] Nevertheless the underlying principle is clear. Second, where the state is already in the business of supporting particular groups, including cultural ones, it must do so in an even-handed manner. To reuse an earlier example, if a liberal state subsidizes string quartets, it must also be willing to subsidize steel bands and mariachi groups. If it grants tax concessions to churches, it must do the same for temples, mosques, and synagogues. In other words, where private culture is concerned, it should follow a principle of equal treatment, whether this means no subsidies for anyone or equivalent subsidies for each group. Third, in the realm of public culture, all groups have an equal claim to be listened to when existing practice is being reviewed or new departures are being contemplated. This might mean anything from the design of the national flag to the content of the public broadcasting media to the position of the established church (if there is one). Finally such matters need to be decided by appeal to the majority, in a democracy, but this ought to be a majority whose views have been enlightened by deliberation with other groups.

Someone might ask at this point why the state should not simply adopt a stance of strict neutrality on all cultural matters, thereby preempting any charge that particular groups are being disadvantaged or "marginalized."[40] One reply is that strict neutrality is in any case impossible. Kymlicka makes this point in relation to language when he notes,

> One of the most important determinants of whether a culture survives is whether its language is the language of government—i.e. the language of public schooling, courts, legislatures, welfare agencies, health services, etc. When the government decides the language of public schooling, it is providing what is probably the most important form of support needed by societal cultures, since it guarantees the passing on of the language and its associated traditions and conventions to the next generation.[41]

Kymlicka here assumes, reasonably enough, that there must *be* a language of government, or at most a small number of official languages. In the same way, there must be a national flag and a national anthem; if there is a public broadcasting service, a government-appointed body must decide what should be given airtime; if there is a national curriculum in schools, another body must decide what it should include, and so forth. None of these decisions is strictly "neutral," from a cultural perspective. As Kymlicka puts it, a policy of "benign neglect" is simply infeasible here.

There are other areas of policy, however, in which benign neglect might be a possibility, but in which there is a legitimate public interest in the state's playing an active role. Take, for example, all of the decisions that have to be made about the use of land: where roads or train tracks should be laid; which areas should be used for industry, which for residential purposes, and which set aside for recreation or conservation; what should be built where, and under what restrictions as to design and appearance, and so forth. In principle the state could wash its hands of these decisions, auction off the available land, and allow the market to run its course: people would bid for the land that they wanted for private, commercial, or cultural purposes, and use it accordingly. But apart perhaps from extreme libertarians, few would regard this as a desirable outcome. The regulated use of land may create a number of public goods, whether these are aesthetic (such as the preservation of areas of outstanding natural beauty or the integrated planning of a town or city), recreational (such as access to public sports facilities or to areas of wilderness), or environmental (such as the conservation of natural resources or the protection of the habitats of endangered species of animals). Such policy decisions inevitably raise questions of culture, in a broad sense. They will reflect the relative value that the people making them attach to goals such as living in beautiful cities or preserving the natural environment, and these are matters over which opinions are likely to differ. A particularly clear example of the cultural significance of public space is provided by the disputes that have erupted when minority religions propose to erect buildings in areas that have traditionally been dominated by Christian churches, reflecting the historic culture of the majority group.[42] On one side stand those who believe that the appearance of public space should continue to reflect their own cultural identity as members of the majority; on the other stand those who believe that it should mirror the diversity of a multicultural society by allowing equal prominence to all forms of religious expression. Although it may be possible to find a pragmatic solution that allows minority cultural symbols to be present in public space without undermining the majority's cultural precedence, this is not "neutrality" in the sense of equal treatment.[43] Instead it represents a fair compromise between the conflicting cultural claims of the majority and the minority groups.

Viewed in this light, what does cultural integration mean? Note first that, in contrast to civic integration, it does not even make sense to think of this as a possible *requirement:* there is no cultural equivalent to the legal acquisition of citizenship. At most, then, cultural integration might be an aspiration, and possibly an expectation, to use Carens's distinction. What does it involve? The immigrant needs both to understand and to recognize the significance of the public culture of the society she has joined. She should acknowledge that expressing or strengthening the public culture is a valid reason in support of a political proposal, and she should also acknowledge that there are contexts in which it is permissible to give that culture symbolic precedence. At the same time she has the right to be heard and taken seriously when some aspect of that culture is being debated. She is also entitled to expect that her private culture should be accommodated and supported in appropriate ways, depending on the case. Thus, to return to the example of the Italian classrooms, a Muslim immigrant to Italy should expect that her female children will be allowed to dress modestly and to wear the headscarf to school, but she should not object to the presence of a crucifix as a representation of Italy's Catholic heritage.[44] Members of minority religions should have the freedom and opportunity to create places of worship that meet their religious needs, but they should not object if in designing these buildings they are required to respect the existing character of public space, by, for example, not overshadowing nearby churches. Full cultural integration requires that members of the indigenous majority understand why the private cultures of immigrants need to be accommodated and offer their ungrudging support for the measures that are needed, and that the immigrants themselves understand and embrace the public culture of the society they have joined.[45]

I began this chapter by presenting integration as the remedy widely proposed for the violent disorders that have sporadically afflicted liberal democracies possessing clustered ethnic minorities of immigrant origin. By distinguishing between social, civic, and cultural integration, I have tried to explain what is valuable about each of these different forms of integration and what measures a liberal state can legitimately take to promote them. I should stress that the integration policies outlined in this chapter and the social justice policies outlined in Chapter 7 are to be taken together. If we say that immigrants should attempt to integrate socially, civically, and culturally, we must at the same time say that they have a right to be included on equal terms in economic and political life and to benefit equally from the services provided by the welfare state. This is the essence of the reciprocal bargain that is struck between immigrant and host community. For immigrants to demand a full array of antidiscrimination and equal opportunity measures while reserving the right to isolate themselves from the wider society in cultural enclaves is unacceptable; but it is equally so for politicians to demand displays of unconditional national loyalty from immigrants without at the same time providing the protection and support that treats them as citizens (or citizens-in-the-making) whose standing is fully equal to that of the native born.

NINE

Conclusion

BARELY A DAY HAS PASSED since I began writing this book when immigration has not featured in the newspapers and the digital media as an issue of topical concern. The largest single event has been the cross-border movement of millions of people fleeing the civil wars in Syria and northern Iraq, described by António Guterres, the UN high commissioner for refugees, as "the biggest humanitarian emergency of our era." The brunt of this human disaster has been borne by states such as Jordan and Turkey that fall outside the main scope of my inquiry, but ripple effects have been felt across Europe as refugees from the fighting have followed precarious routes out of Asia and North Africa: most notoriously hazardous boat trips across the Mediterranean in which thousands of people have lost their lives. Within Europe itself, the principle of free movement of labor has proved increasingly controversial and might yet indeed prove to be the main issue that provokes a British exit from the EU. Meanwhile in the United States, the presence of an estimated eleven million undocumented migrants continues to produce heated political debate between Democrats and Republicans, not least in reaction to President Obama's decision in November 2014 to offer up to five million of these people some legal security under "deferred action" programs.

These events provoke strong reactions: very often moral outrage on the part of those whose sympathies lie with the immigrants, and bitter resentment from those who regard immigrants as welfare-seeking opportunists. Here, for example, is the Liberal Member of Parliament Sarah Teather, the chair of the Parliamentary Group on Refugees, on the day when the British government announced its support for an EU decision sharply to curtail its search-and-rescue operation in the Mediterranean:

> This decision is deeply depressing. We would rather let people drown for nothing other than baseless political motives. It shows that when it comes to immigration, the Government has plumbed new depths of inhumanity.
>
> We cannot pretend this problem has nothing to do with us and wash our hands as people die. It is the policies we are pursuing, attempting to turn Europe into a fortress with no safe routes in, that is forcing migrants into risking their lives. We are forcing people to choose between dying in their own war torn country and drowning in the sea.[1]

Many others within parliament and outside spoke with similar voices. But turn to the right-wing press, and especially the *Daily Mail,* Britain's second most widely read paper, and you find instead a steady stream of articles highlighting the alleged net financial burdens imposed by immigrants, together with disturbing reports of immigrant behavior, such as the following account of the fate awaiting the Queen's swans on a river near Peterborough:

> For the first time, there's irrefutable evidence that swans and vast quantities of fish are being killed by immigrants who have set up camp along the River Nene and are living off the land.
>
> With more than 16,000 new Eastern European immigrants arriving in the past five years, those unable—or unwilling—to pay for accommodation in Peterborough have instead adopted the lifestyle of ancient hunter-gatherers, albeit with a penchant for vast amounts of strong Polish vodka and beer.
>
> Living in crude shelters made of wood and plastic sheeting, scores of immigrants have taken up permanent residence all along the Nene.
>
> Using crude snares and nets, the inhabitants are preying on swans, fish, rabbits, pigeons and even snails—all plundered from this expensively-restored habitat and cooked on open fires.[2]

In such a political climate, working out a coherent and balanced way of thinking about immigration is difficult.[3] Move in one direction and you can be accused of heartlessness toward vulnerable and desperate people; move in the other and you will be called an elitist with no understanding of the impact that immigration can have on working-class communities.[4] The first step is to recognize that there are better and worse reasons in play on both sides of the argument. On the pro-immigration, pro-open-borders side, we find liberal idealists concerned especially for the rights of refugees and others trying to escape from bleak situations; but we also find business leaders, for whom immigrants are a welcome addition to the ranks of what Marxists used to call "the reserve army of the unemployed," helping to push down wages to the minimum. On the side of immigration control, we find narrow-minded bigots opposed to any change in the way that their neighborhood looks or behaves; but we also find thoughtful social democrats who fear the power of global capitalism and see citizen solidarity as the only countervailing force that can be relied on to oppose it. To be in favor of higher immigration is not always to be virtuous, therefore, nor is to be against it always to be merely prejudiced. To avoid descending into caricature, we need to understand both the interests of the different parties affected by immigration—the immigrants themselves, people in the receiving society, and those the migrants leave behind—and the full range of values that are at stake when it is being debated. I have appealed to several of these values as the book has progressed, but without spelling them out explicitly. So let me now remedy this omission, before drawing some general corollaries about how to (and how not to) think about immigration.[5]

My argument has invoked four main values. The first of these is weak moral cosmopolitanism. Immigrants are human beings. However we interact with them, we cannot ignore their moral standing. In particular, we cannot act toward them in ways that violate their human rights, and in many cases we have positive duties to help protect those rights. But weak cosmopolitanism goes further than this. It also requires us to give reasons if we decide to refuse people's demands or requests, even when no rights are at stake. Recall the stranded hiker in need of a good book from Chapter 2. That widening of cosmopolitanism is important because it shows why, even if there is no human right to immigrate, a state's immigration policy must nonetheless be morally defensible, in the sense of giving good reasons for their exclusion to those who are barred from entering.

Although human rights discourse is not popular among those who are inclined to be hawkish about immigration, I doubt if they would repudiate weak cosmopolitanism itself. For example, those who defend the EU's decision in 2014 (later reversed) to devote fewer resources to the rescue of migrants floating in unseaworthy boats on the Mediterranean don't say that they care nothing about the fate of those who drown. Instead they argue that the previous Italian-led search-and-rescue operation created an incentive for people smugglers to invest in the trade, and thereby led to more lives being lost overall. Even if you think that this argument is hypocritical, its underlying premise is cosmopolitan: choose the policy that leads to fewer deaths by drowning, regardless of who the victims are.

The second value is national self-determination. Citizens in a democracy have the right to decide upon the future direction of their society (though within certain bounds set by the weak cosmopolitan restriction just canvassed). Because immigration unavoidably affects that future direction—in part because of the demographic and cultural changes that inward migration brings with it, and in part because most of the new arrivals will themselves become politically active citizens in due course—decisions about whom to admit, how many to admit, and what the terms of admission should be are all important matters for a democracy to decide. In reaching such decisions, citizens should reflect on the goals that they would like to see their society achieve, which need not just be narrowly economic, but might also be sporting, cultural, or environmental. Especially in the case of economic migrants, therefore, national self-determination demands very considerable latitude in choosing an immigration policy that fits with the publicly espoused values of the society in question.

This appeal to national self-determination is likely to be resisted in two ways. One is to challenge the presence of the qualifier "national." Self-determination may be important, many will say, but it should be understood as *citizens'* self-determination, without reference to the national identities of the people who make up the citizen body. This would take much of the heat out of the immigration issue, since questions about immigrant culture and immigrants' capacity to share a national identity with those who already occupy their new home become irrelevant. The issue that then arises is whether self-determination can be understood merely as decision making by a majority of the shifting assemblage of persons who at any moment compose the citizen body, or whether it does not presuppose the existence of a "people" in a more substantive sense—a nation that thinks of itself as a collectivity that endures over time, with a shared past and shared aspirations for the future. In Chapter 4, I offered some arguments in favor of this stronger way of under-standing self-determination.[6]

The second challenge does not deny the value of national self-determination itself, but asserts that it cannot trump the needs and inter-ests of immigrants. Here it is claimed that our obligations of justice toward immigrants, whatever these are, come first, and then our projects of self-determination, cultural or otherwise, can proceed within those limits. This is a harder challenge to meet, because the question it raises is simple but difficult to answer: How much value should we attach to belonging to a political community in which people identify with each other, and also identify with a national project that began sometime in the past and will continue, so it is hoped, well into the future? The correct answer depends partly (but only partly) on how far citizens do actually value being part of such a community.

So the second value I have appealed to is more open to contest than the first. I turn next to the value of fairness, which has informed my discussion in two connected ways. One has to do with social practices and how they are constructed. When the terms of any social practice are being fixed, fair-ness requires that attention be paid to how rights and responsibilities, ben-efits and burdens, are distributed among the participants. This applies as much to a society's immigration regime as it does to any other aspect of so-cial life, the fact that immigrants are new arrivals notwithstanding. So a balance has to be struck between the claims that immigrants can rightfully make and the responsibilities they can reasonably be expected to assume. This rules out, on the one hand, a laissez-faire regime such as prevailed in nineteenth-century Britain and elsewhere, under which immigrants were simply left to fend for themselves unaided by the state,[7] and on the other hand, a regime that would give immigrants generous and unconditional assistance without, for example, imposing a responsibility to integrate (which seems sometimes to be the animating philosophy of immigrant support groups).

The second aspect of fairness is that once a fair social practice has been established, those involved in it must do what the scheme requires of them, and should expect to face sanctions, whether formal or informal, if they do not. So this is fairness as it applies to the individual members of the scheme rather than to its overall design. It means, for example, that when immigrants are admitted conditionally or on a temporary basis, it is reasonable to expect them to respect their terms of admission and not try to evade responsibilities or to use delaying tactics in order to remain in the host society far beyond the agreed date. I should stress that this applies regardless of how they came to join the society—whether on a fully voluntary basis or as refugees moving out of necessity.

Fairness in these two senses is a widely accepted value, although it is not incontestable. Anyone who regards immigration simply as a bargain between two independent parties—the immigrant and the receiving state—will be disposed to think that voluntariness on both sides is all that matters: whatever terms the immigrant is willing to accept are ipso facto just. I suggested in Chapter 1, using Henry Sidgwick as an example, that this was how nineteenth-century liberals thought about immigration (insofar as they thought about it at all). From the other direction, anyone who looks at immigration exclusively through the lens of human rights is likely to believe that the entitlements of immigrants should be treated as unconditional, perhaps with an exception made in the case of those convicted of serious crimes. There is an oddity about this approach: it really does seem to treat immigrants as perfect strangers, since it places them beyond the scope of the principles of fairness and reciprocity that are normally understood to run like threads throughout social life.

The fourth and final value that has informed my discussion is the idea of an integrated society—a society in which people from all walks of life and from diverse ethnic and religious backgrounds live in close proximity to one another, associate with each other for common goals, and interact freely and openly on terms of equality. No society ever lives up to that ideal fully, but it can serve as an aspiration and a guiding beacon. The value of social integration is linked both to national self-determination (because when a society is integrated it becomes easier for all of its members to sense that they are engaged in a common national project) and to fairness (because, as I argued in Chapter 8, opportunities for different groups are not likely to be equal when the groups live largely separate lives), but it goes beyond them, because it speaks directly to the texture of social relationships. Its value, once again, may be contested: it depends on how much weight you attach to promoting social peace and avoiding social conflict. Readers may at this point recall the verdict of Harry Lime in Graham Greene's *The Third Man,* whose proposition is that thirty years of terror and bloodshed under the Borgias produced Michelangelo, Da Vinci, and the Renaissance, while five centuries of peace, democracy, and brotherly love in Switzerland produced the cuckoo clock. A divided, conflictual society may, as Harry suggests, still produce great works of art. Is that justification enough? Moreover integration exacts a price from some immigrant groups, who may have escaped persecution in order to preserve their religious way of life, only to find that they are now being gently encouraged to dilute their beliefs or modify their practices in the name of freedom and equality. Nonetheless, so I maintain, it is a value that should guide our thinking about immigration.

The immigration policy of a liberal democracy, I have argued, should be guided by these four values: weak cosmopolitanism, national self-determination, fairness, and social integration. Unavoidably there will be points at which there is palpable tension between them: for instance, as I suggested in Chapter 8, when we are thinking about the conditions under which immigrants should be entitled to become full citizens, our concerns for fairness and for social integration may begin to pull apart. But before saying more about the practical implications of my approach, I want to underline two ways in which it differs from rival approaches—two strategies of argument in the literature on immigration that I have deliberately *not* adopted.

I begin by echoing what was said at the end of Chapter 1 about the virtues of realism in thinking about immigration.[8] It is very tempting to respond to the acute ethical dilemmas that arise in practical dealings with immigrants—such as the dilemma facing those who command rescue ships in the Mediterranean, if it is indeed the case that a policy of rescue creates incentives for more migrants to embark on hazardous sea journeys—by counterfactually assuming away some of the background conditions that create the dilemma. We should at least salvage all of the refugees, a well-intentioned person might say, while at the same time intervening to tackle the conflicts that continue to produce them in large numbers: there is therefore no real dilemma. But what if there is actually very little that we can do to lessen such conflicts (the civil war in Syria; the brutally repressive regime in Eritrea; the almost complete collapse of political order in Libya, and so on)—if intervention in these places will only make things worse or have unintended side effects? Then by shifting to the ideal level, we avoid having to think hard and make tough choices about what should actually be done: we are no longer forced to ask ourselves which principle or value should be treated as overriding. What does a morally defensible policy of rescue look like, for example? Does it require us, whether as private individuals or as representatives of our state, simply to respond to life-endangering situations when we encounter them as we go about our normal business, or does it mean taking preemptive steps to intervene when we can anticipate that such situations will occur? How far it is permissible to take into account the longer-term consequences of acting on the rescue principle?

As I noted in Chapter 1, a similar evasion occurs if we think about immigration from the standpoint of global justice, and then define a just immigration policy as one that a democratic state should adopt in a world that was also just—one in which human rights were universally protected, for example, and international inequalities were far smaller than those that exist today. In such a world, people would want to move only for personal reasons or because they were attracted by the culture or the climate of a particular society. They would not be moving for pressing economic reasons or because they were in danger of being persecuted by remaining where they were. Because many people attach value to remaining in their communities of origin, we can predict that the volume of migration, even with open borders, would not be great, and the flows would mostly be reciprocal. In these circumstances freedom of movement would surely be the default position, and restrictions would be justified only in special circumstances—to protect ecologically or culturally fragile areas that also happened to be attractive to migrants, for example. But this counterfactual approach does not help us to think about questions such as how to choose, here and now, between different categories of immigrants in circumstances in which borders have to be controlled and the overall numbers coming in have to be limited, for reasons of the kind laid out in Chapter 4. If we are grappling with the problem of whether it's permissible to recruit medical staff from developing countries to plug large gaps in the domestic provision of health care, it is not going to be illuminating to ask what the policy should be in a world where every country had the resources to train and employ sufficient numbers of people to meet its own health needs.

I also want to counsel here against testing an immigration policy by thinking about the way in which it might affect specific individuals who were subject to it. In the literature on immigration, one frequently comes across case studies of immigrants who in one way or another have fallen foul of the prevailing immigration regime and whose stories then serve to reveal its absurdity or inhumanity. These might be people who long ago had failed through oversight to obtain some necessary visa or certificate; or people who despite having entered illegally have turned out to be fine, upstanding members of society; or again people whose circumstances are simply desperate but are being refused admission. Any morally sensitive person will find these individual stories distressing. But one cannot build a coherent immigration policy or regime on such a foundation, any more than good law can be made out of hard cases. Such a policy must apply to large numbers of people and it must take account of the overall consequences of adopting one or other rule with respect to immigrant admission or naturalization, as well as being fair to individual people. As I have been emphasizing throughout this book, our thinking about immigration must be holistic. Admitting immigrants has consequences, which may be good or bad depending on the case, for the overall shape and character of the society that takes them in. What we should learn from these vignettes is that there must be occasions on which immigration officials, judges, and others should allow exceptions to the normal rules in the name of common sense or common humanity; what does not follow is that the rulebook should be thrown out altogether in favor of a free-for-all.

So if we are to think about immigration without counterfactual idealization, and without relying on our intuitions about individual cases, where should we begin? From the realistic premise, I believe, that the immigration regimes of most liberal democracies are under extreme stress, brought about by three main factors: first, the far greater numbers of migrants struggling to be admitted than these states are willing to allow in; second, the premium that is now placed on getting one foot inside the territory, since once a person has managed to cross the relevant border, by whatever means, he gains a range of legal protections that are likely to make it difficult to deport him if he fails to qualify for admission; third, the anxieties, resentments, and prejudices felt by native citizens toward many (though not all) immigrants, creating considerable pressure on governments to cap numbers and further stiffen border controls, and also making it more difficult for the immigrants who are entitled to stay to integrate socially.[9] Such a state of affairs is plainly both ethically and politically unacceptable, leading to human rights violations and social injustices suffered by the immigrants on one side, and a perception of cultural threat and a sense that their home is under invasion on the part of members of the receiving society on the other. And it further distorts democratic politics, as immigration rises toward the top of the agenda, especially for politicians from left of center, North American liberals and European social democrats, whose liberal instincts in the case of immigrants have continually to be reined in to avoid alienating their working and middle-class supporters.

So what should be done? Essentially what is needed is a clear policy on immigration that can be set out and defended publicly, with all the relevant data about how the policy is working also in the public domain. It should cover the overall numbers being accepted, how different categories of immigrants are treated, the criteria of selection being used, and what is expected of immigrants by way of integration. This needs to be accompanied by strong border controls, and rapid assessment of the status of those who are admitted provisionally, as asylum seekers or as a temporary protection measure. No one can pretend that border walls and fences are pleasant things to witness, but if citizens are going to embrace the state's immigration policy, they need to be reassured that the policy is going to be effectively enforced and that the people who are allowed to enter are the people who meet the criteria that it lays down. If one part of the policy covers temporary migration, then it must be transparent that people who are included in the program do actually leave when the program finishes.

What should the content of the policy actually be? Throughout the book I have argued that immigration policy should be developed alongside and in line with the other goals that each society sets for itself, so there cannot be a general answer to this question. If it is a matter of numbers, societies with ample space and/or falling populations and/or labor shortages will be generally pro-immigrant, whereas societies that feel crowded already or whose culture is threatened with erosion will be more restrictive. Societies that are already multicultural, and especially those that have adopted multiculturalism as one of their public policies, will approach both the selection of immigrants and integration policy differently from societies that are relatively homogenous and wish to remain so. When it comes to the selection of economic migrants, the skill shortages in particular industries will likely be a major factor. And so forth.

So there is no single immigration policy that a political philosopher could lay down as the just or correct policy for all the liberal democracies (let alone all societies) to pursue. Nonetheless, I want to argue that its general shape should reflect the four values listed earlier. The position I defend could be described in broad terms as "communitarian" and "social democratic." It places a great deal of weight on social cohesion and social justice and assesses immigration policy from that perspective. Both admission policies and integration policies should aim at ensuring that immigrants become full members of the societies they join, regarded and treated as equal citizens by the indigenous majority, identifying with the society, and participating widely in its social and political life. This does not mean "assimilation." Immigrants are also entitled to retain their specific group–based identities and their cultural differences. But because their rights and opportunities should be exactly the same as those of the native born, it would be a worrying sign if immigrants turned out to achieve markedly different levels of success in spheres such as education, the economy, and politics.

A criticism that is sometimes leveled at this position is that by insisting on full equality for immigrants, it raises the stakes of the original decision about whether or not to admit them. Linda Bosniak characterizes contemporary citizenship policy as *"hard on the outside and soft on the inside."*[10] More colorfully, Kieran Oberman has suggested that contemporary thinking about immigration is dominated by "the coconut consensus," under which tough border controls (the hard shell) separate the few who are admitted from the many who are not, but the chosen few are then treated generously in terms of their rights and status (the softer flesh).[11] What this consensus ignores, it is said, is that there are many migrants who would readily forgo some of the benefits that are currently being provided in order to increase their chances of admission—for instance, they might be happy to remain indefinitely as "denizens" with no prospect of admission to citizenship. (This is sometimes presented as an argument for "soft borders," where crossing a geographical boundary carries less significance in terms of the migrant's entitlements.) Now I have made one concession to these critics by accepting the legitimacy of (properly regulated) temporary migration programs, stepping back from the strong Walzerian position that only full access to citizenship for everyone who enters the society can avoid the risk of domestic tyranny. But I hold firmly to the view that there is something deeply wrong about a society that includes a permanent class of subordinated people, whether these are unauthorized immigrants or people who hold some kind of indefinite probationary status but are potentially subject to expulsion at short notice. Such an arrangement flagrantly violates three of the four values that are guiding my discussion.[12] The fact that the members of this class might accept their position as preferable to the alternatives is not decisive, any more than sweatshop labor can be defended by pointing out that the workers involved choose to engage in it faute de mieux.

Of course all of this depends on the arguments advanced in Chapters 3 and 4 to show that there is no basic right to cross borders, and that states have legitimate grounds for restricting entry. If these arguments are thrown out, then it will no longer be possible to appeal to social justice and cohesion as grounds for limiting immigrant inflows: they will simply be trumped by the immigrants' right to move. But there remains the morally excruciating case of refugees. They do not have an unlimited right to choose where to live, but they do have a right to be offered sanctuary so long as their human rights are under threat in their home countries, and there is no feasible way in which this threat can be removed at source. I handled this issue by arguing that each society was obliged to discharge its fair share of the collective responsibility that all states bear to protect refugees' rights. How that fair share is specified in concrete terms for each state will depend on the international regime that is in place. Where a formal agreement has been reached on the distribution of refugees—either a fully inclusive agreement (the best case) or a partial agreement between a particular group of states—the obligation will be to adjudicate with care all asylum applications that are received, and to take in as many as the agreement requires, passing on the remainder if necessary.[13] Where there is no such agreement, each state needs to make a conscientious effort to work out what its fair share of the refugee burden should be and to admit on that basis. Unavoidably, given the political pressure that governments face to cut back on immigration numbers and the public's somewhat negative attitude toward refugees, there will be an incentive to underestimate what that share amounts to. For this reason, I believe there is a duty to make a good faith attempt to set up an international mechanism to oversee refugee flows, building on the partial success of the existing UN's Office of High Commissioner for Refugees,[14] and to precommit to complying with its recommendations, at least up to an agreed threshold on numbers.

But this approach still leaves two difficult issues unresolved. The first is what should be done if other states fail to live up to the terms of the refugee agreement or otherwise refuse to carry their fair share of responsibility: Must we, as citizens of a compliant state, then step in to "take up the slack," regardless of the numbers involved?[15] The second is what should be done if the number of refugees we are asked to accept *even under a fair distribution* is greater than the number that can be accommodated and/or integrated without serious cost to social justice and cohesion. Since cost considerations are built into the idea of a fair allocation, this second scenario may seem unlikely, the very large refugee flows being generated by recent events in the Middle East notwithstanding. Yet we can imagine a future in which the effects of global warming and resource depletion make large parts of the Earth's surface virtually uninhabitable, and then the searching question is whether the societies that have escaped relatively unscathed would have an obligation to admit refugees in numbers that would transform their own cultures and political institutions. In both cases, I think, the correct answer is that the obligation to admit would in these circumstances be humanitarian in nature, not something that justice demands, which also implies that it would be a matter for the citizens of the receiving society to decide upon—they could not be forced to comply, either by the refugees themselves or by third parties.[16]

These possibilities, even if presently somewhat remote, are what make me describe the refugee issue as "morally excruciating." The dilemma should not be avoided either by wishful thinking to the effect that the number of "genuine" refugees will always be small or by pretending that the cost of absorbing them, even in very large numbers, will always be modest. This cost does of course depend on the way in which those who would have to receive the refugees value cultural or other aspects of their present way of life that would be seriously disrupted by large immigrant inflows. I have assumed throughout that the resistance to large-scale immigration that we see in the public opinion polls is not just an expression of prejudice, but stems from a genuine fear of cultural dislocation as well as from more material worries about jobs and social services.[17]

Having said that the refugee issue may, if things turn out badly, prove to be morally intractable, I want also to say that within the limits set by fairness states have a duty to give precedence to refugees over other categories of immigrant in their admissions policies. This may not be a popular policy choice, but since refugees' claims stem from the threat to their human rights, they must be given priority over those whose claim is simply that their inclusion will benefit the state in one way or another, whether as sports stars, computer programmers or fruit pickers. This would involve a significant shift in policy in the case of countries such as the United Kingdom, so the position I am adopting here by no means amounts to a defense of the status quo. It makes sense when thinking about immigration policy to consider ways of keeping interest and right aligned, so that states can gain something from migration and at the same time discharge their moral responsibilities, but this doesn't mean that they should be allowed simply to cherry-pick the "best" from among those who apply, as they are tempted to do. One constraint is their obligation to refugees, the meeting of which must come first if there is going to be a cap on overall numbers; another is the prohibition on recruiting professionals whose services are vitally needed in the less-developed societies that have educated them; a third relates to legitimate grounds for selection, discussed at some length in Chapter 6. In each case we see that the weak cosmopolitan principle I have posited is far from toothless: it rules out a fair amount of what most of the developed democracies would prefer to do and are actually doing in their treatment of immigrants.

To think clearly and coherently about immigration requires drawing on all of the resources that political philosophy has to offer. It is perhaps not a surprise that (as I noted in Chapter 1) the most influential figure in that field of the late twentieth and early twenty-first centuries—John Rawls—should have sidestepped the issue by postulating that his theory of justice was to apply to a society whose membership was already fixed; and when he later turned to examine questions of international justice, to have stipulated that in his "realistic utopia" the causes that produce mass migration in today's world would simply have disappeared.[18] Abandoning these assumptions would have forced Rawls to confront a series of questions that he managed to avoid: questions about the social and cultural preconditions for a just and democratic political community; questions about the nature of human rights and the obligations that correspond to them; questions about how far morality allows us to favor the interests and justice claims of compatriots over those of strangers. So as we grapple with the contentious and sometimes intractable issues that immigration poses, we also understand better what our fundamental beliefs and values are—what matters most to us when hard choices can no longer be avoided.

Postscript:
The European Migration Crisis of 2015

I FINISHED THE MAIN WRITING OF THIS BOOK at the beginning of 2015, at a moment when developments in North Africa and the Middle East had already begun to put the European migration system under unprecedented stress, but I did not anticipate the extraordinary series of events that were later to unfold, making migration into an almost daily headline issue throughout the continent. The mass movement across the Mediterranean that had previously centered on departures by boat from Libya was now supplemented by an even larger migration across the short sea channel between Turkey and Greece and by land movements across the same border, in both cases unauthorized by the receiving state. Many, though not all, of the new migrants were Syrians, either escaping directly from the civil war or disillusioned by life in the refugee camps established in Lebanon or Jordan.

Some 350,000 people are recorded to have crossed the EU border between January and August 2015, and the actual number may have been considerably larger. Germany, the migrants' main destination of choice, was anticipating having to accommodate as many as 800,000 by the end of the year. For European states that had not traditionally conceived of themselves as "immigrant societies" the numbers arriving appeared very large, and responses differed markedly from state to state, making it impossible for Europe to evolve a collective policy for dealing with the migrants—whether over the best way to prevent people from drowning in the Mediterranean as their unseaworthy boats foundered, or over a scheme for refugee resettlement. State borders that had previously been left open under the Schengen Agreement and the "fundamental" EU principle of freedom of movement were suddenly closed to migrants, leading to scenes of confrontation between police and migrants that for many Europeans were uncomfortably reminiscent of mass deportations in the era of fascism.

My purpose in this short postscript is not to elaborate further on events that are in any case widely reported beyond Europe itself, but to reflect on their implications for the philosophy of immigration set out in this book. Could that philosophy help European citizens and policy makers develop a coherent and principled response to the unauthorized arrival of large numbers of refugees and other migrants, or does the migration crisis simply expose its deficiencies? For some, the main lesson of 2015 is that Europe must open its borders to all those who are sufficiently motivated, or sufficiently desperate, to embrace the evident dangers of reaching them, or it must stand accused of human rights violations on a large scale. The cost of denying people access—whether this means leaving them to drown in the Mediterranean or using coercive means to enforce border controls—is unacceptably high. My purpose in this book has been to defend a qualified right on the part of states to close their borders and to propose principles for selecting immigrants for admission, but my position might seem to collapse when confronted with the physical realities of Europe in late 2015. And although the present crisis is indeed in some ways exceptional, it might be thought to foreshadow similar mass movements of people from people in poor, conflict-ridden societies into the liberal democracies, using whatever access routes are available.

To understand why the 2015 migration crisis is a challenge for my analysis, we need to return to the framework, introduced in this book in Chapter 5, that turns crucially on the distinction between refugees and economic migrants. In this framework, *refugees* are best understood as people whose human rights would be unavoidably threatened if they remain in the place they inhabit, regardless of whether the threat arises from state persecution, state collapse, or natural disaster. The source of the threat does not matter; what does is whether it could be averted *without* the person moving, for example by creating a safe haven within current state borders for those displaced by civil war or by erecting temporary accommodation for earthquake victims. *Economic migrants* are those who have reasons to move but do not qualify for refugee status, a category understood broadly so as to include those escaping routine poverty and those moving for reasons simply of personal inclination.

This distinction is crucial to my analysis, since I argue that states have obligations to refugees that they do not have to economic migrants—primarily the obligation to ensure that those who apply to them for asylum are either taken in or moved to places where their human rights are properly secured. But the events that have created the European migration crisis put this distinction into question. Many of those who have arrived unannounced by land or sea have been escaping conditions of civil war or of political instability in which terrorist groups can operate freely, or else they have been moving out of overcrowded refugee camps where living conditions and opportunities are too sparse to assure their human rights. In most cases they are victims of state failure rather than state persecution. When they attempt to cross a national border, are they then to be counted as refugees on the wider definition that I favor? The problem is that my definition includes a counterfactual element: it asks whether the person in question *could* be adequately protected while remaining in her present country of residence. In the case of someone currently staying in an underfunded refugee camp, for example, the answer to this question is very likely to be yes. What is primarily required to secure the human rights of the people staying there is for richer members of the international community to raise the level of support that they provide. But for the people who are actually living in the camp, the relevant question is whether the resources they need to lead decent lives (including opportunities for education and productive work) will *in fact* be provided so long as they remain where they are. They do not want to wait in hope for ten or twenty years. So they have very strong reasons for moving, but since they are already located in places where their basic rights either are or could be secured, they do not qualify as refugees from the perspective of the states they might move to.

In an influential book, Alexander Betts has proposed that we should introduce the concept of "survival migration" to cover cases like this.[1] Survival migrants, he says, are "persons who are outside their country of origin because of an existential threat for which they have no access to a domestic remedy or resolution."[2] The idea of an existential threat is not self-explanatory, but Betts suggests it might be spelled out by using Henry Shue's conception of basic rights, understood to include a right to subsistence.[3] So a survival migrant must be someone who lacks protection for one or more of his basic rights. But he must also "have no access to a domestic remedy or resolution." What does this mean? It cannot plausibly mean "no access at this very moment." Consider an earthquake survivor. She may need both food and shelter, and it may be some days before these are provided through an international relief effort. Meanwhile she has no access to a domestic remedy because the local authorities are overstretched. Presumably, though, if she decided to cross a frontier it would not be in the spirit of Betts's definition to count her as a survival migrant. What this example shows is that the concept relies on a tacit understanding that conditions in the migrant's country of origin are "unfixable" looking some distance ahead into the future. As such, it inevitably suffers from a considerable degree of indeterminacy. If we say, for example, that people leaving Iraq or Syria will count as survival migrants, we must be making an assumption about what is going to happen in those countries in the future; we are ruling out the possibility of conflict ceasing and the economy recovering in a few years' time.

I do not treat this problem as an objection to the idea of survival migration itself. What it reveals, however, is if the concept is not to be stretched so that it covers everyone who exits a poor country in search of a better life, the people it applies to will also count as refugees on my definition. They will be people whose rights cannot be secured so long as they remain in their countries of origin. This conceptual point matters, because it affects how we see the flood of people crossing the sea and attempting to make their way across land borders to the richer European states. Their situation inevitably makes them look like an undifferentiated mass, desperate people in need of help. But in fact this tide of people is what immigration experts call a "mixed flow." It will include people who count as refugees under the narrow Geneva Convention definition of the term—that is, people who are escaping the threat of persecution. It will include survival migrants coming from places that are unfixable in the medium term and who therefore should be counted as refugees on the wider definition that I favor. And it will also include people moving in search of a decent life but who do not qualify as refugees on either count—for example, those who decided to quit refugee camps in which they were protected against attack but where opportunities to work were inadequate.

For receiving governments having to decide whom to admit, these distinctions matter. With limited resources, they have to be able to set priorities among different applicants, decide whether to admit people temporarily or on a more permanent basis, and so forth. Under normal conditions, this would involve a somewhat lengthy process of investigating the background circumstances of each new arrival. The migration crisis of 2015 is in part a crisis because the numbers arriving have overwhelmed the systems that European states, particularly those bordering the Mediterranean, have put in place to regulate admissions.

There is a further reason why the receiving states ought to look closely at who is coming in. It has been a noticeable (though predictable) feature of the migrant flows into Europe in the recent period that they are disproportionately composed of young men, many of them already having, or seeking, university education. This might bode well for their integration into Germany, Sweden, and the other European societies willing to accept them in substantial numbers, but it also means that the societies they are leaving are being deprived of the very people who are most able to contribute to their rebuilding. In these circumstances, the receiving societies cannot just consider their own needs for skilled labor—see my discussion of "brain drain" in Chapter 6. Paul Collier has recently argued that the central problem with the camps that have taken in refugees from Syria is that they fail to provide work opportunities for the inhabitants. His recommendation is that European states should use part of their support money to create industrial areas near to the camps, so that businesses and jobs can be created that would eventually return to Syria once the civil war ends.[4] Such initiatives, then, would serve a dual purpose: they would reduce the incentive for people to undertake dangerous journeys in the hope of reaching Europe, and they would contribute to the economic regeneration of war-torn societies. If adopted, a large-scale program of this kind would reduce the overall numbers trying to enter Europe and allow the immigration services a much better chance of identifying and welcoming those who are indeed refugees.

If inward mass migration by those who are not refugees is something to be discouraged, what steps can European states legitimately take to deter migrants from entering the borders of the European Union? The crisis has provoked strong disagreement both over search-and-rescue missions that aim to recover people from unseaworthy boats and deliver them to destinations in Europe, and over whether states should allow unauthorized migrants coming from the south to cross their borders and move on to countries farther north. Neither issue is straightforward. In the case of the boat people, all sides recognize that any ship that encounters a boat full of migrants in imminent danger of drowning has a humanitarian duty at least to take them on board and escort them to dry land.[5] However, it seems likely that the prospect of being rescued in this way provides an incentive to migrants to embark on unsafe journeys, and that when states break the link between rescue and access to their territory—as the Australian government has done by adopting a policy whereby migrant boats are either towed back to their point of embarkation or their occupants are assessed in offshore detention centers, with those qualifying for refugee status placed in third countries—the stream of boats rapidly dries up, and with it the loss of life. So here a gulf emerges between what ships, whether naval or commercial, should do when they come across migrant boats and what governments concerned to minimize loss of life should adopt as their policy.

For those who make it to Europe, the main issue is whether they should be allowed to move freely within the continent. Most states now regard such freedom of movement as one of the fundamental principles of the European Union. It might then seem anomalous to extend such a right only to current citizens and not to new arrivals. (One might also recall, from Chapter 3, the idea from Grotius that the right of *passage* across territory was a basic right that survived states' acquisition of territory itself.) However, an adequate response to the current crisis appears to require these states to agree to a burden-sharing scheme for allocating refugees, and a burden-sharing scheme is unlikely to work if refugees, once admitted, are free to move to whichever country they most prefer.

I noted in Chapter 9 that the refugee issue is likely to prove morally excruciating under certain circumstances, and the European crisis appears to confirm that prophecy. No humanitarian could fail to respond to the plight of drowning boat people or of land migrants who find themselves blocked by border fences and without basic means of subsistence. They are the hikers in the desert from Chapter 2. But equally, a coordinated response by states to the crisis must consider the longer-term consequences of what is done now—the signals given and the incentives created for those who might want to move in the future. And where states have developed (justified) policies for different categories of immigrants—refugees, economic migrants, temporary workers, and so forth—these policies should not be torn to shreds because of the current emergency. Citizens and government officials alike have to find a way of reconciling the humanitarian demand with the policy objective. How can they rescue those in need of rescue without turning their borders into a free-for-all?

So what should European states now do? Any adequate response will be financially costly, and there needs first to be a burden-sharing financial arrangement that redistributes resources to those states, such as Italy and Greece, that carry the heaviest responsibility for processing arriving migrants. Probably the best rationale for the European Union itself (beyond the securing of peace in Europe) is that it serves as an insurance mechanism for individual states that find themselves in unexpected difficulties, whether this is a result of global movements of capital or, as in this case, the large-scale movement of people. Second, steps have to be taken to reduce the migrant flows themselves to manageable proportions. This is partly a matter of working with local authorities in the sending states to clamp down on people-smuggling operations and to better police their territorial waters (most relevant in the case of states such as Turkey that are themselves safe havens for refugees), and partly a matter of improving living conditions and providing work opportunities around the camps already established near conflict zones. Finally, in the case of those who do arrive on European soil, receiving states need to agree among themselves on refugee quotas and also on temporary protection schemes for those who should later be encouraged to repatriate to help rebuild the societies (Iraq, Libya, Syria, and the rest) that are currently in a state of collapse. These schemes should be designed to allow the beneficiaries to work and train while they remain in the host societies—they should not be based on providing welfare.

Why should the receiving states do all of this, given how costly it is likely to be? Not because it will be popular with their own citizens. Many ordinary Europeans deserve moral credit for the willingness they have so far shown to extend help to migrants arriving by sea or traveling across the continent. But this generous initial response may not survive the experience of immigrants entering local communities in large numbers and competing for jobs and housing. (It will certainly not survive if it turns out that the migrant flows include a few radicalized Islamists bent on terrorism.) Nor should they do this out of historical guilt. As I have argued earlier, there may indeed be some refugees to whom redress is owed as a result of destructive interventions by Western powers in their home societies. But there is a danger here of a moral double bind, under which the states involved are blamed for the effects of interventions that go wrong (for instance, in Iraq) and at the same time blamed for failing to intervene when intervention seems to be required (for instance, in Syria). Given the difficulty of knowing in advance how any proposed intervention is likely to work out (with hindsight it is of course easy to predict!), the path of blame and guilt should be avoided wherever possible. So the answer has to be that these are comparatively rich states with the capacity to deal with the migration crisis, which by accident of geography makes them the obvious destination for people wanting to move out of failed or malfunctioning states. Once needy people arrive and present themselves, weak cosmopolitanism alone demands a positive response to their entreaties.

Notes

1. INTRODUCTION

1. See http://www.harrisinteractive.com/vault/HI_UK_News_Daily_Mail_Poll -Nov13.pdf.

2. See http://www.theguardian.com/world/2014/feb/09/swiss-referendum-immi gration-quotas. For the widespread preference among Europeans generally for greater restrictions on immigration, see E. Iversflaten, "Threatened by Diversity: Why Re-strictive Asylum and Immigration Policies Appeal to Western Europeans," *Journal of Elections, Public Opinion and Parties* 15 (2005): 21–45.

3. See http://www.gallup.com/poll/163457/americans-pro-immigration-past.aspx. These figures may reflect the contrast between "immigration" and "nonimmigration" societies; see note 38 below.

4. United Nations, Department of Economic and Social Affairs, Population Division, *International Migration Report 2013*, available at http://www.un.org/en /development/desa/population/publications/pdf/migration/migrationreport2013 /Full_Document_final.pdf#zoom=100. See also K. Khoser, *International Migration: A Very Short Introduction* (Oxford: Oxford University Press, 2007), chap. 1.

5. http://www.theguardian.com/news/datablog/2013/sep/26/qatar-migrants -how-changed-the-country.

6. P. Collier, *Exodus: Immigration and Multiculturalism in the 21st Century* (London: Allen Lane, 2013), chap. 2.

7. N. Esipova, J. Ray, and R. Srinivasan, *The World's Potential Migrants: Who They Are, Where They Want to Go, and Why It Matters* (Gallup, 2010–2011). Overall,

40% of those living in the poorest quartile of countries have expressed a wish to migrate; see Collier, *Exodus,* 167.

8. See D. Reimers, *Unwelcome Strangers: American Identity and the Turn against Immigration* (New York: Columbia University Press, 1998), 11–12.

9. See R. Winder, *Bloody Foreigners: The Story of Immigration to Britain* (London: Little, Brown, 2004), chap. 16.

10. Cited in Winder, *Bloody Foreigners,* 118.

11. Cf. the U.S. Supreme Court in 1892: "It is an accepted maxim of international law, that every sovereign nation has the power, as inherent in sovereignty, and essential to self-preservation, to forbid the entrance of foreigners within its dominions, or to admit them only in such cases and upon such conditions as it may see fit to prescribe"; cited in P. Schuck, *Citizens, Strangers, and In-Betweens: Essays on Immigration and Citizenship* (Boulder, CO: Westview Press, 1998), 24.

12. H. Sidgwick, *The Elements of Politics,* 2nd ed. (London: Macmillan, 1897), 248. Sidgwick does, however, go on to say that the state must refrain from *injuring* the aliens it has admitted, or allowing them to be injured by private individuals—in other words it has a duty of care toward them.

13. Sidgwick, *Elements,* 308.

14. Sidgwick thought, however, that the issue would look entirely different if one adopted a cosmopolitan moral perspective, which would mean allowing all human beings access to the natural advantages of any particular territory. This, he said, "is perhaps the ideal of the future." Yet he concluded that "it would not really be in the interest of humanity at large to impose upon civilised states generally, as an absolute international duty, the free admission of immigrants"; Sidgwick, *Elements,* 308–309.

15. To cite some British evidence, asylum seekers and recent immigrants were the two groups most likely to be picked out as getting "unfair priority over you when it comes to public services and state benefits" in a MORI poll, reported in B. Duffy, "Free Rider Phobia," *Prospect* (February 2004): 16–17. The more general theme emerges in an informal study of popular attitudes by the Labour member of Parliament (MP) John Denham. He found that his constituents were strongly wedded to a "fairness code" that is "concerned with what rights you have earned, not just what your needs are today. The assessment of someone's needs should take into account the effort and contribution he or she has made in the past and will make in the future. Public services should be for people who are entitled to them, need them, and use them responsibly"; see J. Denham, "The Fairness Code," *Prospect* (June 2004): 29. It is also possible, however, that perceptions that the welfare state is operating unfairly are driven in part by racial prejudice. On this topic, see R. Ford, "Prejudice and White Majority Welfare Attitudes in the UK," *Journal of Elections, Public Opinion and Parties* 16 (2006): 141–156. For evidence that Americans hold similar beliefs— that people who make no effort to contribute shouldn't receive welfare, with blacks

picked out as the prime undeserving group—see M. Gilens, *Why Americans Hate Welfare: Race, Media, and the Politics of Antipoverty Policy* (Chicago: University of Chicago Press, 1999), chap. 3.

16. For evidence of the negative impact of ethnic diversity on social trust, see, e.g., A. Alesina and E. La Ferrara, "Who Trusts Others?," *Journal of Public Economics* 85 (2002): 207–234; J. Delhey and K. Newton, "Predicting Cross-National Levels of Social Trust: Global Pattern or Nordic Exceptionalism?," *European Sociological Review* 21 (2005): 311–327; R. Putnam, *"E Pluribus Unum:* Diversity and Community in the Twenty-first Century," *Scandinavian Political Studies* 30 (2007): 137–174. There are, however, some dissenting voices, including M. Crepaz, *Trust beyond Borders: Immigration, the Welfare State, and Identity in Modern Societies* (Ann Arbor: University of Michigan Press, 2008), chap. 3; N. Letki, "Does Diversity Erode Social Cohesion? Social Capital and Race in British Neighbourhoods," *Political Studies* 56 (2008): 99–126.

17. For discussion of the relationship between ethnic diversity and support for the welfare state, see S. Soroka, R. Johnston, and K. Banting, "Ethnicity, Trust and the Welfare State," in *Cultural Diversity versus Economic Solidarity,* ed. P. Van Parijs (Brussels: De Boeck, 2004).

18. S. Soroka, K. Banting, and R. Johnston, "Immigration and Redistribution in a Global Era," in *Globalization and Egalitarian Redistribution,* ed. P. Bardhan, S. Bowles, and M. Wallerstein (Princeton, NJ: Princeton University Press / New York: Russell Sage Foundation, 2006), 278.

19. For analysis of the United States, see G. Borjas, *Heaven's Door: Immigration Policy and the American Economy* (Princeton, NJ: Princeton University Press, 1999), esp. chap. 5; for an opposing view, see D. Card, "Is the New Immigration Really So Bad?," *Economic Journal* 115 (2005): 300–323. For analysis of the United Kingdom, see S. Nickell and J. Saleheen, "The Impact of Immigration on Occupational Wages: Evidence from Britain," Federal Reserve Bank of Boston Working Papers, No. 08-6 (Boston, 2008); C. Dustmann, T. Frattini, and I. Preston, "The Effect of Immigration along the Distribution of Wages," *Review of Economic Studies* 80 (2013), 145–173.

20. See F. Docquier, C. Ozden, and G. Peri, "The Labour Market Effects of Immigration and Emigration in OECD Countries," *Economic Journal* 124 (2014): 1106–1145.

21. See, e.g., Collier, *Exodus,* 60–61.

22. See http://articles.latimes.com/2004/mar/14/news/adna-dwork14.

23. See http://www.theguardian.com/commentisfree/2014/feb/03/morecambe -bay-cockle-pickers-tragedy.

24. See Iversflaten, "Threatened by Diversity," for evidence about the role played by concerns over language, religion, and traditions in accounting for opposition to high levels of immigration.

25. I. Kant, *Perpetual Peace: A Philosophical Sketch,* in *Kant's Political Writings,* ed. H. Reiss (Cambridge: Cambridge University Press, 1971).

26. See S. Benhabib, *The Rights of Others: Aliens, Residents and Citizens* (Cambridge: Cambridge University Press, 2004), esp. chap. 1; I. Valdez, "Perpetual What? Injury, Sovereignty, and a Cosmopolitan View of Immigration," *Political Studies* 60 (2012): 95–114.

27. Kant, *Perpetual Peace,* 105–106.

28. In Chapter 3 I will examine whether this idea can be developed to justify a universal right to move across state borders.

29. J. Rawls, *A Theory of Justice* (Cambridge, MA: Harvard University Press, 1971), esp. sec. 2.

30. J. Rawls, "Kantian Constructivism in Moral Theory," in J. Rawls, *Collected Papers,* ed. S. Freeman (Cambridge, MA: Harvard University Press, 1999), 323.

31. J. Rawls, *The Law of Peoples* (Cambridge, MA: Harvard University Press, 1999), 9.

32. Rawls, *Theory of Justice,* 4.

33. J. Carens, *The Ethics of Immigration* (New York: Oxford University Press, 2013). Carens's version of cosmopolitanism is not extreme, inasmuch as it allows states to give some priority to the interests of their own citizens over those of foreigners. Nevertheless, Carens believes that basic liberal principles of free movement and equal opportunity must be applied on a global scale, which directly entails unimpeded migration across state borders. I discuss these arguments in Chapter 3.

34. I have discussed this problem of inconsistency in relation to Carens in D. Miller, "Das Carensproblem," *Political Theory* 43 (2015): 387–393.

35. I put "distributively just" in scare quotes because this is not how I understand global justice myself. I am gesturing toward a cosmopolitan view of immigration that asks how we would think about it if global justice, here understood in egalitarian terms, prevailed.

36. I am assuming here a view about the purpose of political philosophy that I have defended elsewhere; see D. Miller, "Political Philosophy for Earthlings," in *Political Theory: Methods and Approaches,* ed. D. Leopold and M. Stears (Oxford: Oxford University Press, 2008), repr., D. Miller, *Justice for Earthlings: Essays in Political Philosophy* (Cambridge: Cambridge University Press, 2013).

37. I take it from an old article by my doctoral supervisor, John Plamenatz; J. Plamenatz, "Strangers in Our Midst," *Race* 7 (1965): 1–16. These are the reflections of a sensitive liberal philosopher on an earlier moment at which the arrival of immigrants (in this case black and brown immigrants from the British Commonwealth) provoked heated reactions among the public. Little read now, it is still instructive.

38. A contrast is sometimes drawn at this point between the "New World" societies of North America and the Antipodes, which historically have understood themselves to be immigrant societies, and the "Old World" societies of Europe and elsewhere. It might then be asked whether it is possible to propose a way of thinking about

immigration that holds good in both these settings. My own view is that for some time now the societies of immigration have been changing in ways that bring them closer to the Old World, both in terms of public policy and of public attitudes. It remains true that the actual pattern of immigration varies considerably from country to country, which also means that the issues that are seen as most pressing are likely to be country specific. Although I have tried to avoid parochialism, readers are entitled to judge how far the arguments I make in this book are influenced by the national context in which it is written.

2. COSMOPOLITANISM, COMPATRIOT PARTIALITY, AND HUMAN RIGHTS

1. See D. Miller, *On Nationality* (Oxford: Clarendon Press, 1995), esp. chap. 3; D. Miller, *National Responsibility and Global Justice* (Oxford: Oxford University Press, 2007), esp. chap. 2.

2. See esp. M. Blake, "We Are All Cosmopolitans Now," in *Cosmopolitanism versus Non-Cosmopolitanism: Critiques, Defences, Reconceptualizations,* ed. G. Brock (Oxford: Oxford University Press, 2013). Among others who have noted the ambiguity of "cosmopolitanism" are C. Beitz, "Cosmopolitanism and Global Justice," *Journal of Ethics* 9 (2005): 11–27; S. Scheffler, "Conceptions of Cosmopolitanism," in *Boundaries and Allegiances* (Oxford: Oxford University Press, 2001), chap. 7.

3. For a much-cited defense of cosmopolitanism as a form of personal identity, see J. Waldron, "Minority Cultures and the Cosmopolitan Alternative," *University of Michigan Journal of Law Reform* 25 (1991–1992): 751–793, repr., *The Rights of Minority Cultures,* ed. W. Kymlicka (Oxford: Oxford University Press, 1995).

4. Thomas Pogge has given a more elaborate three-part definition that is widely cited: "First, *individualism:* the ultimate units of concern are *human beings,* or *persons*—rather than, say, family lines, tribes, ethnic, cultural, or religious communities, nations, or states. . . . Second, *universality:* the status of ultimate unit of concern attaches to every living human being *equally* . . . —not merely to some subset such as men, aristocrats, Aryans, whites, or Muslims. Third, *generality:* this special status has global force. Persons are ultimate units of concern *for everyone*—not only for their compatriots, fellow religionists, or such like"; T. Pogge, *World Poverty and Human Rights* (Cambridge: Polity Press, 2002), 169.

5. I use the example as a concrete way of explaining what weak cosmopolitanism demands of us, at a minimum. I don't intend to suggest that it captures everything that we might owe to people who are not our fellow citizens. Indeed there are many circumstances in which we will owe more than I describe, e.g., as a result of past transactions with the people in question. Later in this chapter, I will ask how our obligations to strangers change when their human rights are at stake.

6. For examples of this approach, see R. Goodin, "What Is So Special about Our Fellow Countrymen?" *Ethics* 98 (1987–1988): 663–686; P. Singer, "Outsiders:

Our Obligations to Those beyond Our Borders," in *The Ethics of Assistance,* ed. D. Chatterjee (Cambridge: Cambridge University Press, 2004); L. Ypi, "Statist Cosmopolitanism," *Journal of Political Philosophy* 16 (2008): 48–71.

7. Bernard Williams famously expressed this idea by saying that the person who chooses to rescue his spouse in preference to a stranger and justifies this choice by thinking that the world will go better in general if each person similarly prefers their own partner has had "one thought too many"; B. Williams, "Persons, Character, and Morality," in *Moral Luck: Philosophical Papers, 1973–1980* (Cambridge: Cambridge University Press, 1981), 18.

8. For discussions of associative obligations, see R. Dworkin, *Law's Empire* (London: Fontana, 1986), 195–215; S. Scheffler, "Families, Nations, and Strangers," in Scheffler, *Boundaries and Allegiances;* M. Moore, "Is Patriotism an Associative Duty?," *Journal of Ethics* 13 (2009): 383–399; S. Lazar, "The Justification of Associative Duties," *Journal of Moral Philosophy* 13 (2016): 28–55. The fullest treatment is J. Seglow, *Defending Associative Duties* (Abingdon, UK: Routledge, 2013).

9. This third strand in the relationship may not extend to all citizens, but even those who don't share in the national identity must recognize that for their compatriots this cultural and historical identification is an important (and morally relevant) form of commonality.

10. Some readers might think that this too-rosy picture of the modern democratic state violates my injunction in Chapter 1 to inject a strong dose of realism into our thinking about immigration. I concede that I am here identifying goods that actual states only realize partially, at most. But I don't believe that the obstacles to justice and self-determination that currently exist are of the kind that makes the quest to overcome them a hopeless one. The nearer we get to realizing these ideals, the greater the value of this form of association.

11. For doubts about whether nationality can serve as an independent ground of associative duties, see A. Mason, "Special Obligations to Compatriots," *Ethics* 107 (1997): 427–447; Moore, "Is Patriotism an Associative Duty?"; S. Lazar, "A Liberal Defence of (Some) Duties to Compatriots," *Journal of Applied Philosophy* 27 (2010): 246–257.

12. Here I am thinking about the simple case where all or at least most citizens share a single national identity. Things become more complicated when the state also houses national minorities because then there will be reasons of identity pushing in both directions—toward maintaining state unity and toward secession.

13. See D. Miller and S. Ali, "Testing the National Identity Argument," *European Political Science Review* 6 (2014): 237–259, in which we survey the evidence that has so far been collected.

14. Important contributions include M. Blake, "Distributive Justice, State Coercion, and Autonomy," *Philosophy and Public Affairs* 30 (2001): 257–296; T. Nagel, "The Problem of Global Justice," *Philosophy and Public Affairs* 33 (2005): 113–147;

A. Sangiovanni, "Global Justice, Reciprocity and the State." *Philosophy and Public Affairs* 35 (2007): 3–39; A. Abizadeh, "Cooperation, Pervasive Impact, and Coercion: On the Scope (Not the Site) of Distributive Justice," *Philosophy and Public Affairs* 35 (2007): 318–358. For a critical overview from a cosmopolitan perspective, see C. Barry and L. Valentini, "Egalitarian Challenges to Global Egalitarianism: A Critique," *Review of International Studies* 35 (2009): 485–512.

15. I have defended this approach in "Justice and Boundaries," *Politics, Philosophy and Economics* 8 (2009): 291–309, repr., D. Miller, *Justice for Earthlings: Essays in Political Philosophy* (Cambridge: Cambridge University Press, 2013). See also M. Risse, *On Global Justice* (Princeton, NJ: Princeton University Press, 2012), chaps. 1–3.

16. Questions about fairness between states do, however, arise when we are considering the issue of how to allocate the responsibility for taking in refugees. I discuss these questions in Chapter 5.

17. These documents are conveniently reprinted as appendices in J. Nickel, *Making Sense of Human Rights* (Malden, MA: Blackwell, 2007).

18. I present here my preferred way of understanding human rights, that grounds them on basic needs shared by all human beings; for a fuller statement, see D. Miller, "Grounding Human Rights," *Critical Review of International Social and Political Philosophy* 15 (2012): 407–427. Other widely cited accounts of human rights appeal instead to human interests or to human agency. On human interests, see, e.g., Nickel, *Making Sense of Human Rights,* chap. 4; J. Tasioulas, "On the Foundations of Human Rights," in *Philosophical Foundations of Human Rights,* ed. R. Cruft, M. Liao, and M. Renzo (Oxford: Oxford University Press, 2015). On human agency, see J. Griffin, *On Human Rights* (Oxford: Oxford University Press, 2008), esp. chap. 2. These philosophically contrasting approaches tend to generate overlapping, but not identical, lists of rights. I have discussed the differences between my view and Griffin's in D. Miller, "Personhood versus Human Needs as Grounds for Human Rights," in *Griffin on Human Rights,* ed. R. Crisp (Oxford: Oxford University Press, 2014).

19. I shall not here enter the debate among human rights theorists on whether human rights have to be attributable to human beings throughout the course of history, or whether their scope should be limited to the denizens of modern societies. For contrasting views, see Griffin, *On Human Rights,* esp. chaps. 2, 7; J. Tasioulas, "The Moral Reality of Human Rights," in *Freedom from Poverty as a Human Right,* ed. T. Pogge (Oxford: Oxford University Press, 2007); C. Beitz, *The Idea of Human Rights* (Oxford: Oxford University Press, 2009), chaps. 2–3.

20. But do they arise even then? Someone might doubt this, holding that obligations always arise in the context of specific social practices and not outside them. Here it is difficult to do more than appeal to our moral intuitions. Return to the example of the dehydrated hiker introduced previously. There is some danger that unless I share my water with her she will die. It is surely not enough to say that I have

a reason to give her a drink; I *must* give her some of my water. If I refuse to do so, she, or someone else passing by, can *make* me do it. Admittedly, this is an extreme case. But what it shows is that there is nothing ridiculous about the idea of obligations that arise simply from the urgency of a person's claim, even if nothing connects me to the person apart from my ability to respond to it.

21. See, e.g., O. O'Neill, *Towards Justice and Virtue* (Cambridge: Cambridge University Press, 1996), chap. 5. O'Neill's claim is that positive rights such as rights to welfare can only exist when they have been institutionalized, for instance by a state.

22. Here I summarize a position set out more fully in D. Miller, "Distributing Responsibilities," *Journal of Political Philosophy* 9 (2001): 453–471, and in revised form in *National Responsibility and Global Justice,* chap. 4.

23. I have defended a position of this second type in "Taking Up the Slack? Responsibility and Justice in Situations of Partial Compliance," in *Responsibility and Distributive Justice,* ed. C. Knight and Z. Stemplowska (Oxford: Oxford University Press, 2010), repr., Miller, *Justice for Earthlings.*

24. Cicero, *On Duties,* ed. M. Griffin and E. Atkins (Cambridge: Cambridge University Press, 1991), 22.

3. OPEN BORDERS

1. The relationship between Grotius's idea of common ownership and Kant's is not straightforward. For an analysis, see K. Flikschuh, *Kant and Modern Political Philosophy* (Cambridge: Cambridge University Press, 2000), chap. 5.

2. H. Grotius, *The Rights of War and Peace,* ed. R. Tuck (Indianapolis: Liberty Fund, 2005), bk. 2, chap. 2, sec. 2. For relevant discussion of Grotius, see M. Risse, *On Global Justice* (Princeton, NJ: Princeton University Press, 2012), chap. 5; J. Salter, "Hugo Grotius: Property and Consent," *Political Theory* 29 (2001), 537–555; S. Buckle, *Natural Law and the Theory of Property: Grotius to Hume* (Oxford: Clarendon Press, 1991), chap. 1.

3. Grotius, *Rights of War and Peace,* 2, 434–437.

4. Grotius, *Rights of War and Peace,* 2, 438–449.

5. H. Sidgwick, *The Elements of Politics,* 2nd ed. (London: Macmillan, 1897), 255; M. Walzer, *Spheres of Justice* (Oxford: Martin Robertson, 1983), 46–47.

6. Grotius, *Rights of War and Peace,* 2, 432–433.

7. M. Risse, *On Global Justice* (Princeton, NJ: Princeton University Press, 2012), chap. 6.

8. I. Kant, *The Metaphysics of Morals,* ed. M. Gregor (Cambridge: Cambridge University Press, 1996), 121.

9. There are further objections to joint ownership that I shall not consider here. As Risse argues, "what is really troublesome is that if each person must *be asked* about any use of the collective property, she must also *ask* about any such use. So others can

veto uses that satisfy basic needs"; Risse, *On Global Justice,* 121. This echoes Locke's charge that if my taking of "Acorns or Apples" from nature requires the consent of all others, "Man had starved, notwithstanding the Plenty God had given him"; J. Locke, *Two Treatises of Government,* ed. P. Laslett (Cambridge: Cambridge University Press, 1988), bk. 2, sec. 28, p. 288.

10. The main defender of this position in the recent past has been Hillel Steiner. See H. Steiner, "Liberty and Equality," *Political Studies* 29 (1981): 555–569; H. Steiner, "Slavery, Socialism, and Private Property," in *Nomos XXII: Property,* ed. J. R. Pennock and J. W. Chapman (New York: New York University Press, 1980); H. Steiner, "Capitalism, Justice and Equal Starts," *Social Philosophy and Policy* 5 (1987), 49–71; H. Steiner, *An Essay on Rights* (Oxford: Blackwell, 1994), chaps. 7–8; H. Steiner, "Territorial Justice and Global Redistribution," in *The Political Philosophy of Cosmopolitanism,* ed. G. Brock and H. Brighouse (Cambridge: Cambridge University Press, 2005).

11. See, e.g., Steiner, "Territorial Justice and Global Redistribution," 35–36.

12. I have discussed this question at greater length in *National Responsibility and Global Justice* (Oxford: Oxford University Press, 2007), chap. 3, sec. 2, and with specific reference to Steiner in "Property and Territory: Locke, Kant, and Steiner," *Journal of Political Philosophy* 19 (2011): 90–109.

13. See, e.g., J. Carens, *The Ethics of Immigration* (New York: Oxford University Press, 2013), 227–228, 233–236.

14. See B. Boxhill, "Global Equality of Opportunity and National Integrity," *Social Philosophy and Policy* 5 (1987): 143–168.

15. For this reply, see S. Caney, "Cosmopolitan Justice and Equalizing Opportunities," *Metaphilosophy* 32 (2001): 113–134. Sen has developed the capabilities approach in many works, including A. Sen, *Commodities and Capabilities* (Amsterdam: North-Holland, 1985); A. Sen, *Inequality Reexamined* (Oxford: Clarendon Press, 1992); A. Sen, "Capability and Well-Being," in *The Quality of Life,* ed. M. Nussbaum and A. Sen (Oxford: Clarendon Press, 1993); A. Sen, *Development as Freedom* (Oxford: Oxford University Press, 1999).

16. See, e.g., Sen, *Inequality Reexamined,* chap. 3.

17. The problem has been widely recognized in the literature on the capabilities approach, but no solution has appeared from within. For a critical appraisal of the approach in which this appears as one among several problems, see T. Pogge, "A Critique of the Capability Approach," in *Measuring Justice: Primary Goods and Capabilities,* ed. H. Brighouse and I. Robeyns (Cambridge: Cambridge University Press, 2010). One of its main defenders, Martha Nussbaum, has described cases in which basic capabilities cannot all be realized simultaneously as involving "tragic choices"; see M. Nussbaum, *Creating Capabilities: The Human Development Approach* (Cambridge, MA: Harvard University Press, 2011), chap. 2. For a good overview of the current state of play, see I. Robeyns, "The Capability Approach (and Social Justice),"

in *The Routledge Companion to Social and Political Philosophy,* ed. G. Gaus and F. D'Agostino (New York: Routledge, 2013).

18. Defenders of a human right to immigrate include Carens, *Ethics of Immigration,* chap. 11; K. Oberman, "Immigration as a Human Right," in *Migration in Political Theory: The Ethics of Movement and Membership,* ed. S. Fine and L. Ypi (Oxford: Oxford University Press, 2016). Michael Dummett draws back from claiming that there is a strong right to immigrate on the grounds that a genuine obligation-imposing right must be unconditional (whereas he acknowledges that there might be cases in which states could justifiably limit immigration), but he defends such a right in a "weaker, conditional sense"; see M. Dummett, *On Immigration and Refugees* (London: Routledge, 2001), chap. 3.

19. Joseph Carens has embraced this way of describing his rights-based argument for open borders in Carens, *Ethics of Immigration,* chap. 11, esp. 237–245. The cantilever strategy does of course rely on the assumption that the right being cantilevered out from is justified, but its advantage is that we need not agree on why it is justified before embarking on the cantilever argument.

20. In what follows I attempt to be ecumenical, since defenders of a human right to immigrate may interpret the grounds for that right in different ways if they choose to employ the direct strategy.

21. See Oberman, "Immigration as a Human Right."

22. A possible response here is that the generic interest in question is the interest in freedom itself. But freedom unqualified—the absence of all constraints on the actions a person might take—could not plausibly serve as a ground of human rights, not least because one person's freedom in this unrestricted sense will unavoidably collide with the equal freedom of everyone else.

23. For arguments that the first right implies the second, see P. Cole, *Philosophies of Exclusion: Liberal Political Theory and Immigration* (Edinburgh: Edinburgh University Press, 2000), chap. 3; A. Dummett, "The Transnational Migration of People Seen from within a Natural Law Perspective," in *Free Movement: Ethical Issues in the Transnational Migration of People and of Money,* ed. B. Barry and R. Goodin (Hemel Hempstead, UK: Harvester Wheatsheaf, 1992).

24. P. Collier, *Exodus: Immigration and Multiculturalism in the 21st Century* (London: Allen Lane, 2013), 199–200.

25. Carens, *Ethics of Immigration,* 239.

26. This is certainly the case if we are thinking about the developed democracies. It may well be less true of rapidly developing societies such as Brazil and China in which gross inequalities between the countryside and the city create incentives for mass migration to the latter.

27. In early 2013, and in the face of alarm about the number of Romanians and Bulgarians who might migrate to the United Kingdom once EU freedom of movement rules were extended at the beginning of 2014, the British government was

widely reported to be considering an advertising campaign highlighting the negative aspects of life in the UK: rainy weather, disorder on the streets, lack of jobs, and so forth. Wiser counsels prevailed, however, and the government eventually decided simply to tighten up the eligibility requirements for social security and other benefits for all EU migrants.

28. I emphasize here the negative role played by the right of free movement against potential threats coming from the state, but one might also highlight its positive role in creating a well-functioning democracy. For this argument, see A. Hosein, "Immigration and Freedom of Movement," *Ethics and Global Politics* 6 (2013): 25–37.

29. See, e.g., the account of the Venetian ghettos in R. Sennett, *Flesh and Stone: The Body and the City in Western Civilization* (London: Penguin, 2002), chap. 7.

30. On the special settlements, see L. Viola, *The Unknown Gulag: The Lost World of Stalin's Special Settlements* (New York: Oxford University Press, 2007).

31. Someone might ask how the examples I have cited, which all involve the oppression of already vulnerable groups, can explain why the right to free movement extends, say, to affluent Californians wanting to move to New York. But human rights are general claims directed (in the first place) to a state on behalf of all its citizens. That some might not need the protection provided by particular rights—a very rich person may be able to do without the right to vote because he can adequately protect his interests in other ways—does not mean that we should retrench on their universality. As essential safeguards, they must be available to everyone, whether or not they are needed at this moment.

4. CLOSED BORDERS

1. For a vivid description of how borders are defended in practice, see J. Harding, *Border Vigils: Keeping Migrants Out of the Rich World* (London: Verso, 2012).

2. I follow here the analysis in F. H. Hinsley, *Sovereignty,* 2nd ed. (Cambridge: Cambridge University Press, 1986), chap. 1; A. James, "The Practice of Sovereign Statehood in Contemporary International Society," *Political Studies* 47 (1999): 457–473.

3. I say a little more about these advantages in *National Responsibility and Global Justice* (Oxford: Oxford University Press, 2007), chap. 8.

4. Here I follow Henry Sidgwick: "The main justification for the appropriation of territory to governments is that the prevention of mutual mischief among the human beings using it cannot otherwise be adequately secured"; H. Sidgwick, *The Elements of Politics,* 2nd ed. (London: Macmillan, 2007), 252. For a fuller exploration of the human rights requirement for political legitimacy, see A. Buchanan, *Justice, Legitimacy, and Self-Determination* (Oxford: Oxford University Press, 2004), pt. 2. See also A. Altman and C. Wellman, *A Liberal Theory of International Justice* (Oxford: Oxford University Press, 2009), chap. 1.

5. The only source of challenge that I can imagine would be a claim about the common ownership of the earth, but in the previous chapter I considered and rejected versions of that idea (joint ownership and equal ownership) that might be used to mount a challenge.

6. Important contributions to this debate include A. Kolers, *Land, Conflict and Justice* (Cambridge: Cambridge University Press, 2009); T. Meisels, *Territorial Rights*, 2nd ed. (Dordrecht: Springer, 2009); M. Moore, *A Political Theory of Territory* (Oxford: Oxford University Press, 2015); C. Nine, *Global Justice and Territory* (Oxford: Oxford University Press, 2012); A. J. Simmons, "On the Territorial Rights of States," *Philosophical Issues* 11 (2001): 300–326; H. Steiner, "Territorial Justice and Global Redistribution," in *The Political Philosophy of Cosmopolitanism*, ed. G. Brock and H. Brighouse (Cambridge: Cambridge University Press, 2005); A. Stilz, "Why Do States Have Territorial Rights?," *International Theory* 1 (2009): 185–213. For an overview of the debate, see D. Miller and M. Moore, "Territorial Rights," in *Global Political Theory*, ed. D. Held and P. Maffetone (Cambridge: Polity Press, forthcoming).

7. Most fully in D. Miller, "Territorial Rights: Concept and Justification," *Political Studies* 60 (2012): 252–268.

8. As I explained in Chapter 2, in this context we can think of human rights as a subdomain of citizenship rights.

9. Michael Blake has appealed to this idea to develop an argument for the state's right to exclude immigrants that hinges on the right to refuse to take on unwanted obligations, namely those that might be incurred in providing for the immigrants' basic rights. See M. Blake, "Immigration, Jurisdiction, and Exclusion," *Philosophy and Public Affairs* 41 (2013): 103–130.

10. A somewhat different argument for the right to close borders that also appeals to self-determination has been developed by Kit Wellman. Wellman's strategy is to argue that self-determination entails enjoying the right to freedom of association, including the freedom *not* to associate with unwanted persons. In explaining why the freedom not to associate should matter at state level as well as within smaller, more intimate communities, however, he appeals to some of the same considerations that I give here—for example, the unwelcome cultural changes that incomers might introduce. So our arguments share some common ground, despite Wellman's different starting point. See C. Wellman, "Immigration and Freedom of Association," *Ethics* 119 (2008–2009): 109–141; C. Wellman and P. Cole, *Debating the Ethics of Immigration: Is There a Right to Exclude?* (New York: Oxford University Press, 2011), chap. 1. For challenges to Wellman, see S. Fine, "Freedom of Association Is Not the Answer," *Ethics* 120 (2009–2010): 338–356; M. Blake, "Immigration, Association, and Anti-Discrimination," *Ethics* 122 (2011–2012): 748–762; S. Fine and A. Sangiovanni, "Immigration," in *The Routledge Handbook of Global Ethics*, ed. D. Moellendorf and H. Widdows (Abingdon: Routledge, 2014). My own reasons for

rejecting Wellman's approach can be found in *National Responsibility and Global Justice,* 210–211.

11. But, it may be said, immigrants will generate sufficient taxable income to pay for the public services they require. This may indeed happen—or it may not. Recall here that we are not considering a carefully crafted immigration policy that selects a certain number of immigrants on the basis of their future employment prospects, but the possible consequences of an open borders policy implemented by a modern liberal state.

12. This point is pressed in S. Scheffler, "Immigration and the Significance of Culture," *Philosophy and Public Affairs* 35 (2007): 93–125, repr., S. Scheffler, *Equality and Tradition* (New York: Oxford University Press, 2010). Scheffler refers to our descendants as "immigrants from the future."

13. For an account of cultural transmission that highlights the role played by "formative institutions and practices," see A. Patten, *Equal Recognition: The Moral Foundations of Minority Rights* (Princeton, NJ: Princeton University Press, 2014), chap. 2.

14. For discussion and evidence about the way the presence or absence of generalized trust affects the functioning of democracy, see R. Putnam, *Making Democracy Work: Civic Traditions in Modern Italy* (Princeton, NJ: Princeton University Press, 1993); T. Tyler, "Trust and Democratic Governance," in *Trust and Governance,* ed. M. Levi and V. Braithwaite (New York: Russell Sage Foundation, 1998); M. Warren, "Democratic Theory and Trust," in *Democracy and Trust,* ed. M. Warren (Cambridge: Cambridge University Press, 1999); P. Lenard, *Trust, Democracy, and Multicultural Challenges* (University Park: Pennsylvania State University Press, 2012), esp. chap. 2.

15. For evidence about the effects of ethnic diversity on public goods provision, see A. Alesina, R. Baqir, and W. Easterly, "Public Goods and Ethnic Divisions," *Quarterly Journal of Economics* 114 (1999): 1243–1284.

16. See the sources cited in Chap. 1, n. 16.

17. See M. Marschall and D. Stolle, "Race in the City: Neighbourhood Context and the Development of Generalised Trust," *Political Behavior* 26 (2004): 125–153. The now-classic study of the effects of declining levels of civic engagement (in the United States) on social trust is R. Putnam, *Bowling Alone: The Collapse and Revival of American Community* (New York: Simon and Schuster, 2000).

18. For a much more extended argument about the relationship between immigration control and population size, see P. Cafaro, *How Many Is Too Many? The Progressive Argument for Reducing Immigration into the United States* (Chicago and London: University of Chicago Press, 2015).

19. This challenge has been mounted not only by open-borders advocates but by some of those who regard immigration controls as justified, including Michael Blake and Ryan Pevnick; M. Blake, "Immigration," in *A Companion to Applied Ethics,*

ed. R. Frey and C. Wellman (Oxford: Blackwell, 2003), 232–234; R. Pevnick, *Immigration and the Constraints of Justice* (Cambridge: Cambridge University Press, 2011), chap. 6. Both authors also contend that invoking culture as a ground for restrictions risks demeaning current citizens who do not form part of the majority culture. See also the discussion in J. Carens, *The Ethics of Immigration* (New York: Oxford University Press, 2013), chap. 12.

20. For different versions of this challenge, see S. Fine, "The Ethics of Immigration: Self-Determination and the Right to Exclude," *Philosophy Compass* 8 (2013), 262–264; Fine and Sangiovanni, "Immigration," 199; J. Hidalgo, "Freedom, Immigration, and Adequate Options," *Critical Review of International Social and Political Philosophy* 17 (2014): 212–234.

21. This challenge has been made especially by Arash Abizadeh in A. Abizadeh, "Democratic Theory and Border Coercion: No Right to Unilaterally Control Your Own Borders," *Political Theory* 36 (2008): 37–65.

22. So long, that is, as neither side wishes to impose its convictions on the other.

23. The phrase "parallel societies" was popularized by Thomas Meyer in T. Meyer, "Parallelgesellschaft und Demokratie," in *Die Bürgergesellschaft: Perspektiven für Bürgerbeteiligung und Bürgerkommunikation,* ed. T. Meyer and R. Weil (Bonn: Dietz, 2002). I do not take a stand here on how strong the tendency for immigrants to create parallel societies really is. For a helpful overview of immigrant residential segregation in North America and western Europe (which reveals considerable variation between communities), see R. Alba and N. Foner, *Strangers No More: Immigration and the Challenges of Integration in North America and Western Europe* (Princeton, NJ: Princeton University Press, 2015), chap. 4.

24. J. S. Mill, *Utilitarianism,* in *Utilitarianism: On Liberty; Representative Government,* ed. H. B. Acton (London: Dent, 1972), 32.

25. The question of competing interests is pressed by Fine, "Ethics of Immigration"; Fine and Sangiovanni, "Immigration."

26. This point is overlooked in the otherwise perceptive discussion of the issue in Hidalgo, "Freedom, Immigration, and Adequate Options." Hidalgo concedes that states have a *right* to exclude immigrants, but argues that the interests they typically have in being admitted show that it is morally wrong to exclude them. This assumes that these interests must weigh heavily *for the citizens of the receiving state.* (Hidalgo also assumes that the exclusion of immigrants is a coercive act, which is discussed later in this chapter.)

27. I focus on Abizadeh here, but the view that immigration controls are coercive has been accepted by a number of authors, including some who wish to defend border restrictions. See, e.g., M. Blake, "Distributive Justice, State Coercion and Autonomy," *Philosophy and Public Affairs* 30 (2001): 257–296; Blake, "Immigration, Jurisdiction, and Exclusion"; T. Nagel, "The Problem of Global Justice," *Philosophy and Public Affairs* 33 (2005): 113–146, esp. 129–130.

28. Abizadeh, "Democratic Theory and Border Coercion," 48.

29. It is sometimes argued that in such cases the inebriated individual has tacitly given his consent to being coerced in the circumstances described, but I do not see why it is necessary to assume this. It is surely sufficient that I can avert a potential catastrophe by driving my drunken friend home against his will.

30. I grant this point for purposes of argument, even though I am doubtful that it is true. Earlier in the chapter, I sketched a view of legitimate state jurisdiction that did not require democracy as one of its components, but instead the weaker requirement that the state should represent the people over whom it is exercising its jurisdiction.

31. In what follows I draw on my much more detailed discussion in D. Miller, "Why Immigration Controls Are Not Coercive: A Reply to Arash Abizadeh," *Political Theory* 38 (2010): 111–120. Abizadeh's response can be found in A. Abizadeh, "Democratic Legitimacy and State Coercion: A Reply to David Miller," *Political Theory* 38 (2010): 121–130.

32. Coercion is a difficult concept to pin down precisely, so this specification is intended only as a rough characterization. For more thoroughgoing attempts to analyze it, see R. Nozick, "Coercion," in *Philosophy, Politics and Society,* ed. P. Laslett, W. G. Runciman, and Q. Skinner, 4th ser. (Oxford, UK: Blackwell, 1972); M. Bayles, "A Concept of Coercion," in *Nomos XIV: Coercion,* ed. J. R. Pennock and J. W. Chapman (Chicago: Aldine Atherton, 1972); A. Wertheimer, *Coercion* (Princeton, NJ: Princeton University Press, 1987), pt. 2.

33. What if it turns out that there is no other country that will allow him to enter? Refusing entry is still not a case of coercion, because the state that refuses does not intend that the person in question should be confined to his home country. Still, it may be said, to bar entry in these circumstances is *as bad as* coercion because the practical result will be the same in either case. This shows that prevention too requires justification, especially in cases where preventing somebody will have dire consequences. As we will see in Chapter 5, there may be an obligation to admit immigrants whose human rights are under threat in their current state of residence. But this is not a reason to conflate coercion and prevention or to suppose that exclusion always requires the democratic consent of the excluded.

34. See Abizadeh, "Democratic Theory and Border Coercion," 54–56.

5. REFUGEES

1. I shall shortly examine in much greater detail what qualifies somebody to be counted as a refugee.

2. Thus "economic" here has to be understood in a broad sense to include people moving for personal reasons that are not economic in the narrower sense, such as finding a more lucrative job. It might be better to use "voluntary migrants" as an umbrella term for this second group, but "economic" has become accepted usage.

3. E.g., the Ugandan Asians who held British passports but whose right to immigrate was abruptly removed by the Immigration Act of 1971. When Idi Amin came to power and threatened to expel them at short notice, the British government recognized its obligation and allowed them to enter. The episode is described in R. Winder, *Bloody Foreigners: The Story of Immigration to Britain* (London: Little Brown, 2004), chap. 22.

4. Consider the case of the Nepalese Gurkhas who, after serving in the British army, have sought the right to reside in Britain after retiring. This right was granted to them by a High Court decision in 2008. According to the actress Joanna Lumley who spearheaded their campaign, "The whole campaign has been based on the belief that those who have fought and been prepared to die for our country should have the right to live in our country"; http://www.gurkhajustice.org.uk.

5. I am also correcting my own rather casual treatment of the definitional issue in *National Responsibility and Global Justice* (Oxford: Oxford University Press, 2007), chap. 8.

6. "The principle of *non-refoulement* prescribes, broadly, that no refugee should be returned to any country where he or she is likely to face persecution, other ill-treatment, or torture"; G. Goodwin-Gill and J. McAdam, *The Refugee in International Law,* 3rd ed. (Oxford: Oxford University Press, 2007), 201. The interpretation of this principle in international law is a complex matter. See J. Hathaway, *The Rights of Refugees under International Law* (Cambridge: Cambridge University Press, 2005), 307–370.

7. I have learned here from the discussion in M. Lister, "Who Are Refugees?," *Law and Philosophy* 32 (2013): 645–671.

8. Cited in Hathaway, *Rights of Refugees,* 96–97. A further clause extends refugee status to people in a similar situation who have no nationality.

9. M. Dummett, *On Immigration and Refugees* (London: Routledge, 2001), 37.

10. I shall not discuss the condition that the refugee must already be "outside the country of his nationality." It does not seem important to me whether a person is currently trying to escape her country, has reached the border of another country, or has already crossed the border. What matters is the kind of threat she faces by remaining or being sent back. As Souter puts it, "If asylum fundamentally consists in surrogate protection, then it is the lack of protection within refugees' state of origin, rather than the fact of their flight across a border per se, that grounds their moral entitlement to asylum"; J. Souter, "Towards a Theory of Asylum as Reparation for Past Injustice," *Political Studies* 62 (2014): 328.

11. See M. Foster, *International Refugee Law and Socio-Economic Rights* (Cambridge: Cambridge University Press, 2007), for a full treatment of this topic.

12. See Goodwin-Gill and McAdam, *Refugee in International Law,* 98–100.

13. A strong argument in favor of maintaining the link to persecution is mounted by Matthew Price in M. Price, *Rethinking Asylum: History, Purpose and Limits* (Cam-

bridge: Cambridge University Press, 2009). Price draws a distinction between asylum and a broader refugee status and argues that the granting of asylum serves an expressive as well as a protective purpose: it signals condemnation of the behavior of the persecuting state.

14. A. Shacknove, "Who Is a Refugee?," *Ethics* 95 (1984–1985), 277.

15. J. Carens, *The Ethics of Immigration* (New York: Oxford University Press, 2013), 201.

16. This estimate is provided by the Office of the United Nations High Commissioner for Refugees (UNHCR) for 2015, though in the light of my earlier discussion, one should also include the 38.5 million "internally displaced persons" who have fled war or persecution but have not crossed an international frontier, bringing the overall total close to 60 million. See http://www.unhcr.org/558193896.html.

17. E.g., the people of Montserrat, two-thirds of whom were forced to leave their island following a volcanic eruption in 1995 that devastated the southern part of the island.

18. Price, *Rethinking Asylum*, 248.

19. For a thoughtful discussion of the conditions under which the repatriation of refugees, either voluntary or mandatory, can be justified, see M. Bradley, *Refugee Repatriation: Justice, Responsibility and Redress* (Cambridge: Cambridge University Press, 2013), chaps. 2–3. Bradley underlines the need to provide redress for the material and psychological costs of displacement as one essential condition.

20. The United States offers temporary protected status only to nationals from a small group of designated countries.

21. The argument for not counting "climate change refugees" as refugees except in the special case when their human rights are being threatened by discriminatory behavior on the part of their home state is well set out in J. McAdam, *Climate Change, Forced Migration, and International Law* (Oxford: Oxford University Press, 2012), chap. 2. McAdam also draws attention to the forceful rejection of the refugee label by those whose territory is vulnerable to the effects of climate change, e.g., the people of the island states of Kiribati and Tuvalu. Matthew Lister, in contrast, argues that the term can properly be applied to "the subset of those displaced by climate change or other environmental disruptions of expected indefinite duration, where international movement is necessitated, and where the threat is not just to a favored or traditional way of life, but to the possibility of a decent life at all"; M. Lister, "Climate Change Refugees," *Critical Review of International Social and Political Philosophy* 17 (2014): 621.

22. See L. Ferracioli, "The Appeal and Danger of a New Refugee Convention," *Social Theory and Practice* 40 (2014): 123–144. Carens, although recognizing the concern, ends up favoring a wide definition according to which anyone who flees their country in response to a threat to their human rights counts as a refugee, even if it would be possible to protect them in situ; see Carens, *Ethics of Immigration*, 200–202.

23. For Matthew Gibney, e.g., refugees are "people in need of a new state of residence, either temporarily or permanently, because if forced to return home or remain where they are they would—as a result of either the brutality or inadequacy of their state—be persecuted *or* seriously jeopardize their physical security or vital subsistence needs"; M. Gibney, *The Ethics and Politics of Asylum: Liberal Democracy and the Response to Refugees* (Cambridge: Cambridge University Press, 2004), 7.

24. See D. Miller, "Distributing Responsibilities," *Journal of Political Philosophy* 9 (2001): 453–471; Miller, *National Responsibility and Global Justice,* chap. 4.

25. Cf. Gibney, *Ethics and Politics of Asylum,* 55.

26. E.g., see, respectively, P. and R. Singer, "The Ethics of Refugee Policy," in *Open Borders? Closed Societies?: The Ethical and Political Issues,* ed. M. Gibney (New York: Greenwood Press, 1988); T. Pogge, "Migration and Poverty," in *Citizenship and Exclusion,* ed. V. Bader (Basingstoke, UK: Macmillan, 1997).

27. The ethical position I am adopting here may be contested. As a thought experiment to test it, suppose that I am confronted with a situation in which I must choose between rescuing A, who I have promised to help should the need ever arise, and five others together, who may be rescued by other people, though this is uncertain. I believe that my first priority should be to rescue A, despite the greater number on the other side (the case becomes more difficult if I am the only possible rescuer).

28. For a careful analysis of the economic and social costs of admitting refugees, see S. Martin, A. Schoenholtz, and D. Fisher, "The Impact of Asylum on Receiving Countries," in *Poverty, International Migration and Asylum,* ed. G. Borjas and J. Crisp (Basingstoke, UK: Palgrave Macmillan, 2005). The authors note that the overall net cost depends on government policies toward asylum seekers that vary considerably between countries.

29. For a description of these methods, see M. Gibney, "'A Thousand Little Guantanamos': Western States and Measures to Prevent the Arrival of Refugees," in *Displacement, Asylum, Migration: The Oxford Amnesty Lectures 2004,* ed. K. Tunstall (Oxford: Oxford University Press, 2006).

30. For such a recommendation, see J. Hathaway and R. Neve, "Making Internal Refugee Law Relevant Again: A Proposal for Collectivised and Solution-Oriented Protection," *Harvard Human Rights Journal* 10 (1997): 115–211. For reasons why regional schemes for responsibility sharing are more plausible than a global scheme, see A. Hans and A. Suhrke, "Responsibility Sharing," in *Reconceiving International Refugee Law,* ed. J. Hathaway (The Hague: Martinus Nijhoff, 1997).

31. For a review of these and other proposed criteria, see T. Kritzman-Amir, "Not in My Backyard: On the Morality of Responsibility Sharing in Refugee Law," *Brooklyn Journal of International Law* 34 (2009): 355–393, pt. 3.

32. For an illuminating discussion of the special conditions under which successful burden-sharing schemes have emerged, together with reasons why these are unlikely to be present elsewhere, see A. Suhrke, "Burden-sharing during Refugee

Emergencies: The Logic of Collective versus National Action," *Journal of Refugee Studies* 11 (1998): 396–415.

33. For a proposal of this kind, see P. Schuck, "Refugee Burden-Sharing: A Modest Proposal," *Yale Journal of International Law* 22 (1997): 243–297.

34. Schuck, "Refugee Burden-Sharing," argues in favor of using "national wealth" as the sole criterion for setting quotas.

35. For the general charge, see, e.g., D. Anker, J. Fitzpatrick, and A. Shacknove, "Crisis and Cure: A Reply to Hathaway/Neve and Schuck," *Harvard Human Rights Journal* 11 (1998): 295–310.

36. M. Sandel, *What Money Can't Buy: The Moral Limits of Markets* (London: Allen Lane, 2012), 64.

37. M. Gibney, "Forced Migration, Engineered Regionalism and Justice between States," in *New Regionalism and Asylum-Seekers: Challenges Ahead,* ed. S. Kneebone and F. Rawlings-Sanaei (Oxford: Berghahn, 2007). For a different response to Gibney's argument, see J. Kuosmanen, "What (If Anything) Is Wrong with Trading Refugee Quotas?," *Res Publica* 19 (2013): 103–119.

38. Souter, in "Asylum as Reparation for Past Injustice," provides a detailed analysis of the conditions under which asylum claims of this kind are valid. I consider the more general case of immigrants who have reparative claims to advance in Chapter 7.

39. Souter, "Asylum as Reparation for Past Injustice," 335–336.

40. Carens, *Ethics of Immigration,* 214.

41. This description applies except in cases where it is outside intervention that has brought about the refugee crisis, as noted earlier. In such cases the responsible state would lie under a stricter obligation to admit the refugees it has helped to create.

42. For further policy suggestions on these lines, see Gibney, '"A Thousand Little Guantanamos,'" 162–167.

43. Here I assume that where there is a burden of this kind to be shared between a number of parties, justice only requires each party to discharge their own portion. Anything that goes beyond this is a matter of benevolence or humanity, and performance cannot be demanded. For my defense, see D. Miller, "Taking up the Slack? Responsibility and Justice in Situations of Partial Compliance," in *Responsibility and Distributive Justice,* ed. C. Knight and Z. Stemplowska (Oxford: Oxford University Press, 2011), repr., D. Miller, *Justice for Earthlings: Essays in Political Philosophy* (Cambridge: Cambridge University Press, 2013). For the contrary view, see A. Karnein, "Putting Fairness in Its Place: Why There Is a Duty to Take Up the Slack," *Journal of Philosophy* 111 (2014): 593–607.

44. I have reflected more fully on this "protection gap" in D. Miller, "The Responsibility to Protect Human Rights," in *Legitimacy, Justice and Public International Law,* ed. L. Meyer (Cambridge: Cambridge University Press, 2009).

6. ECONOMIC MIGRANTS

1. E.g., in the year ending March 2014, around 560,000 people migrated to Britain, of whom only less than 24,000 were admitted as asylum seekers (the total figure does, however, include 177,000 students). See http://www.theguardian.com /uk-news/2014/aug/28/uk-net-migration-soars-to-243000-theresa-may.

2. See M. Ruhs, *The Price of Rights: Regulating International Labour Migration* (Princeton, NJ: Princeton University Press, 2013), 124.

3. The big exception is of course the temporary migration of international students. I am going to leave these aside here because the questions that may be asked about them are somewhat different and arguably less important for the general themes of this book.

4. These categories are best regarded as ideal types for the purposes of teasing out the normative questions that they raise. The policies that states actually adopt may bridge between the three categories.

5. M. Walzer, *Spheres of Justice* (Oxford: Martin Robertson, 1983), chap. 2. Metics were resident aliens sponsored by citizens, who worked in Athens and were given some protection by the courts but could not, e.g., own houses or land or participate in the *ekklesia* or the other organs of Athenian democracy.

6. In fact these were far from being the worst examples of people in guest-worker status, as Hahamovitch's comparative historical survey shows; see C. Hahamovitch, "Creating Perfect Immigrants: Guestworkers of the World in Historical Perspective," *Labor History* 44 (2003): 69–94.

7. Walzer, *Spheres of Justice*, 61.

8. I rely in this paragraph on Hahamovitch, "Creating Perfect Immigrants."

9. I assume that such restrictions are permissible, provided the duration of the program is relatively short, e.g., as in the case of seasonal programs for agricultural workers.

10. Daniel Attas appeals to the Rawlsian principle of fair play to argue that although temporary migrants are not full citizens, they participate in the economy on the same basis as other residents and should therefore be granted equal economic rights; see D. Attas, "The Case of Guest Workers: Exploitation, Citizenship and Economic Rights," *Res Publica* 6 (2000): 73–92. However, this view overlooks the fact that they are not engaged in a cooperative enterprise that spans the whole of a human life, including childhood and retirement, as citizens anticipate being. They do not, e.g., expect to advance up a career ladder or to pay into a pension pot in the host society. So they participate in the economy on a somewhat different basis. I do, however, partially accept one of the corollaries that Attas draws—that temporary migrants are entitled to freedom of occupation—for different reasons as set out later.

11. For a more sustained defense of the view that temporary migration programs should pay attention to the nature of the migrants' own projects when they participate (and should therefore not impose conditions that would only be appropriate in

the case of citizens), see V. Ottonelli and T. Torresi, "Inclusivist Egalitarian Liberalism and Temporary Migration: A Dilemma," *Journal of Political Philosophy* 20 (2012): 202–224.

12. This point is forcefully made in J. Carens, *The Ethics of Immigration* (New York: Oxford University Press, 2013), chap. 6.

13. Participants in the Canadian Live-in Caregiver Programme have the right to move to permanent resident status after two years, e.g., but this provision is unusual. For discussion, see J. Carens, "Live-in Domestics, Seasonal Workers, and Others Hard to Locate on the Map of Democracy," *Journal of Political Philosophy* 16 (2008): 419–445.

14. For supporting evidence, see D. Bell and N. Piper, "Justice for Migrant Workers? The Case of Foreign Domestic Workers in Hong Kong and Singapore," in *Multiculturalism in Asia,* ed. W. Kymlicka and B. He (Oxford: Oxford University Press, 2005); Ruhs, *Price of Rights,* chap. 6.

15. Another way to think about this problem is to say that people *do* give their voluntary consent to arrangements that are beneficial to them, provided the terms of these arrangements are fair ones, even if they lack any reasonable alternatives. This line of thinking is pursued in A. Patten, *Equal Recognition: The Moral Foundations of Minority Rights* (Princeton, NJ: Princeton University Press, 2014), chap. 8, in relation to immigrants' surrender of some of their cultural rights on entering the host society. However, it rests on making the voluntariness of a choice depend on whether it alters the claims that the chooser can legitimately make, and this seems to put the cart before the horse. We normally think that a choice's being voluntary is what *explains* why the chooser may forfeit certain rights in consequence.

16. Isn't it objectionable paternalism on the state's part to prevent immigrants from choosing their terms of employment? Suppose an employer offers to pay more for work that involves risks that would be prohibited under normal employment law, and the immigrant, knowing the risks but eager to earn more, agrees to take it on. Why should the state intervene? The state is responsible for ensuring that human rights are adequately protected wherever its authority runs. It may therefore sometimes have to enact policies that can be labeled as paternalist, for its own citizens as well as for other residents.

17. This argument is made in P. Lenard and C. Straehle, "Temporary Labour Migration, Global Redistribution, and Democratic Justice," *Politics, Philosophy and Economics* 11 (2012): 206–230.

18. Lenard and Straehle, "Temporary Labour Migration," 215.

19. Lenard and Straehle echo this claim when they argue that "the existence of partial members, whose access to the political environment is restricted, is *our* failure to live up to the democratic principles we claim to uphold. We are perpetuating injustice, in other words, and this constitutes harm to *us*"; Lenard and Straehle, "Temporary Labour Migration," 216.

20. These exclusions are sometimes challenged, but even their opponents would hesitate to describe them as "tyrannical."

21. Walzer concedes in a footnote that his argument seems not to apply to "privileged guests: technical advisors, visiting professors, and so on"; Walzer, *Spheres of Justice,* 60. This suggests that what is really driving it is not the headline principle of democracy, but the powerless and unprotected status of those who, historically at least, have participated in guest-worker programs.

22. Others who have argued that temporary migration programs may involve an acceptable trade-off between the migrants' own interests and other values include Bell and Piper, "Justice for Migrant Workers?"; R. Mayer, "Guestworkers and Exploitation," *Review of Politics* 67 (2005): 311–334.

23. Might the same be said about the admission of refugees who are denied permanent residence on the grounds that they should be expected to repatriate once it is safe for them to do so? They too may face an extended period in limbo. However, given the difficulty of inducing states to take in their fair share of refugees (see Chapter 5), this may be the lesser of two evils. If states were required to grant all refugees rights of permanent residence, they would be willing to admit fewer still.

24. Carens frames his discussion of this question by means of a distinction between "criteria of exclusion" and "criteria of selection"; see Carens, *Ethics of Immigration,* chap. 9. I can see some merit in this, but here I treat qualifying and disqualifying factors simply as two portions of the same scale, so if "being skilled" is a reason for admission, "being unskilled" is a reason for rejection. My discussion is less comprehensive than his.

25. For this transformation, see C. Joppke, *Selecting by Origin: Ethnic Migration and the Liberal State* (Cambridge, MA: Harvard University Press, 2005).

26. M. Blake, "Immigration and Political Equality," *San Diego Law Review* 45 (2008): 970.

27. Carens argues that selecting immigrants on grounds of race or ethnicity is inconsistent with any "plausible interpretation of liberal democratic principles"; J. Carens, "Who Should Get In? The Ethics of Immigration Admissions," *Ethics and International Affairs* 17 (2003): 105. But this again assumes that such principles apply in the same way to the state's treatment of those who are not yet subject to its authority as they do to its treatment of its own citizens, and this is what needs to be shown.

28. I. Brownlie and G. Goodwin-Gill, eds., *Basic Documents on Human Rights,* 5th ed. (Oxford: Oxford University Press, 2006), 366.

29. I explore reasons for thinking that the human right against discrimination might apply to immigration policies in greater depth in D. Miller, "Border Regimes and Human Rights," *Law and Ethics of Human Rights* 7 (2013): 6–27.

30. It is followed in Carens, "Who Should Get In?," and at greater length in M. Blake, "Discretionary Immigration," *Philosophical Topics* 30 (2002): 273–289; M. Blake, "Immigration," in *A Companion to Applied Ethics,* ed. R. Frey and C. Wellman (Oxford: Blackwell, 2003). I also used the argument in an earlier discussion;

D. Miller, *National Responsibility and Global Justice* (Oxford: Oxford University Press, 2007), chap. 8.

31. Blake, "Discretionary Immigration," 284.

32. This is conceded by Blake in Blake, "Discretionary Immigration," 285. See also Walzer, *Spheres of Justice,* 35–51, and the discussion in Blake, "Immigration."

33. Suppose the selection were to be made using a lottery: Might this be acceptable? Only, I think, if the receiving state could plausibly claim that it was using the lottery to choose among preselected candidates who could not reliably be distinguished from one another on the basis of criteria such as skills, professional qualifications, and so on.

34. A rather similar position is taken in Blake, "Immigration and Political Equality," where it is formulated in the language of "reasons that immigrants could not reasonably reject" (971).

35. I rely here on an intuitive understanding of which social goals it is legitimate for the state to pursue, and which it is not—e.g., that cultural cohesion is a legitimate goal while racial purity is not (to say that cultural cohesion is a legitimate goal is to say that it is one that the state *may choose* to pursue, not one that it *should* pursue). It is revealing, I think, that those who in the past have advocated racist immigration policies have always felt obliged to appeal to something beyond race itself—e.g., to the alleged differences in moral character between those belonging to different races.

36. Carens, *Ethics of Immigration,* chap. 9.

37. I ask this question without myself being sure of the answer. Since my underlying assumption, defended in Chapter 2, is that states *do* owe more to their own citizens than to strangers, one could argue that the toleration that liberal democracies extend to their dissident citizens need not be granted to those applying to join the political community.

38. As Carens puts it, "the problem is not with any single immigrant's views, but with the collective effect of ideas hostile to democracy"; Carens, *Ethics of Immigration,* 176.

39. Relevant discussions include D. Kapur and J. McHale, *Give Us Your Best and Brightest: The Global Hunt for Talent and Its Impact on the Developing World* (Washington, DC: Center for Global Development, 2005); D. Kapur and J. McHale, "Should a Cosmopolitan Worry about the 'Brain Drain'?," *Ethics and International Affairs* 20 (2006): 305–320; C. Packer, V. Runnels, and R. Labonte, "Does the Migration of Health Workers Bring Benefits to the Countries They Leave Behind?," in *The International Migration of Health Workers,* ed. R. Shah (Basingstoke: Palgrave Macmillan, 2010); F. Docquier and H. Rapoport, "Globalization, Brain Drain, and Development," *Journal of Economic Literature* 50 (2012): 681–730; P. Collier, *Exodus: Immigration and Multiculturalism in the 21st Century* (London: Allen Lane, 2013), pt. 4.

40. See Docquier and Rapoport, "Globalization, Brain Drain, and Development," 701–703; Collier, *Exodus,* 199–203.

41. See Kapur and McHale, *Give Us Your Best and Brightest,* 25–29. However, one should not neglect the impact that free movement within the EU has had on countries such as Poland and Bulgaria, who have seen many of their professionals and skilled workers leave for jobs elsewhere in Europe. See, e.g., K. Connolly, "As Poland Loses Its Doctors and Builders, 'Euro-orphans' Are Left at Home to Suffer," http://www.theguardian.com/world/2015/mar/15/euro-orphans-fastest-shrinking -town-poland-radom; I. Krastev, "Britain's Gain Is East Europe's Brain Drain," http://www.theguardian.com/commentisfree/2015/mar/24/britain-east-europe -brain-drain-bulgaria.

42. Here I follow K. Oberman, "Can Brain Drain Justify Immigration Restrictions?," *Ethics* 123 (2013): 434–437. See also Brock's argument in G. Brock and M. Blake, *Debating Brain Drain: May Governments Restrict Emigration?* (Oxford: Oxford University Press, 2015), chap. 4.

43. How this obligation should be understood will depend on where one stands on the wider question of associative obligations, discussed in Chapter 2. But even strong cosmopolitans may argue that the fact of proximity together with various practical considerations may mean that skilled workers do have a special obligation to meet the needs of fellow citizens; see the discussion in Oberman, "Can Brain Drain Justify Immigration Restrictions?," 437–438.

44. The right of exit is rarely challenged, but see L. Ypi, "Justice in Migration: A Closed Borders Utopia?," *Journal of Political Philosophy* 16 (2008): 391–418, for one example. For a strong defense, see Blake's contribution to Brock and Blake, *Debating Brain Drain,* chap. 9.

45. I can envisage circumstances in which a government faced with a large-scale natural disaster—an earthquake or a volcanic eruption—might *temporarily* restrict the exit rights of those able to contribute to the rescue operation.

46. A government may decide that the professionals it educates should be contractually obliged to work in the home country for a certain number of years and demand financial repayment from those who leave without having discharged their obligations. Depending on the details of the scheme and the background circumstances, this may be justifiable; see Brock's argument in Brock and Blake, *Debating Brain Drain,* chap. 4. This permission, however, does not extend to physically preventing their departure.

47. Luara Ferracioli argues that rich states that open their borders to skilled workers whose skills are needed to avoid deprivation in their home countries are best described as "enabling harm" by their actions. See L. Ferracioli, "Immigration, Self-Determination and the Brain Drain," *Review of International Studies* 41 (2014): 99–115. She adds, correctly, that this is on the assumption that conditions in the sending states are not so bad that their skills cannot be used there.

48. A number of possible methods are discussed in Kapur and McHale, *Give Us Your Best and Brightest,* chap. 10.

49. Oberman argues that this is the policy that must be pursued in preference to imposing immigration restrictions. He concedes that "it is unfair if rich states have to provide extra assistance to make up for a failure by skilled workers to fulfil their duties to their poor compatriots," but argues that this unfairness must be borne because "the freedom to cross borders is a basic liberty"; Oberman, "Can Brain Drain Justify Immigration Restrictions?," 443. This illustrates how policy responses to brain-drain problems depend on the underlying principles we accept, in this case whether we acknowledge a basic human right to immigrate.

50. To avoid misunderstanding, I am not claiming that policies such as these have no independent merit. They may be valuable ways of supplying aid to poor countries. My claim is just that rich countries are not *required* to pursue them as an alternative to restricting the inward migration of health workers and others.

51. However, for many members of this group moving may not be feasible; see the discussion in Collier, *Exodus,* chap. 6.

7. THE RIGHTS OF IMMIGRANTS

1. I take the phrase "irregular migrants" from Carens and will use it in what follows despite some qualms; see J. Carens, "The Rights of Irregular Migrants," *Ethics and International Affairs* 2 (2008): 163–186; J. Carens, *The Ethics of Immigration* (New York: Oxford University Press, 2013), chap. 7. Carens argues that it more accurately reflects the position of unauthorized immigrants: although they have no legal right to be present on the state's territory, they should not be regarded as criminals on that account alone. It is also true that people who fall into this category range from those who have crossed a border covertly in full knowledge that they were doing so to avoid normal immigration procedures to those whose unauthorized status is due to some legal technicality, such as a parent having failed to register them for citizenship. My qualms about "irregular migrants" are that it suggests too strongly that the people we are talking about are *merely* in breach of some formal rule.

2. Here I follow M. Lister, "Immigration, Association and the Family," *Law and Philosophy* 29 (2010): 717–745.

3. It follows that irregular migrants cannot make family reunification claims. What is more moot is the position of temporary migrants. Because a main aim of temporary migration programs is to allow participants to accumulate resources that can then be sent back to their families abroad, it makes sense that these programs do not normally allow the migrants to bring their families with them. What may be at issue is the amount of time for which such a restriction can be imposed. For contrasting views on this, see J. Carens, "Live-in Domestics, Seasonal Workers, and Others Hard to Locate on the Map of Democracy," *Journal of Political Philosophy* 16 (2008): 423–424; M. Ruhs, *The Price of Rights: Regulating International Labour Migration* (Princeton, NJ: Princeton University Press, 2013), 175–176.

4. There is an illuminating discussion in Carens, *Ethics of Immigration*, 186–191. A more radical approach has been adopted by Luara Ferracioli, who argues that liberal states committed to a principle of neutrality cannot justify extending reunification rights only to those in romantic and/or familial relationships; see L. Ferracioli, "Family Migration Schemes and Liberal Neutrality: A Dilemma," *Journal of Moral Philosophy* (forthcoming).

5. J. Souter, "Towards a Theory of Asylum as Reparation for Past Injustice," *Political Studies* 62 (2014): 326–342.

6. Against this proposal, Souter argues that reparation in the form of asylum provides *immediate* protection of rights, whereas programs of aid and development (and the same would apply to restoration programs of the kind discussed here) take longer to implement; Souter, "Towards a Theory of Asylum," 337–338. This shows, however, that on-site reparation would need to be accompanied by forms of compensation to cover the victim's short-term losses if it is to be morally preferable to asylum.

7. Are there indeed any other examples? We might think of people who have made a significant political contribution to the state, by supporting a revolution or helping to draft a constitution: Benjamin Franklin and Thomas Paine were both awarded French citizenship on such grounds. Or we might think of those who have helped to make or restore a cultural artifact of national significance.

8. See http://www.legion-recrute.com/en/faq.php#f4.

9. Or as the legion's own statement puts it, "La République peut-elle mieux témoigner sa reconnaissance qu'en offrant à ces combattants étrangers touchés dans leur chair de devenir Français à part entière?"; http://www.legion-etrangere.com/modules/info_seul.php?id=165.

10. See "Was Lumley Campaign Good for Gurkhas?," at http://www.bbc.co.uk/news/world-south-asia-13372026.

11. This principle has been recognized in American constitutional doctrine, which holds that a person who has entered U.S. territory unlawfully is nevertheless entitled to the equal protection of the laws for as long as he remains on that territory. For relevant Supreme Court judgments, see L. Bosniak, *The Citizen and the Alien: Dilemmas of Contemporary Membership* (Princeton, NJ: Princeton University Press, 2006), 53–56.

12. See my discussion in D. Miller, "Are Human Rights Conditional?," in *Human Rights and Global Justice: The 10th Kobe Lectures, July 2011*, ed. T. Sakurai and M. Usami (Stuttgart: Franz Steiner Verlag, 2014); C. Wellman, "The Rights-Forfeiture Theory of Punishment," *Ethics* 122 (2012): 371–393.

13. Carens, *Ethics of Immigration*, 133.

14. See Bosniak, *Citizen and the Alien*, chap. 3.

15. It is a moot point whether the firewall idea can be coherently implemented in a modern state, but I am assuming for present purposes that it could be. For discussion, see C. Boswell, "The Elusive Rights of an Invisible Population," *Ethics and International Affairs* 22 (2008): 187–192.

16. The illegal crossing of a border is treated as a criminal act in both the United States and the United Kingdom (in the United States it is classified as a misdemeanor). However, among those present without authorization at any time there will be asylum seekers whose claims have not yet been resolved, people attempting to renew temporary visas, and so forth. So some but not all irregular migrants will be chargeable with criminal offenses.

17. Carens, "Rights of Irregular Migrants," 167.

18. See Carens, *Ethics of immigration,* 143–145. Carens believes, however, that there may still be public policy reasons for having a firewall in place with respect to these rights.

19. I leave aside incentive considerations—the state's legitimate wish not to attract further irregular migrants.

20. J. Rawls, "Kantian Constructivism in Moral Theory," in *Collected Papers,* ed. S. Freeman (Cambridge, MA: Harvard University Press, 1999), 323.

21. Prominent among them are Carens, *Ethics of Immigration,* chaps. 5 and 7; R. Rubio-Marin, *Immigration as a Democratic Challenge: Citizenship and Inclusion in Germany and the United States* (Cambridge: Cambridge University Press, 2000), esp. chaps. 2 and 5; A. Shachar, *The Birthright Lottery: Citizenship and Global Inequality* (Cambridge, MA: Harvard University Press, 2009), chap. 6.

22. "The claim advanced here is that at least all those who are permanently subject to the law and deeply affected by the political process should be automatically and unconditionally included. As societal members, settled immigrants (whatever their legally recognized status) qualify for full democratic membership"; Rubio-Marin, *Immigration as a Democratic Challenge,* 84.

23. T. Nagel, "The Problem of Global Justice," *Philosophy and Public Affairs* 33 (2005): 133. Nagel's aim in this article is to explain why obligations of distributive justice apply among the citizens of a political community but not between citizens and strangers.

24. See, e.g., A. Sangiovanni, "The Irrelevance of Coercion, Imposition, and Framing to Distributive Justice," *Philosophy and Public Affairs* 40 (2012): 79–110; J. Cohen and C. Sabel, "Extra Rempublicam Nulla Justitia?," *Philosophy and Public Affairs* 34 (2006): 147–175; D. Miller, "Justice and Boundaries," *Politics, Philosophy and Economics* 8 (2009): 291–309, repr., D. Miller, *Justice for Earthlings: Essays in Political Philosophy* (Cambridge: Cambridge University Press, 2013).

25. I am distinguishing between chosen and unchosen membership, and "native-born" should therefore be read to include children raised in a society regardless of their precise place of birth.

26. Shachar, *Birthright Lottery,* 184–188. This appeal, it should be noted, is not Shachar's main argument for granting immigrants permanent rights of residence, which I discuss below under the heading of "social membership." In fact it seems somewhat at odds with the latter, for whereas adverse possession would suggest that the right to remain should follow automatically after sufficient time has elapsed, the

social membership argument points us toward "earned citizenship," which depends on the degree to which the immigrant has integrated in and contributed to the society she has joined. On the latter, see A. Shachar, "Earned Citizenship: Property Lessons for Immigration Reform," *Yale Journal of Law and the Humanities* 23 (2011): 110–158.

27. For discussion of the doctrine, see J. Stake, "The Uneasy Case for Adverse Possession," *Georgetown Law Journal* 89 (2000–2001): 2419–2474.

28. Shachar suggests that the authorities may have "chosen to turn a blind eye to the 'adverse possession' by millions of unauthorized migrants who settled within their territory"; Shachar, *Birthright Lottery,* 186. Were this indeed so, the argument for legalization would be very strong. However, in the case of the United States, the immigration authorities deported four million people between 2001 and 2013, with the numbers per annum increasing over time; see http://www.pewresearch.org/fact-tank/2014/10/02/u-s-deportations-of-immigrants-reach-record-high-in-2013. Estimates of the cost vary, but one source gives a figure of $23,482 per deportee; https://www.americanprogress.org/wp-content/uploads/issues/2010/03/pdf/cost_of_deportation_execsumm.pdf. Although an estimated eleven million unauthorized migrants remain, it is hard to present this as a case of turning a blind eye.

29. Carens, *Ethics of Immigration,* 164.

30. This will also be true of some refugees, those admitted initially simply on grounds of their threatened status, but who are still unable to return safely to their homelands after some time has elapsed. These people must be granted permanent residence and full inclusion. But what sets them apart from irregular migrants is that the state in granting asylum to refugees recognizes an obligation toward them that includes citizenship as a possible final outcome.

31. J. Carens, "The Case for Amnesty," ' in J. Carens, *Immigrants and the Right to Stay* (Cambridge, MA: MIT Press, 2010), 25–26; Carens, *Ethics of Immigration,* 164–168. Carens suggests an analogy with the right to vote, where a fixed age is set for acquiring the right despite empirical evidence of significant variance in children's political capacity: "Some children are highly responsible at 12, others still not at 30" (165). Yet the analogy overlooks the fundamental principle of equal treatment of citizens, which would be breached if some were declared more competent than others by being enfranchised at an earlier age, whereas the decision to grant permanent residence is a material decision about who deserves to stay and who does not (just as admission decisions generally are decisions about who deserves to enter and who does not).

32. It might be said that being turned down for legal residence—and therefore being rendered liable for deportation—is a greater cost for the person concerned than simply being refused admission, and therefore stricter safeguards are needed. Yet this will depend on what the consequences are of being denied full inclusion: for example, someone who is rejected might nonetheless be granted temporary leave to remain and allowed to reapply.

33. Shachar, *Birthright Lottery,* 177–178.

34. L. Bosniak, "Amnesty in Immigration: Forgetting, Forgiving, Freedom," *Critical Review of International Social and Political Philosophy* 16 (2013): 344–365.

35. Bosniak adds a third possibility: "amnesty as vindication." On this reading, granting amnesty is an acknowledgment that the original acts of the government wronged the victims. In the present context, this would have to mean that the border controls that the migrants evaded were illegitimate.

36. M. Walzer, *Spheres of Justice* (Oxford: Martin Robertson, 1983), 52–63.

37. See, e.g., Bosniak, *Citizen and the Alien,* chap. 6, where she attacks what she calls "hard outside, soft inside" conceptions of citizenship on empirical grounds; K. Oberman, "What Is Wrong with Permanent Alienage?" (October 29, 2012), http://ssrn.com/abstract=2168271, where he argues that the consent of voluntary migrants would be sufficient to justify their permanent alienage if there were no human right to immigrate.

38. T. H. Marshall, *Citizenship and Social Class,* ed. T. Bottomore (London: Pluto Press, 1992).

39. M. Helbling, "Contentious Citizenship Attribution in a Federal State," *Journal of Ethnic and Migration Studies* 36 (2010): 793–809.

8. INTEGRATING IMMIGRANTS

1. For general reflection on the pervasive use, in Europe especially, of "integration" as the umbrella concept for discussing relationships between indigenous citizens and immigrants, see A. Favell, "Integration Nations: The Nation-State and Research on Immigrants in Western Europe," in *International Migration Research,* ed. M. Bommes and E. Morawska (Aldershot, UK: Ashgate, 2005).

2. *Community Cohesion: A Report of the Independent Review Team* (London: Home Office, 2001), 9.

3. *Oldham Independent Review,* sec. 2.8, http://resources.cohesioninstitute.org .uk/Publications/Documents/Document/DownloadDocumentsFile.aspx?recordId =97&file=PDFversion.

4. Another specific aim that has been prominent in recent debates about integration has been preventing home-grown terrorism. Without in any way denying its importance, I am looking here at reasons for valuing integration that transcend such immediately pressing issues.

5. E. Anderson, *The Imperative of Integration* (Princeton, NJ: Princeton University Press, 2010), 116.

6. Anderson, *Imperative of Integration,* 116.

7. Moreover, it is possible for civic integration to occur without much social integration, e.g., as happened with Jewish communities in Britain in the early part of the twentieth century or with Chinese communities in Malaysia and Indonesia. These are special cases, however, and a state that wants to promote civic

integration would generally be well advised to tackle social segregation as part of its strategy.

8. A broader argument in favor of "voluntary separation" is mounted in M. Merry, *Equality, Citizenship and Segregation: A Defense of Separation* (New York: Palgrave Macmillan, 2013). Merry emphasizes, however, that the benefits of separation he identifies are highly contingent and arise only under "non-ideal" circumstances of social inequality.

9. J. Carens, "The Integration of Immigrants," *Journal of Moral Philosophy* 2 (2005): 30.

10. Carens, "Integration of Immigrants," 30–31.

11. This is the practice whereby an unscrupulous real estate agent will scare house owners by telling them that members of an ethnic minority are moving into their neighborhood, encouraging them to sell at a deflated price and confirming the prediction by selling at a reinflated price to minority buyers.

12. For discussion of integration contracts in different European countries, see C. Joppke, "Beyond National Models: Civic Integration Policies for Immigrants in Western Europe," *West European Politics* 30 (2007): 1–22; S. Goodman, "Integration Requirements for Integration's Sake? Identifying, Categorising and Comparing Civic Integration Policies," *Journal of Ethnic and Migration Studies,* 36 (2010): 753–772; S. Goodman, "Fortifying Citizenship: Policy Strategies for Civic Integration in Western Europe," *World Politics* 64 (2012): 659–698.

13. For a wide-ranging analysis of the shift toward the use of citizenship tests in European states, including the United Kingdom, see the essays collected in *A Redefinition of Belonging? Language and Integration Tests in Europe,* ed. R. van Oers, E. Ersboll, and D. Kostakopolou (Leiden: Martinus Nijhoff, 2010).

14. For recent data, see https://www.gov.uk/government/publications/life-in-the-uk-test-data-january-2010-to-october-2013; see also Goodman, "Fortifying Citizenship," 689–690. The Canadian test has a pass rate of over 80% and the American test a pass rate of over 90%.

15. This charge is leveled in Joppke, "Beyond National Models," 14–19.

16. For surveys, see D. Kerr, "Citizenship Education: An International Comparison," in *Education for Citizenship,* ed. D. Lawton, J. Cairns, and R. Gardner (London: Continuum, 2000); O. Ichilov, ed., *Citizenship and Citizenship Education in a Changing World* (London: Woburn Press, 1998).

17. J. Wales, *Life in the United Kingdom: The Official Study Guide* (Norwich, UK: Stationery Office, 2013). The UK test in its present form is clearly intended to be a vehicle of cultural as well as civic integration. Although it refers occasionally to immigrant cultures (e.g., non-Christian religious festivals), the booklet covers in some detail the work of British artists, writers, musicians, etc., both historical and contemporary, and invites the reader to take note of major points of cultural reference.

18. J. Carens, *The Ethics of Immigration* (New York: Oxford University Press, 2013), 59.

19. The United Kingdom introduced a revised test in 2013, Canada in 2010, the United States in 2008.

20. See the figures cited in H. de Schutter and L. Ypi, "Mandatory Citizenship for Immigrants," *British Journal of Political Science* 45 (2015): 235–251, p. 237. For liberal democracies, the proportion of noncitizen residents ranges between 7% and 20%. Of course these snapshot figures are likely to be overestimates since they include people who will eventually progress to citizenship.

21. De Schutter and Ypi, "Mandatory Citizenship for Immigrants."

22. They also suggest an interesting democratic argument, which holds that because everyone living in society will behave in ways that affect other people (such as engaging in a particular set of religious practices), they should be expected to engage in democratic deliberation with those they affect. Limitations of space prevent me from considering this further.

23. J. Rawls, *A Theory of Justice* (Cambridge, MA: Harvard University Press, 1971), 342–343. It is of course possible that some of those who currently decline the opportunity to become citizens may do so because they believe that the scheme they are being invited to join is *not* fair.

24. See http://www.theglobeandmail.com/news/national/appeal-court-upholds -oath-to-queen-in-citizenship-case/article20032155.

25. A possible way round this problem would be to replace the citizenship test with compulsory citizenship classes, which, presumably, every incoming resident would be able to attend. Many people, however, would likely find this a more burdensome requirement than the test itself.

26. The obvious analogy here is with military service. If the state is fighting a just war, citizens may have a moral obligation to join up, and this obligation may justifiably be made legally enforceable if circumstances warrant. But people who can demonstrate that they have reasons of conscience for not engaging in armed conflict should be allowed to serve in other ways.

27. For evidence of this disagreement, see P. Conover, I. Crewe, and D. Searing, "The Nature of Citizenship in the United States and Great Britain: Empirical Comments on Theoretical Themes," *Journal of Politics* 53 (1991): 800–832.

28. W. Kymlicka, *Multicultural Citizenship* (Oxford: Clarendon Press, 1995), 76.

29. More radical forms of multiculturalism may, however, argue against the need for any common cultural framework as the setting for democratic politics. See, e.g., my critical discussion of Iris Young's *Justice and the Politics of Difference* in D. Miller, *On Nationality* (Oxford: Clarendon Press, 1995), chap. 5.

30. K. Banting and W. Kymlicka, "Do Multiculturalism Policies Erode the Welfare State?," in *Cultural Diversity versus Economic Solidarity,* ed. P. Van Parijs (Brussels: Deboeck Université Press, 2004), 251–252. I shall not comment here on

the alleged "death of multiculturalism" in popular political debate over the last decade, except to say that the form of multiculturalism that is being targeted when its death is pronounced is very different from Kymlicka's. For examples of the recent attack on multiculturalism, see T. Modood, *Multiculturalism,* 2nd ed. (Cambridge: Polity Press, 2013), chap. 1.

31. There is nonetheless a difference between understanding a culture and identifying with it—between being able to grasp points of cultural reference and actually valuing the culture's contents. If full cultural integration requires the latter, then the argument presented here does not go so far. Perhaps, though, we should understand "sharing a cultural identity" in a weaker sense that allows for diversity in the way that individual people view the culture's defining symbols and practices.

32. All of these are included in the latest version of the UK citizenship study guide and the test that it prepares for.

33. On Britain's Armistice Day in November 2010, a group of Muslims burnt a giant poppy (the symbol of remembrance) in protest against British involvement in Iraq and Afghanistan, with predictable results. It is difficult to believe that they would have chosen to do this had they understood the meaning that day holds for almost all British people (they might have chosen instead to wear white poppies, a long-standing pacifist symbol that commemorates the war dead while expressing the hope that there will be no more wars).

34. Anderson, *Imperative of Integration,* 116.

35. I have discussed some of these in D. Miller, " 'Are They *My* Poor?': The Problem of Altruism in a World of Strangers," *Critical Review of International Social and Political Philosophy* 5 (2002): 106–127, repr., D. Miller, *Justice for Earthlings: Essays in Political Philosophy* (Cambridge: Cambridge University Press, 2013).

36. See D. Miller and S. Ali, "Testing the National Identity Argument," *European Political Science Review* 6 (2014): 237–259; E. Theiss-Morse, *Who Counts as an American? The Boundaries of National Identity* (New York: Cambridge University Press, 2009), esp. chap. 4.

37. See M. Nussbaum, introduction to *Liberty of Conscience: In Defense of America's Tradition of Religious Equality* (New York: Basic Books, 2008). Nussbaum concedes, however, that in some European countries with "few religious differences that inspire real passion" it may be acceptable to permit an established church to exist for historical reasons (13).

38. Nussbaum, *Liberty of Conscience,* 18.

39. See my discussion in D. Miller, "Liberalism, Equal Opportunities and Cultural Commitments," in *Multiculturalism Reconsidered,* ed. P. Kelly (Cambridge: Polity Press, 2002), repr., Miller, *Justice for Earthlings.*

40. Because I am not defending neutrality, I do not need to explain what it means, but for a good discussion of the concept, see A. Patten, "Liberal Neutrality: A

Reinterpretation and Defense," *Journal of Political Philosophy* 20 (2012): 249–272; A. Patten, *Equal Recognition: The Moral Foundations of Minority Rights* (Princeton, NJ: Princeton University Press, 2014), chap. 4.

41. Kymlicka, *Multicultural Citizenship,* 111.

42. I have studied in some detail the Swiss debate about the building of Islamic minarets, culminating in a referendum decision to ban them, in D. Miller, "Majorities and Minarets: Religious Freedom and Public Space," *British Journal of Political Science* (forthcoming).

43. Thus one solution to conflicts over the building of Islamic minarets in Christian-heritage countries has been to permit minarets but to limit their height so that existing churches remain the dominant features of the skyline.

44. Immigrants may in any case prefer that the schools their children attend should have a religious character: they may see secularism as a greater threat to their own identity than the mild and tolerant versions of Christianity that most liberal democracies now formally espouse.

45. What does it mean to embrace a culture that is not your own—e.g., for a Jew or a Muslim to embrace Christianity as the established religion of his adopted country? Clearly it cannot mean accepting the distinctive beliefs embedded in that culture oneself. But it does mean, e.g., being a willing participant in national ceremonies whose form reflects the religion (investitures, state funerals, etc.). This is not so different from a Scot who dislikes the sound of the bagpipes herself nevertheless thinking it fitting for that instrument to be played on certain occasions, as a way of expressing their distinctively Scottish character.

9. CONCLUSION

1. http://www.catholicherald.co.uk/news/2014/10/28/catholic-charity-critical -of-governments-refusal-to-support-future-migrant-rescues/.

2. http://www.dailymail.co.uk/news/article-1261044/Slaughter-swans-As -carcasses-pile-crude-camps-built-river-banks-residents-frightened-visit-park -Peterborough.html.

3. For another example, on the day that the report *The Fiscal Impact of Immigration to the UK* by economists at University College, London, was published, the main headline of the left-leaning *Guardian* read "UK Gains £20bn from EU Migrants," and the main headline in the right-leaning *Daily Telegraph* read "Immigration from Outside Europe Cost £120 Billion." Both claims could be substantiated on the basis of the researchers' evidence, but it would take considerable detective work to uncover their real significance. Meanwhile, everyone can take comfort in having their prejudices confirmed.

4. Professors are much more likely to hear the first charge, but they should be aware of the second too. Indeed they should be more reflective about their own position

within the social order, as belonging to the class most likely to benefit from, rather than be harmed by, freedom of international movement.

5. One value I shall not discuss is economic efficiency, even though this is often invoked in defense of the free movement of labor. I shall not discuss it because, as I noted in Chapter 1, there is much debate among economists not only about the net gains that might arise from migration, but also about how its costs and benefits are distributed between different groups.

6. National identity can also be linked to a concern about democratic representation: "In a world in which there are constant changes in the individual composition of the members—due to immigration, emigration, births and deaths—it is vital that all see themselves as members of a shared enterprise, as having an identity that can unify the whole and so render the political representatives legitimate. In our (contemporary) world, national identities provide the basis for this sense of shared membership and unity"; M. Moore, *The Ethics of Nationalism* (Oxford: Oxford University Press, 2001), 88. Moore also credits M. Canovan, *Nationhood and Political Theory* (Cheltenham, UK: Edward Elgar, 1996), for this insight.

7. An approach memorably summed up in the words of the Chartist Joshua Harney that I cited near the beginning of Chapter 1.

8. I don't use "realism" here with the technical meaning that is sometimes now given to it in political philosophy, but simply to signal an approach that starts by looking at the world as it is, with its manifold inequalities and injustices, and asks what range of immigration policies may legitimately be pursued by democratic states under these circumstances.

9. Governments, however, are cross-pressured because although voters generally want immigrant numbers reduced, big business can lobby effectively both to recruit (allegedly) scarce talent at one end of the scale and cheap unskilled labor at the other.

10. L. Bosniak, *The Citizen and the Alien: Dilemmas of Contemporary Membership* (Princeton, NJ: Princeton University Press, 2006), 4.

11. Kieran Oberman, in a lecture to the Refugee Studies Centre, University of Oxford, October 2012. He credits Costica Dumbrava with first use of the phrase; he now prefers "cantaloupe consensus" on the grounds that the insides of coconuts are insufficiently soft.

12. It violates fairness and social integration for obvious reasons. It violates national self-determination because that principle assumes that everyone in the society can identify with the nation and participate in making its decisions, which the subaltern group clearly cannot do.

13. Of course the difficulties in reaching such an agreement should not be underestimated, as my discussion in Chapter 5 should have made clear.

14. For discussion of its achievements and limitations, see G. Loescher and J. Milner, "UNHCR and the Global Governance of Refugees," in *Global Migration Governance,* ed. A. Betts (Oxford: Oxford University Press, 2011).

15. For the general question of what justice requires when we are asked to take up the slack that others have left, see my essay "Taking Up the Slack? Responsibility and Justice in Situations of Partial Compliance," in *Responsibility and Distributive Justice,* ed. C. Knight and Z. Stemplowska (Oxford: Oxford University Press, 2010), repr., D. Miller, *Justice for Earthlings: Essays in Political Philosophy* (Cambridge: Cambridge University Press, 2013).

16. The reason, however, is different in the two cases. In the first case, the excluded refugees have a claim of justice against the states that refuse to carry their fair share of the collective task, and this is what makes the residual obligation of compliant states only a humanitarian one. In the second case, the reason is the excessive cost of doing what justice otherwise demands—so the position is similar to that of an individual person who finds herself in a situation where she has to decide whether to carry out a rescue that involves her taking a significant risk. However, the position alters if the receiving state is partly responsible for the global warming or the resource depletion that produces the refugees—it will then have an obligation to compensate for the harm it has inflicted regardless of the cost of doing so, and this might mean taking in large numbers of unwanted refugees.

17. That popular resistance to immigration is driven more by concerns about the loss of cultural identity than by economic self-interest is the main thesis of the study of Dutch society in P. Sniderman and L. Hagendoorn, *When Ways of Life Collide: Multiculturalism and Its Discontents in the Netherlands* (Princeton, NJ: Princeton University Press, 2007).

18. "The problem of immigration is not, then, simply left aside, but is eliminated as a serious problem in a realistic utopia"; J. Rawls, *The Law of Peoples* (Cambridge, MA; Harvard University Press, 1999), 9.

POSTSCRIPT: THE EUROPEAN MIGRATION CRISIS OF 2015

1. A. Betts, *Survival Migration: Failed Governance and the Crisis of Displacement* (Ithaca and London: Cornell University Press, 2013).

2. Betts, *Survival Migration*, 23.

3. H. Shue, *Basic Rights: Subsistence, Affluence and U.S. Foreign Policy* (Princeton, NJ: Princeton University Press, 1980).

4. P. Collier, "If You Really Want to Help Refugees, Look Beyond the Mediterranean," *The Spectator*, August 8, 2015.

5. This is also a legal duty under the international law of the sea. However that law was not designed to for circumstances of the kind we encounter in the case of the boat people. I have explored the issue in much greater depth in a forthcoming paper, "The Duty to Rescue Boat People."

Acknowledgments

I began thinking intensively about immigration over ten years ago, and I should like to begin by thanking Andrew Cohen and Kit Wellman for providing the initial spur, in the form of an invitation to contribute an essay to Blackwell's *Contemporary Debates in Applied Ethics,* with a clear mandate: defend the right of states to close their borders to immigrants! That foray was followed by a number of papers refining and buttressing the original argument, and the present book attempts to distill what I have learned over that decade into a concise statement of my views. Along the way I have accumulated many debts.

One is to SIAS, a consortium of Institutes of Advanced Study that in 2007 and 2008 provided generous support for two Summer Institutes on Citizenship and Migration, one in Berlin and one in Palo Alto. My co-convenor Eamonn Callan and I were given a free hand to pick twenty of the most talented young scholars from Europe and North America, working in different disciplines but the same broad field, and to invite distinguished visiting speakers to address them over the course of a two-week workshop. This was an enriching experience for me personally, and I have remained in close touch with many of the participants, as the list of names that follows will reveal.

There have been many occasions to try out preliminary versions of the ideas presented here in lectures, seminars, and workshops, so I should like to thank all those who participated in events held at the following institutions: the University of Amsterdam; Cambridge University; Trinity College, Dublin; the European University Institute; the Hebrew University, Jerusalem; University College, London;

the University of Melbourne; Ohio State University; the University of Ottawa; the University of Palermo; Princeton University; the University of Rijeka; the University of St. Gallen; Sciences Po, Paris; the University of Stockholm; the Academic Centre for Law and Business, Tel Aviv; and Yale University. Closer to home, Oxford University's internal pluralism means that I have been able to try out thoughts at the Centre for the Study of Social Justice, the Centre on Migration, Policy and Society, the Refugee Studies Centre, and last but not least, Nuffield College, whose Political Theory Workshop, running every week for thirty years, provides an unparalleled opportunity for work in progress to be scrutinized.

With apologies to those I have inadvertently omitted from the list, I should particularly like to record my thanks to the following for illuminating discussions about topics connected to immigration: Arash Abizadeh, Rainer Bauböck, Gillian Brock, Daniel Butt, Eamonn Callan, Simon Caney, Paul Collier, Cathryn Costello, Avner de Shalit, Helder de Schutter, Gabriella Elgenius, David Enoch, Paulina Ochoa Espejo, Cécile Fabre, Sarah Fine, Gina Gustavsson, Ronit Kedar, Avery Kolers, Tally Kritzman-Amir, Chandran Kukathas, Cécile Laborde, Patti Lenard, Meira Levinson, Terry Macdonald, David Owen, Alan Patten, Hans Roth, Martin Ruhs, Zosia Stemplowska, Anna Stilz, Christine Straehle, John Tasioulas, Tiziana Torresi, Philippe van Parijs, Ashwini Vasanthakumar, Kit Wellman, and Lea Ypi.

Some people deserve special mention. I begin with Joseph Carens, whose writing about immigration, sustained over a quarter century and culminating in 2013 with *The Ethics of Immigration,* has been a constant source of inspiration. Readers will observe how much I have learned from reading Joe's work, even while dissenting sharply from some of the positions he takes. Joe is the most courteous of interlocutors and has provided generous comments on the book's manuscript. Matthew Gibney has been a valuable source of advice whenever I needed guidance on what to read about immigration policy, as well as of reassurance about the result. Elizabeth Finneron-Burns and Caleb Yong provided research assistance along the way, and Caleb also provided detailed comments on the manuscript. In doing this he was joined by Michael Blake, Luara Ferracioli, Margaret Moore, Kieran Oberman, and the two reviewers for Harvard University Press. My thanks to all of these for their suggestions, and my apologies for not always having followed their recommendations.

Margaret is also owed thanks of a different kind, having come into my life as the book was nearing completion and provided encouragement and distraction, both equally welcome. The book is dedicated to her.

Index